# Mathematics and Gender

# Mathematics and Gender

*Edited by*
**ELIZABETH FENNEMA**
**GILAH C. LEDER**

**TEACHERS COLLEGE PRESS**

Teachers College, Columbia University
New York and London

Published by Teachers College Press, 1234 Amsterdam Avenue
New York, NY 10027

*Library of Congress Cataloging-in-Publication Data*

Mathematics and gender: influences on teachers and students / edited
    by Elizabeth Fennema, Gilah C. Leder.
        p.    cm.
    Includes bibliographical references.
    ISBN 0-8077-3002-5 (alk. paper). — ISBN 0-8077-3001-7 (pbk. :
alk. paper)
    1. Women in mathematics.    2. Sex differences in education.
    3. Mathematics — Study and teaching.    I. Fennema, Elizabeth.
    II. Leder, Gilah C.
    QA27.5.M38    1990                                              89-49117
    510′.7 — dc20                                                      CIP

Printed on acid-free paper

Manufactured in the United States of America

96  95  94  93                        8  7  6  5  4  3  2

# Contents

**8**
**Teachers' Beliefs and Gender Differences in Mathematics**
    *Elizabeth Fennema*

**9**
**Gender Differences in Mathematics: A Synthesis**
    *Gilah C. Leder and Elizabeth Fennema*

# Acknowledgments

Whenever research is done and a book is written, there are many who contribute. We gratefully acknowledge the help of these people, both in the United States and in Australia, without whom the work could never have been accomplished:

Our cheerful and expert typist, Chris Kruger
Our thoughtful and professional assistant, Susan Lamon
Those who helped with data collection: Laurie Hart,
    William R. Vilberg, and Ingrid Leonard
All the teachers who let us watch them teach
All the learners who helped us understand
The governmental agencies who supported the research: Australian
    Research Grants Scheme and the National Science Foundation
    of the United States

# Justice, Equity, and Mathematics Education

ELIZABETH FENNEMA

A basic belief underlying this book is that there should be justice for females and males in mathematics education. This is not a new belief nor one that needs defending. Partly as a result of this belief, gender differences in mathematics have been studied intensely for about 20 years. In many countries, the incentive for such study has been the recognition that lack of mathematical learning and negative beliefs about themselves and mathematics hampers females from achieving equity with males. It appears that these studies have been based on the idea that females' achievement and beliefs about themselves should be compared to males'. Studies based on this type of thinking, which use male behavior as the standard against which female behavior is measured, are not unusual and have been severely attacked by many. In what is perhaps the best known discussion of this, Gilligan (1982) points out that using the male standard as a benchmark against which to measure female behavior has resulted in a psychology that is both inaccurate and misleading. It has been shown that the resulting generalizations about the human condition are often lacking in validity where females are concerned.

The use of the male standard is particularly evident in the study of gender differences in mathematics. In part such studies have been undertaken to explain the facts that females' mathematics achievement has not been as high as males' and that females have not elected to participate in advanced mathematics courses or in mathematics-related careers at the same level as have males. This male bias, however, has only exacerbated the difficulty in exposing the full implication of mathematics achievement for females. Reality shows that females' social learning and beliefs about themselves with regard to mathematics have been particularly detrimental both to society as a whole and to females as a group. While it can be argued that mathematics achievement and participation should be increased for everyone, lower achievement and participation of females in mathematics-related careers is partially the cause of the economic problems faced by many women. Mathematics has been and continues to be a "critical filter" that successfully inhibits participation in many occupations and in career advancement and change.

There are reasons other than economic ones for continued concern about gender differences in mathematics. Females have made contributions to our knowledge of mathematics in the past (Osen, 1974; Perl, 1979), but such contributions have been inhibited because of societal attitudes toward females as mathematicians. It has been suggested that females could make a unique contribution to our mathematical way of thinking if only given the chance (see Mura, 1987, for a complete discussion of this). The entire field of mathematics might be enriched if more young females were given the opportunity to grow into mathematical scholars.

Mathematics is a unique product of human culture. Permitting females to understand this culture is important both for their own appreciation of the beauty of mathematics and the transmission of this culture to future generations.


## DEFINING EQUITY

Research is always value laden, and nowhere are values more evident than in research dealing with gender and mathematics. The goal of most studies is to gain information that will promote equity in mathematics. Dictionary definitions of equity use the terms *fairness* and *impartiality*, yet there is no consensus on what this might mean for the field of mathematics. According to Secada (1989), equity involves "our judgments about whether or not a given state of affairs is just" (p. 68). (See Secada, 1989, for a complete discussion of equity in education.) To help in deciding whether or not there is justice for males and females, three definitions of equity will be discussed here: (1) equity as equal educational opportunity, (2) equity as equal educational treatment, and (3) equity as equal educational outcome.

### Equity As Equal Opportunity to Learn Mathematics

In many countries it is assumed that there is equal opportunity for males and females to learn mathematics. In the United States, for example, females and males in elementary school are not segregated when it is time to learn mathematics. Teachers usually teach the entire class at one time and do not make conscious decisions about teaching boys and girls differently or identically. As children move up the educational ladder, a different pattern appears. Learners are either placed in different tracks or are given the option to study mathematics. Neither these tracking decisions nor the range of opportunities opened to students is overtly determined by sex. In most coed schools in European countries and Australia, the situation is similar (see Chapter 2, by Leder). Many believe that providing equal opportunity to elect mathematics and not tracking by sex ensures that equity in mathematics is achieved. However, when data are examined about who actually elects to take the most advanced mathematics courses in secondary schools, there are clear differences by sex, with males electing to take such courses more often than do females. After secondary school, the discrepancy in the number of females and males studying mathematics or preparing for mathematics-related careers is even more dramatic.

In legal terms, equity is construed as equal opportunity, though this definition is always expanding as more court cases are being decided. The argument here, however, is that, even when legal equity exists, an examination of actual practice reveals that equality in mathematics has not been achieved. As Secada (1989) explained, "Equity goes beyond following . . . rules, even if we have agreed that they are intended to achieve justice" (p. 68). Thus, this definition of educational equity does not seem sufficient to achieve justice for females and males.

## Equity As Equal Educational Treatment

Another definition presents equity as equality of educational treatment or equality of mathematical experiences in schools. In particular, it focuses on equal treatment in the mathematics classroom. If equity satisfying this definition were reached, it would be impossible to detect any differences in teachers' treatment of males and females. While teachers would treat individuals differently, differential treatment of males and females as groups would not exist. Females would be talked to by the teacher as much as would males. Females would be asked to solve problems as many times as would males. Females would be rewarded in the same way for the same kind of responses, and they would be scolded as much as would males. In fact, if one believes that equity in mathematics education means equal treatment within classrooms, there would be no difference in the way that teachers interact with males as compared to females.

There is much evidence that equality in treatment of the sexes does not exist in most classrooms. Males interact more frequently with teachers than do females, and females have many more days in which they do not interact at all with the teacher than do males. Teachers initiate more contacts with males than with females. Males receive more discipline contacts as well as more praise. Teachers respond more frequently to requests for help from males than from females and tend to criticize females more than males for the academic quality of their work (Fennema & Peterson, 1987). Grieb and Easley (1984) report that teachers allow some males to exert their independence overtly and prohibit females from doing so (see Chapter 6, by Koehler, and Chapter 7, by Leder, for a complete discussion of this).

There have been many studies that have documented unequal treatment, and much has been written about it. Many writers have strongly inferred or even stated that if this differential treatment were eliminated, then equity in mathematics education would be achieved. Either they consider equal treatment an end in itself or they believe that if equal treatment were accorded both sexes, gender differences in mathematics would be eliminated.

## Equity As Equal Educational Outcomes

If equity in mathematics education were achieved using the definition of equal educational outcomes, there would be no differences in the attainment of important educational outcomes for males and females. At the end of public education, there would be no gender differences in achievement or in how males and females felt about themselves and mathematics. (Chapters 2, 4, and 5 explore the outcomes of mathematics education for females and males thoroughly.) It is clear that, at the end of secondary school, males have learned more and different mathematics than have females. Males, more than females, are able to transfer their learning to the solution of complex problems, even when both sexes have participated in the same mathematics courses. In addition, males have personal belief systems that enable them to pursue mathematics-related careers. Females, more than males, report less confidence, exhibit an attributional style that inhibits persistence and other achievement-related behaviors, and fail to perceive mathematics as a useful pursuit. Thus, it is clear that, if justice is equity in outcomes of mathematics education, justice for the sexes has not yet been achieved.

## WHAT IS JUSTICE?

Does justice in mathematics mean that everyone should learn the same thing, or does it mean that everyone should have equal opportunity to participate in mathematics courses? Does it mean that everyone should be treated identically by teachers, or does it mean that teachers should systematically vary their teaching to adapt to the way that each individual learns mathematics best? Does it mean that females and males should learn in the same classrooms or in separate ones? Does it mean that when females and males complete their public school education they should have the same mathematical knowledge, skills, and personal belief systems about mathematics?

This book clearly demonstrates that, with the possible exception of legal equity (equality in the right to choose mathematics courses), justice for the sexes has not been served according to any definition of equity. We must conclude that, while there is a semblance of equal opportunity to learn mathematics in today's world, mere semblance is not enough. Females are not learning and participating in mathematics at the same level as are males. Do females even recognize that there is equal opportunity to learn? Females and males do not develop the same internal belief systems to support their learning of mathematics (see Chapters 4 and 5). Does the school have a responsibility to respond to these differential belief systems? Is overt equality enough, or are there other levels of equality that must be enforced if equity in mathematics is to be achieved? Are there less obvious ways in which inequality exists, such as scheduling problems, that discourage females from participating in upper-level courses in mathematics? Do gender differences in mathematics exist because females and males actually participate in different learning activities or because they apply different cognitive processes to mathematical problems?

Legally enforcing equity is obviously a prerequisite to the achievement of equity; but it is not a sufficient condition. (See Isaacson, 1986, for a complete discussion.) Without the power of the law, many would resist changing the status quo in the schools; however, legal equity alone will not achieve justice. Justice in mathematics will not be achieved until the goals of education are met equally by both sexes. Educators must take it upon themselves to do whatever is needed to achieve true justice.

At the end of schooling, there should be no differences in what females and males have learned, nor should there be any gender differences in how students feel about themselves as learners of mathematics. Males and females should be equally willing to pursue mathematics-related careers and should be equally able to learn new mathematics as it is required. The definition of equity as the achievement of equal outcomes offers the greatest promise for achieving true justice.

Achieving equivalent outcomes in mathematics education for males and females may require that teachers actually treat the sexes differently. It could be that the most effective teaching for males is different from that for females. For example, there is some evidence that classes organized to provide competition result in somewhat better learning for males, while classrooms that encourage cooperation are better for females (see Fennema & Peterson, 1987, and Peterson & Fennema, 1985, for a complete discussion). However, the question of whether effective teaching is the same for both sexes cannot be answered simply. Fennema and Peterson (1987) suggest that several dimensions of classroom instruction hold promise for decreasing gender-related differences in mathematics. As noted, teachers might place more stress on cooperative mathematics activities than on competitive ones. Teachers should not tacitly accept socializing by females during mathematics class; teachers should ensure that both females and males fully attend to mathematics tasks. Teachers need to increase their interactions with females on high-cognitive-level mathematics activities, expect females to be able to figure out mathematics answers, and then praise them for doing so. Further, when females respond incorrectly in mathematics class, the teacher needs to encourage divergent and independent thinking by giving them hints on alternate strategies, rather than telling them the answers. Perhaps the most important thing that a teacher can do is to expect females to work independently, encouraging them to engage in independent learning behavior and praising them for participating in and performing well on high-cognitive-level mathematics tasks. The learning of mathematics, particularly the skills required to perform high-level tasks, does not occur quickly and all at once. Rather, students develop these skills over many years by repeatedly choosing, persisting at, and succeeding in the activities necessary for performing high-level tasks.

If educators take these guidelines to heart, then gender differences in mathematics achievement may diminish. Moreover, if the differences are reduced, females' beliefs about themselves and mathematics will improve. Educators are important change agents, and they, more than anyone else, can help females to achieve equity in mathematics.

## CLASSROOMS AS MEDIATORS OF
## GENDER DIFFERENCES IN MATHEMATICS

Mathematics is learned, for the most part, in classrooms. While the environment outside of the school undoubtedly contributes to what is learned, most mathematical knowledge is built upon classroom experiences. Classroom interactions and class-related homework assignments provide students with the activities to learn mathematics. The degree to which the student participates in them have a major impact on what is learned. Such an obvious truism needs little support, but support can be readily found. Begle (1979) reported that, when a textbook used by learners emphasized understanding of mathematical ideas, learners performed at higher levels on tasks that measure understanding. Good, Grouws, and Ebmeier (1983) found that, when more time was spent in classroom activities that developed the reasons for mathematical ideas, children performed at higher levels on tests that measured concepts.

It is not only overt participation in learning activities that determines what is learned. The mental activity that takes place during the activity by each individual is as important as what the individual appears to be doing. The knowledge that is brought to the activity, the confidence that one feels about successful completion of the activity, the control that is felt in doing the activity, and the interest in the activity all affect the quality of one's participation and, ultimately, what is learned from doing that activity.

This explanation of learning is consistent with a cognitive constructivist epistemology. Constructivism hypothesizes that knowledge is subjective; it is the "individual's conceptual organization of the individual's experience" (Von Glasersfeld, 1987, p. 16).

In 1985, Fennema and Peterson proposed the Autonomous Learning Behavior model (discussed at length by Meyer and Koehler in Chapter 4; see Figure 4.2) as a possible explanation of the development of gender differences in mathematics. This model suggests that gender differences in mathematics are caused by females' lowered participation in autonomous learning behaviors (ALBs), which both require and develop one's ability to work independently in high-cognitive-level activities. Fennema and Peterson further suggest that these traits do not develop when one becomes an adult; instead, they are formed over a period of years as a person grows and develops. The traits are learned as one is allowed, forced, or expected to exhibit them. In other words, participation in ALBs allows one to be independent in constructing one's own knowledge in mathematics. Autonomous learning activity is the active and willing participation in mathematical tasks that require knowledge and independent thinking. ALBs are, in fact, the processes through which individuals construct their own knowledge.

The ALB model also indicates some influences on females' and males' participation in such behaviors in the mathematics classroom. An internal belief system is hypothesized to influence willingness to work independently. Its components are confidence in one's ability to learn and perform in mathematics, perception of usefulness of mathematics, a pattern of causal attributions of successes and failures in mathematics, and sex-role identity. Interacting with this internal belief system (and also directly influencing participation in ALBs) are external influences such as teachers, peers, and parents.

The components of the ALB model are not necessarily sufficient explanations for gender differences; however, they — and their relationships — are useful in planning research designed to increase understanding of gender differences in mathematics. In particular, consideration of the interaction between internal beliefs and external influences as they impact on the learning activities of mathematics will provide increased knowledge. This book explicates the ALB model and expands our understanding of it. In Chapter 2 Leder presents current knowledge about where gender differences in mathematics exist. Tartre, in Chapter 3, adds a dimension of internal influence not usually addressed in connection with the model. She suggests that spatial skills of a well-defined kind may be an internal influence on learning activities which involve mathematics represented spatially. Chapters 4 and 5 explore the internal belief system as it influences participation in mathematical learning activities. Chapters 6, 7, and 8 report studies dealing with classrooms and teachers, important external influences on the learning of mathematics. In the final chapter, Leder and I synthesize the work presented in this book and discuss areas for future research.

This book reports on various studies that have increased our understanding of why females and males learn different kinds and amounts of mathematics. A great deal of knowledge has been gained in the last two decades about where gender differences in mathematics exist. In addition, we have well-replicated information about variables that relate to male/female differences. Perhaps future consideration of the relationships suggested in the ALB model will prove fruitful in ensuring that both sexes learn mathematics equally and acquire positive feelings about themselves and mathematics. Then, and not until then, will justice in mathematics education be achieved.

## REFERENCES

Begle, E. G. (1979). *Critical variables in mathematics education: Findings from a survey of the empirical literature.* Washington, DC: Mathematical Association of America and National Council of Teachers of Mathematics.

Fennema, E., & Peterson, P. L. (1985). Autonomous learning behavior: A possible explanation of gender-related differences in mathematics. In L. C. Wilkinson & C. B. Marrett (Eds.), *Gender-related differences in classroom interactions* (pp. 17–35). New York: Academic Press.

Fennema, E., & Peterson, P. L. (1987). Effective teaching for girls and boys: The same or different? In D. C. Berliner & B. V. Rosenshine (Eds.), *Talks to teachers* (pp. 111–125). New York: Random House.

Gilligan, C. (1982). *In a different voice*. Cambridge, MA: Harvard University Press.

Good, T. L., Grouws, D. A., & Ebmeier, H. (1983). *Active mathematics teaching*. New York: Longman.

Grieb, H., & Easley, J. (1984). A primary school impediment to mathematical equity: Case studies in role-dependent socialization. In M. Steincamp & M. L. Maehr (Eds.), *Women in science. Vol. 2: Advances in motivation and achievement* (pp. 317–362). Greenwich, CT: JAI Press.

Isaacson, Z. (1986). Freedom and girls' education: A philosophical discussion with particular references to mathematics. In L. Burton (Ed.), *Girls into maths can go* (pp. 223–240). London: Holt, Rinehart and Winston.

Mura, R. (1987). Feminist views on mathematics. *International Organization of Women and Mathematics Education Newsletter, 3*(2), 6–11.

Osen, L. (1974). *Women and mathematics*. Cambridge, MA: MIT Press.

Perl, T. H. (1979). *Discriminating factors and sex differences in electing mathematics*. Unpublished doctoral dissertation, Stanford University, Stanford, CA.

Peterson, P. L., & Fennema, E. (1985). Effective teaching, student engagement in classroom activities, and sex-related differences in learning mathematics. *American Educational Research Journal, 22*(3), 309–335.

Secada, W. G. (1989). Educational equity versus equality of education: An alternative conception (pp. 68–88). In W. G. Secada (Ed.), *Equity in education*. London: Falmer Press.

Von Glasersfeld, E. (1987). Learning as a constructive activity. In C. Janvier (Ed.), *Problems of representation in the teaching and learning of mathematics* (pp. 3–17). Hillsdale, NJ: Lawrence Erlbaum.

# 2 Gender Differences in Mathematics: An Overview

## GILAH C. LEDER

*This chapter provides the context for the studies described in subsequent chapters in two different ways. First, Leder outlines the nature and extent of gender-related problems by examining participation and performance statistics. In addition, she provides a general overview of literature relevant to gender differences in mathematics learning.*

Special government grants and programs are indicators of widespread concerns about the educational needs of females. Funds provided by the Women's Educational Equity Act and the Ford and National Science Foundations in the United States, and by the Projects of National Significance and the Participation and Equity programs in Australia, for example, testify to a willingness on the part of governments to go beyond rhetoric. A poignant illustration of the way such initiatives are sometimes organized is provided by the report of the influential Cockcroft (1982) committee in the United Kingdom. Its purposes were "to consider the teaching of mathematics in primary and secondary schools in England and Wales, with particular regard to the mathematics required in further and higher education, employment, and adult life generally, and to make recommendations" (p. ix). While the body of the report contains some references to the mathematical performance of females, the bulk of the relevant information is given in the special appendix, "Differences in Mathematical Performance Between Girls and Boys." In contrast, reviews of existing research on the teaching and learning of mathematics were apparently commissioned early enough for their findings to be integrated fully in the text.

From time to time, governments' long-term plans to improve educational provisions for females are published in reports and special publications. It is instructive to compare two state documents published a decade apart in the United States and Australia, respectively.

> School administrators should take whatever action is necessary to provide equal educational opportunities for both sexes and to actively oppose sex role stereotyping which develops within the school and in the larger society. . . . Schools may have to develop programs to inform parents of the need for increased mathematical training for all students. In combination, the school and parents may successfully combat the development of negative mathematics orientations found in many children, orientations which may serve to limit the child's opportunities as an adult. [Allen & Chambers, 1977, p. 12]

> A national policy for the education of girls has been endorsed by the Commonwealth Government. . . . It will consider how major changes to school curriculum and organization can contribute to more equal outcomes between males and females. Four broad areas have been proposed: the raising of awareness of the educational needs [of] girls, equal access to, and participation in, appropriate curriculum, supportive school environment, and equitable resource allocation. [State Board of Education, 1986, pp. 46–47]

Schildkamp-Kundiger's (1982) review of international data on gender and mathematics confirms the existence of similar concerns in many other countries.

## EXAMINATION OF PERTINENT DATA

Discussion of participation and performance data will illustrate more specifically the nature of the disadvantages faced by females. Participation rates are considered first.

### Participation

Recent years have seen an increased tendency for more females than males to stay at school until the end of secondary schooling. Official public examination data confirm this for Australia and the United Kingdom, while results from the National Assessment of Educational Progress (NAEP) illustrate it for U.S. youth. Given that fewer females than males opt out of formal education, the educational disadvantage faced by females does not lie in the retention domain. Substantial anomalies appear, however, when retention in specific subject areas is considered. Fewer U.S. females than males enroll for more advanced mathematics courses such as trigonometry, precalculus, and calculus, and the same is true for intensive and advanced mathematics courses in the United Kingdom and Australia. Schildkamp-Kundiger's (1982) review again testifies to the generalizability of this trend to other countries, though the severity of the gender differences in participation rates does vary among countries. The conclusion reached by Keeves in 1973 is still pertinent today:

> The range of differences across countries is too great for a simple explanation to be advanced as to why such sex differences should have been observed. . . . Nevertheless, it is clear from this evidence that girls tend to be less well-prepared to enter occupations and careers that require a prior knowledge of mathematics and science. To this extent, inequalities between males and females are built into educational systems. [p. 57]

The consequences of the differences in participation rates of males and females in mathematics and science subjects are far-reaching. Mathematical qualifications are commonly used as a critical entry barrier to apprenticeships, further training, and tertiary courses (Sells, 1973). According to one Australian survey (Hansen, 1981) 67% of almost 500 unskilled or semiskilled jobs required Grade-9 mathematics, 89% of more than 150 trades investigated required a passing grade in mathematics at the Grade-10 level, while 75% of more than 200 tertiary courses reviewed required a passing grade in Grade-12 mathematics. Females, it appears, are disadvantaged with respect to further educational and career opportunities because, all too frequently, they self-select out of mathematics courses once they are no longer compulsory. The need to enhance our understanding of why this occurs, as well as a desire to achieve more equitable educational outcomes, has motivated many studies.

## Performance

Neither the governmental concerns and initiatives described nor the considerable research attention directed at the issue of gender differences in mathematics participation and achievement have enabled agreement to be reached on the relative importance of contributing factors. A careful reading of U.S., Australian, and British studies reveals an inconsistency of findings, with males performing better in some studies and females in others. Few consistent differences in performance in mathematics are found at the early primary school level. There is, however, a substantial body of evidence to suggest that, from the beginning of secondary schooling, males frequently outperform females in mathematics. For example, data from successive NAEP testings continue to reveal few performance differences between males and females at either 9 or 13 years of age, but consistent though relatively small differences in favor of males at the 17-year-old level (Fennema & Carpenter, 1981; NAEP, 1983; Meyer, 1989). There is, in fact, much overlap in the performance in mathematics of males and females. Consistent between-gender differences are dwarfed by within-group differences. When found, the former seem to depend on the content and format of the test administered (Armstrong, 1985; Marshall, 1983; NAEP, 1983; Senk & Usiskin, 1985; Smith & Walker, 1988) and the age level at which the testing takes place (Fennema & Carpenter, 1981; NAEP, 1983; Meyer, 1989). However, between-gender differences are particularly marked when above-average performance is considered, with males achieving at higher levels (Benbow & Stanley, 1980; Fennema & Carpenter, 1981; Fox & Cohn, 1980; Leder, in press; NAEP, 1983). A recent meta-analysis of 100 studies both confirms these findings and indicates that gender differences have declined in recent years (Hyde, Fennema, & Lamon, in press).

Variations in the samples being tested and the nature of the tasks to be performed make cross-study comparisons difficult. Yet findings of the lower performance of females, compared with males, in public examinations and large-scale testings that have emerged from U.S. studies (Marshall, 1983; NAEP, 1983) are frequently replicated in other countries. British (Cockcroft, 1982; Shuard, 1986) and Australian data (Leder, 1984b; Moss, 1982; Yates & Firkin, 1986) also show such gender differences in mathematics performance. Differences in the proportions of males and females who score exceptionally well are particularly striking, as Joffe and Foxman (1986) report:

> Nearly all the differences in performance between boys and girls at both ages [11 and 15 years] are accounted for by the top 10 to 20 percent of attainers in most topics. . . . The proportion of boys to girls among 15-year-old pupils obtaining the highest 10 percent of scores on APU [Assessment of Performance Unit] concepts and skills tests is 61 to 39 percent. [pp. 48–49]

Similar findings for the Australian context have been reported by Leder (1984b). The similarities in the patterns of postcompulsory participation in mathematics and achievement in mathematics in the three countries discussed are noteworthy.

## POSSIBLE EXPLANATIONS

A large number of explanations have been put forward to account for gender differences in mathematics. The fact that workers from a variety of disciplines have been attracted to the area, each intent on examining those aspects of the problem most congruent with their particular research perspective, has led to considerable fragmentation of the field. The tendency to concentrate on one or perhaps a small set of variables, and to ascribe differences obtained to these variables alone, has at times given rise to unproductive and largely artificial controversies. These appear to be a consequence of the delineation of the issue, rather than genuinely conflicting results. Yet a sensitive interpretation of the findings obtained, the ability to distinguish between extension and replication studies, together with a willingness to synthesize rather than polarize results from investigations that have evolved from different research perspectives can lead to a fuller and deeper understanding of the many facets that affect mathematics learning. Provided the constraints imposed by different disciplines are recognized, the diversity of approaches helps to describe more accurately and constructively the complex interaction of individuals with their environment. It is useful to highlight the variables of particular importance to the authors of this book. Such a representation is given in Figure 2.1.

Many of the variables linked to gender differences in mathematics learning are discussed in later chapters of this book. Of necessity, in each chapter emphasis is placed on those most pertinent to the study or studies described. While the importance of societal and home influences is recognized, much of the research described in this book focuses on variables more susceptible to the educational process. To provide a context for the research presented here, a brief but general overview of relevant literature is presented.

### School Variables

There are a number of ways in which schools, and teachers within the schools, differentiate between students on the basis of gender. The former do so through their organizational procedures, the latter through their behavior, expectations, and beliefs.

Until recently, gender-segregated education was viewed as an anachronism, reflective of outmoded beliefs that males and females have different educational needs. Coeducation was assumed to be the avenue through which similarity of treatment of the two could be achieved, while the degree to which a community provided for educa-

Figure 2.1   Variables studied in relation to gender
differences in mathematics

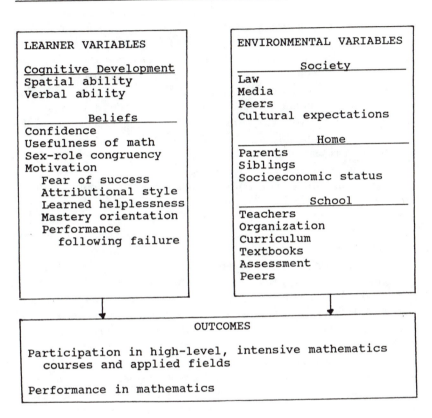

tion in sex-segregated settings was considered to be a measure of the
extent to which males and females were believed to require different
preparations for different adult roles. The extensive amount of research
evidence that coeducation does not signify equity or equality in policy
or practice has brought about a reexamination of this assumption. Researchers have experimented with single-sex settings for various school-
and system-level interventions aimed at improving the learning climate
for females (Fox & Cohn, 1980; Lockheed, 1985; Stage, Kreinberg,
Eccles, & Becker, 1985). Collectively, these studies suggest that carefully
timed, organized, and implemented programs may indeed lead to qualitative if not quantitative benefits in the learning of mathematics for
some females. As important, they have highlighted the many subtle

ways (including time-tabling decisions, curriculum selection, counsel-
ors' advice, and administrators' advocacy of certain instructional policies) in which females may be disadvantaged in a coeducational setting.

On the other hand, a graphic illustration of the inequities still
produced by single-sex schooling emerged from a recent test case in
Australia. A family living in a suburb of Sydney sent their daughter,
Melissa, to an all-females' school and her twin brother to a neighboring
all-males' school. Concerned by the more limited curriculum selection
available at her school, Melissa claimed discrimination, fought her case
in the courts, and won on a number of points. The implications of the
verdicts reached are still not fully explored (a fuller discussion of this
benchmark case can be found in Shorten, 1987).

It should be stressed again that the research evidence to date does
not warrant an unreservedly enthusiastic advocacy or adoption of long-
term gender-segregated mathematics classes. While some (Assessment of
Performance Unit, 1982; Cockcroft, 1982; Harding, 1981; and Ormerod, 1981) argue that females studying mathematics and science
seem to be disadvantaged in a mixed school setting, others (Bone, 1983;
Dale, 1974; Marsh, Owens, Myers, & Smith, 1989; Smith, 1986; and
Steedman, 1983) report that females in coeducational schools perform
at least as well in mathematics as those in single-sex schools. An examination of students' reflections about their experiences in segregated and
coeducational classes (Eales, 1986) highlights the importance attached
by students to having close friends in their class, irrespective of other
organizational arrangements.

Care must be taken when subject preferences and performance are
compared across different school systems in which equipment available,
staffing, and class sizes may not be comparable. In both England and
Australia, where sections of the school population are still educated in
single-sex schools (though in both countries there is an increasing trend
toward coeducation for economic as well as educational considerations),
many of those schools cater to children from higher socioeconomic stra-
ta. The effect of parents' educational and occupational level on their
children's mathematics learning cannot be discounted (Armstrong,
1985; Brush, 1985; Husen, 1967; Wise, 1985). Most of the studies that
have examined the apparent benefits or disadvantages of long-term education in a gender-segregated environment have not controlled adequately for socioeconomic factors.

## Teachers

Whatever the formal organization of the mathematics lessons,
teachers play a vital role in carrying out school policies. The ways in

which teacher beliefs are reflected in classroom practices is explored by Fennema in Chapter 8. Also discussed in this volume, in Chapters 6 and 7, are teacher/student interactions. Earlier research has indicated that teachers often interact differently with their male and female students, with males attracting more and qualitatively different interactions. Support for this assertion with respect to mathematics classes in the United States is provided by Becker (1981); Brophy (1985); Brophy and Good (1974); Eccles and Blumenfeld (1985); Fennema, Reyes, Perl, Konsin, and Drakenberg (1980); and Peterson and Fennema (1985). Making the same case in British classrooms are Galton, Simon, and Croll (1980) and Walden and Walkerdine (1985); for Australian classrooms, Dunkin and Doenau (1982).

## Peers

Along with teachers, the peer group is another important variable to be considered. It acts as an important reference for childhood and adolescent socialization and further perpetuates sex-role differentiation through gender-typed leisure activities, friendship patterns, subject preferences, and career intentions. Peer influence operates in both society at large and in the classroom.

The preference of males for active games and pastimes concerned with skills and mastery of objects, and the preference of females for play in which they practice skills related to mastery over people and interpersonal relations, has been frequently documented and conforms with adults' expectations. It has also been argued (Horner, 1968; Leder 1986b; Stein & Bailey, 1973; Walden & Walkerdine, 1985) that females differ in the areas in which they strive or are expected to aim for success. While males favor achievement in the traditionally highly valued areas of intellectual expertise and leadership skills, females are considered more likely to aim for excellence in areas congruent with their traditional role, that is, areas that require social skills. Thus mathematics' frequent stereotyping as a male domain (Boswell, 1985; Fox, Brody, & Tobin, 1985; Joffe & Foxman, 1986; Leder, 1986a; Sherman & Fennema, 1977) has often been used to explain females' lower performance and participation in postcompulsory mathematics courses. Minimizing stereotypes; increasing exposure to a wide range of ideas, experiences, and models; teaching skills for choice, problem solving, and evaluation; and providing experiences conducive to self-differentiation and self-knowledge are strategies advocated by Nash (1979) to minimize the constraining effects of sex role on cognitive functioning.

Differences in leisure-time activities and particularly in attitudes toward mathematics (Boswell, 1985; Fennema & Sherman, 1977; Fox et al., 1985; Joffe & Foxman; 1986, Leder, 1988; Sherman, 1980; Sherman & Fennema, 1977) are reflected in the career expectations of females and males. Their occupational intentions indicate that competence in mathematics is a more important prerequisite for the attainment of the career ambitions of males than females. In a number of studies (Eccles et al., 1985; Kelly, 1986; Leder, 1988; Pedro, Wolleat, Fennema, & Becker, 1981; Wolleat, Pedro, Becker, & Fennema, 1980) this view is expressed explicitly by males and females. More generally, Maines (1985) has argued that "the ideology of men enables them to select mathematics as a meaningful area of activity and their life structures enable them to pursue it as a career. The ideology of women deflects them away from focused attention on mathematics and their life structures militate against their career pursuit of it" (p. 317).

The pervasiveness of such beliefs is illustrated by reference throughout this section to U.S., British, and Australian data. Their self-perpetuating and reinforcing nature is highlighted by Lockheed (1985):

> Self-selected sex segregation is well documented as a widespread phenomenon among elementary and junior high school-aged children. It has been demonstrated in studies of student friendship choices and work partner preferences that utilize sociometric techniques, in surveys of student attitudes, and by direct observation. . . . Students identify same-sex but not cross-sex classmates as friends . . . , choose to work with same-sex but not cross-sex classmates . . . , sit or work in same-sex but not cross-sex age groups . . . , and engage in many more same-sex than cross-sex verbal exchanges. [p. 168]

The subtle ways in which students who contravene prevailing norms are sanctioned by the peer group have been described by Spender and Sarah (1980); Webb and Kenderski (1985); and Wilkinson, Lindow, and Chiang (1985).

### Learner Variables

The review so far has highlighted factors outside the learner. The consequences of different school and teacher practices and of teacher and peer-group expectations and beliefs discussed so far are compounding and far-reaching. They are often accompanied by affective differences in the ways males and females regard themselves as learners of mathematics. Such differences further reinforce and perpetuate gender-related inequalities, as is illustrated, for example, in the model of academic choice proposed by Meece, Eccles, Futterman, Goff, and Kaczala (1982). They argue that, when choices are available, the path selected is influenced not simply by reality but also by the individual's perceptions and interpretations of reality. Thus students capable of continuing with mathematics but who *believe* that the study of mathematics is inappropriate for them may select themselves out of mathematics or perform at a level they believe others consider appropriate for them. In this section I want to address within-learner variables linked to gender differences in mathematics learning.

It is convenient to distinguish between cognitive and internal belief variables. In line with the thrust of this book, the bulk of this section focuses on the latter. It should be pointed out, however, that past performance in mathematics is generally accepted to be the best predictor of future achievement in mathematics. Given the considerable overlap between measures of mathematical ability and tests of general intelligence, students who do well on intelligence tests tend to perform better in mathematics than those whose general intelligence score is lower. The findings on the contribution made by spatial abilities to mathematics performance are less consistent. It is now recognized that the way in which spatial abilities are operationally defined and measured influences whether or not gender differences in these abilities are reported (Maccoby & Jacklin, 1974; Petersen & Wittig, 1979). Presmeg (1986) argues that teachers may have most difficulty catering adequately to students who rely heavily on spatial skills for problem solving. (The link between spatial abilities and mathematics learning is pursued further in Chapter 3.)

The gender differences in peer group values outlined in the previous section are reflected in students' beliefs about their own performance and long-term expectations. One noteworthy finding that emerged from the Fennema and Sherman studies (1977, 1978) was that males in Grades 6 through 12 consistently showed greater confidence than females in their ability to learn mathematics. Initially those differences were not reflected in differences in achievement; however, for the older students, confidence in mathematics was a good predictor of performance for females but not for males. (Meyer and Koehler take up this issue in more detail in Chapter 4.) I have also reported gender differences in attitudes about mathematics, including confidence in ability to do mathematics, without attendant differences in performance for seventh-grade males and females (Leder, 1988). Joffe and Foxman (1986), on the other hand, found that males' and females' differing attitudes toward mathematics were paralleled by differences in the test performance of the two groups. Differences in performance, however, were minimal except in the top attainment bands. "Nearly all the differences in performance between boys and girls at both ages [11 and 15 years] are accounted for by the 10 to 20 percent of attainers in most topics" (p. 48).

Research on the motive to avoid success, also known as the "fear-of-success" construct, is particularly relevant to gender differences in performance among high achievers. This construct was postulated (Horner, 1968) in an attempt to explain gender differences in studies that explored achievement motivation. Because of Western culture's assumption that attainment of success in certain areas is more congruent with the male than the female role, attainment of success by females in these areas may be accompanied by negative consequences such as unpopularity, guilt, abuse, or doubt about their femininity. The prediction that success in mathematics, an area typically stereotyped as a male domain, may evoke ambivalence or anxiety about success — particularly among the most able, achievement-oriented females — has received research support (Clarkson & Leder, 1984; Horner, 1968; Leder, 1982b) and is consistent with the lower confidence expressed by females in their ability to do mathematics, the uncertainty about the appropriateness of their doing mathematics (Boswell, 1985; Fox et al., 1985; Sherman & Fennema, 1977), and ultimately their lower performance in mathematics. Studies such as these suggest that females' lower performance in mathematics is a function not so much of ability per se as of internalization of, and conforming to, the expectations of others.

Closely related to the work on fear of success — and building on the expectancy value theory of achievement motivation — are studies that consider attributions of success and failure on certain tasks. Those who have concentrated on success and failure attributions in a mathematics setting (Fennema, 1985; Gitelson, Petersen, & Tobin-Richards, 1982; Leder, 1982a, 1984a; Pedro et al., 1981; Wolleat et al., 1980) have typically reported less functional attributions of success and failure in mathematics by females as compared with males. For example, one indicator of fear of success is the image or feeling that females must work harder than males to have their achievements recognized. It is echoed by females' tendency to attribute success to effort while males attribute success to ability, and by males' attributing failure to effort while females attribute it to ability. These findings reflect a pattern of attributions most likely to lead, according to Weiner (1972, 1980), to cognitive, motivational, and/or emotional deficits. (In Chapter 5, Kloosterman explores this issue in more detail.)

There are other related indicators that may help not only explain gender differences in mathematics learning but also point to ways in which a reexamination of class organization and teaching practices could facilitate females' learning of mathematics. As will be discussed more fully in the chapters that follow, there is considerable evidence that females, on average, are reinforced and encouraged less than males to work independently and persistently, especially in difficult high-level mathematics tasks. In their three-year study of British classrooms, Walden and Walkerdine (1985) wrote,

> While good girls like SMILE [Secondary Mathematics Individualized Learning Experiment] work, good boys dislike it or find it boring. The reasons why girls like it relate to its safety and continuity with the practices of the primary school. The safety is precisely what allows them to continue in the hard work/feminine/helpful constellation, and precisely what leads to pejorative evaluations by the teachers. . . . It is the reason why teachers prefer girls to take CSE rather than 0 level [i.e., the Certificate of Secondary Education rather than the more demanding General Certificate of Education Ordinary level]. CSE is school-based, more importantly it is course-work based, it is safer, requiring less pushing. The circularity with which practices, teachers' evaluations, and the self evaluation of the girls fit together is extremely important. The first-year boys want to leave the practices of the primary school behind and dislike SMILE for that reason. This, of course, allows for the development of a different participation in the classroom. [p. 81]

This passage clearly conveys the teachers' beliefs (and, by extension, those of the wider society that have shaped prevalent school and teacher practices) that their female students are more dependent on confirmation by others and less capable of risk taking, independent work, and handling complex mathematics. Implied, too, is the extent to which the students themselves have accepted and internalized these expectations and beliefs.

## CONCLUSION

The issue of gender differences in mathematics learning is complex, and there are many perspectives from which it can be explored. The clusters presented in Figure 2.1 suggest at least one approach. The emphasis on variables that are potentially modifiable is a constructive one for educators. The omission of biological factors, thought to be unchangeable and certainly beyond the control of teachers, administrators, and schools, is deliberate. Implicit in our approach is the recognition that the practices, values, expectations, and beliefs of both individuals and society must be examined if the currently existing gender differences in mathematics participation and performance are to be understood and changed.

## REFERENCES

Allen, R. H., & Chambers, D. L. (1977). *A comparison of the mathematics achievement of males and females.* Madison, WI: Department of Public Instruction.

Armstrong, J. M. (1985). A national assessment of participation and achievement of women in mathematics. In S. F. Chipman, L. R. Brush, & D. M. Wilson (Eds.), *Women and mathematics: Balancing the equation* (pp. 59–94). Hillsdale, NJ: Lawrence Erlbaum.

Assessment of Performance Unit. (1982) *Mathematical development* (Secondary Survey Report No. 3). London: HMSO.

Becker, J. (1981). Differential treatment of females and males in mathematics classes. *Journal for Research in Mathematics Education, 12,* 40–53.

Benbow, C. P., & Stanley, J. C. (1980). Sex differences in mathematical ability: Fact or artifact? *Science, 210,* 1262–1264.

Bone, A. (1983). *Girls and girls only schools: A review of evidence.* London: Equal Opportunities Commission.

Boswell, S. L. (1985). The influence of sex-role stereotyping on women's attitudes and achievement in mathematics. In S. F. Chipman, L. R. Brush, & D. M. Wilson (Eds.), *Women and mathematics: Balancing the equation* (pp. 175–198). Hillsdale, NJ: Lawrence Erlbaum.

Brophy, J. (1985). Interactions of male and female students with male and female teachers. In L. C. Wilkinson & C. B. Marrett (Eds.), *Gender influences in classroom interaction* (pp. 115–142). New York: Academic Press.

Brophy, J., & Good, T. (1974). *Teacher-student relationships: Causes and consequences.* New York: Holt, Rinehart & Winston.

Brush, L. R. (1985). Cognitive and affective determinants of course preferences and plans. In S. F. Chipman, L. R. Brush, & D. M. Wilson, (Eds.), *Women and mathematics: Balancing the equation* (pp. 123–150). Hillsdale, NJ: Lawrence Erlbaum.

Clarkson, P., & Leder, G. C. (1984). Causal attributions for success and failure in mathematics: A cross-cultural perspective. *Educational Studies in Mathematics, 15,* 413–422.

Cockcroft, W. H. (1982). *Mathematics counts.* London: HMSO.

Dale, R. (1974). *Mixed or single sex schools?* (Vol. 3). London: Routledge & Kegan Paul.

Dunkin, M. J., & Doenau, S. J. (1982). Ethnicity, classroom interaction, and student achievement. *Australian Journal of Education, 26,* 171–189.

Eales, A. (1986). Girls and mathematics at Oadby Beauchamp College. In L. Burton (Ed.), *Girls into maths can go* (pp. 163–186). London: Holt, Rinehart and Winston.

Eccles, J. S., Adler, T. F., Futterman, R., Goff, S. B., Kaczala, C. M., Meece, J. L., & Midgley, C. (1985). Self-perceptions, task perceptions, socializing influences, and the decision to enroll in mathematics. In S. F. Chipman,

L. R. Brush, & D. M. Wilson (Eds.), *Women and mathematics: Balancing the equation* (pp. 95–121). Hillsdale, NJ: Lawrence Erlbaum.

Eccles, J. S., & Blumenfeld, P. (1985). Classroom experience and student gender: Are there differences and do they matter? In L. C. Wilkinson & C. B. Marrett (Eds.), *Gender influences in classroom interaction* (pp. 79–114). New York: Academic Press.

Fennema, E. (1985). Attribution theory and achievement in mathematics. In S. R. Yussen (Ed.), *The development of reflections.* New York: Academic Press.

Fennema, E., & Carpenter, T. (1981). The second national assessment and sex-related differences in mathematics. *Mathematics Teacher, 74,* 554–559.

Fennema, E., Reyes, L. H., Perl, T. H., Konsin, M. A., & Drakenberg, M. (1980, April). *Cognitive and affective influences on the development of sex-related differences in mathematics.* Paper presented at the annual meeting of the American Educational Research Association, Boston.

Fennema, E., & Sherman, J. A. (1977). Sex-related differences in mathematics achievement, spatial visualization and affective factors. *American Educational Research Journal, 14,* 51–71.

Fennema, E., & Sherman, J. A. (1978). Sex-related differences in mathematics achievement, spatial visualization, and related factors: A further study. *Journal for Research in Mathematics Education, 9,* 189–203.

Fox, L. H., Brody, L., & Tobin, D. (1985). The impact of early intervention programs upon course-taking and attitudes in high school. In S. F. Chipman, L. R. Brush, & D. M. Wilson (Eds.), *Women and mathematics: Balancing the equation* (pp. 249–274). Hillsdale, NJ: Lawrence Erlbaum.

Fox, L. H., & Cohn, S. J. (1980). Sex differences in the development of precocious mathematical talent. In L. H. Fox, L. Brody, & D. Tobin (Eds.), *Women and the mathematical mystique* (pp. 94–111). Baltimore: Johns Hopkins University Press.

Galton, M., Simon, B., & Croll, P. (1980). *Inside the primary classroom.* London: Routledge & Kegan Paul.

Gitelson, I. B., Petersen, A. C., & Tobin-Richards, M. H. (1982). Adolescents' expectancies of success, self-evaluations, and attributions about performance on spatial and verbal tasks. *Sex Roles, 8,* 411–420.

Hansen, C. (1981). Maths and jobs. *Vinculum, 18,* 8–13.

Harding, J. (1981). Sex differences in science examination. In A. Kelly (Ed.), *The missing half* (pp. 192–204). Manchester, England: Manchester University Press.

Horner, M. S. (1968). *Sex differences in achievement motivation and performance in competitive and non-competitive situations.* Unpublished doctoral dissertation, University of Michigan, Ann Arbor.

Husen, T. (Ed.) (1967). *International study of achievement in mathematics: A comparison in twelve countries.* Stockholm, Sweden: Almquist & Wiksell.

Hyde, J. S., Fennema, E., & Lamon, S. J. (in press). Gender differences in mathematics performance: A meta-analysis. *Psychological Bulletin.*

Joffe, L., & Foxman, D. (1986). Attitudes and sex differences: Some APU findings. In L. Burton (Ed.), *Girls into maths can go* (pp. 38-50). London: Holt, Rinehart and Winston.

Keeves, J. (1973). Differences between the sexes in mathematics and science courses. *International Review of Education, 19*, 47-63.

Kelly, A. (1986). Gender roles at home and school. In L. Burton (Ed.), *Girls into maths can go* (pp. 90-109). London: Holt, Rinehart and Winston.

Leder, G. C. (1982a). Learned helplessness in the classroom: A further look. *Research in Mathematics Education in Australia, 2*, 40-55.

Leder, G. C. (1982b). Mathematics achievement and fear of success. *Journal for Research in Mathematics Education, 13*, 124-135.

Leder, G. C. (1984a). Sex differences in attributions of success and failure. *Psychological Reports, 54*, 57-58.

Leder, G. C. (1984b, August). *Sex differences in participation and performance in Australia*. Paper presented at the Fifth International Congress on Mathematical Education, Adelaide, S.A., Australia.

Leder, G. C. (1986a). Mathematics: Stereotyped as a male domain? *Psychological Reports, 59*, 955-958.

Leder, G. C. (1986b). Successful females: Print media profiles and their implications. *Journal of Psychology, 120*, 239-248.

Leder, G. C. (1988). Teacher-student interactions: The mathematics classroom. *Unicorn, 14*, 161-166.

Leder, G. C. (in press). Critical variables: Gender. In D. A. Grouws (Ed.), *Handbook of research on teaching and learning*. New York: Macmillan.

Lockheed, M. E. (1985). Some determinants and consequences of sex segregation in the classroom. In L. C. Wilkinson & C. B. Marrett (Eds.), *Gender influences in classroom interaction* (pp. 167-184). New York: Academic Press.

Maccoby, E. E., & Jacklin, C. N. (1974). *The psychology of sex differences*. London: Oxford University Press.

Maines, D. R. (1985). Preliminary notes on a theory of informal barriers for women in mathematics. *Educational Studies in Mathematics, 16*, 314-320.

Marsh, H. W., Owens, L., Myers, M. R., & Smith, I. D. (1989). From single-sex to coed schools. In G. C. Leder & S. N. Sampson (Eds.), *Educating girls: Practice and research* (pp. 144-157). Sydney, Australia: Allen & Unwin.

Marshall, S. P. (1983). Sex differences in mathematical errors: An analysis of distractor choices. *Journal for Research in Mathematics Education, 14*, 325-336.

Meece, J. L., Eccles, J., Futterman, R., Goff, S. B., & Kaczala, C. M. (1982). Sex differences in math achievement: Towards a model of academic choice. *Psychological Bulletin, 91*, 324-348.

Meyer, M. R. (1989). Gender differences in mathematics. In M. M. Lindquist (Ed.), *Results from the Fourth Mathematics Assessment*. Reston, VA: National Council of Teachers of Mathematics.

Moss, J. D. (1982). *Toward equality: Progress by girls in mathematics in Australian secondary schools* (Occasional Paper No. 16). Hawthorn, Vic.: Australian Council for Educational Research.

Nash, S. C. (1979). Sex role as a mediator of intellectual functioning. In M. A. Wittig & A. C. Petersen (Eds.), *Sex-related differences in cognitive functioning* (pp. 263–302). New York: Academic Press.

National Assessment of Education Progress. (1983) *The third national mathematics assessment: Results, trends and issues.* Denver: Education Commission of the States.

Ormerod, M. B. (1981). Factors differentially affecting the science subject preferences, choices and attitudes of girls and boys. In A. Kelly (Ed.), *The missing half* (pp. 100–112). Manchester, England: Manchester University Press.

Pedro, J. D., Wolleat, P., Fennema, E., & Becker, A. D. (1981). Election of high school mathematics by females and males: Attributions and attitudes. *American Educational Research Journal, 18,* 207–218.

Petersen, A. C., & Wittig, M. A. (1979). Sex related differences in cognitive functioning: An overview. In M. A. Wittig & A. C. Petersen (Eds.), *Sex-related differences in cognitive functioning* (pp. 1–17). New York: Academic Press.

Peterson, P. L., & Fennema, E. (1985). Effective teaching. Student engagement in classroom activities and sex-related differences in learning mathematics. *American Educational Research Journal, 22,* 309–335.

Presmeg, N. C. (1986). Visualization and mathematical giftedness. *Educational Studies in Mathematics, 17*(3), 297–311.

Schildkamp-Kundiger, E. (1982). An international review of gender and mathematics. Columbus, OH: ERIC Clearinghouse for Science, Mathematics, and Environmental Education.

Sells, L. (1973). *High school mathematics as the critical filter in the job market.* Berkeley: University of California. (ERIC Document Reproduction Service No. ED 080 351).

Senk, S., & Usiskin, Z. (1985). Geometry proof-writing: A new view of sex differences in mathematics ability. *American Journal of Education, 91,* 187–201.

Sherman, J. (1980). Mathematics, spatial visualiation and related factors: Changes in girls and boys, grades 8–11. *Journal of Educational Psychology, 72,* 476–482.

Sherman, J., & Fennema, E. (1977). The study of mathematics by high school girls and boys: Related variables. *American Educational Research Journal, 14,* 159–168.

Shorten, A. (1987, November). *Ripples on the pond.* Paper presented at conference on "The education of girls: Research and beyond," at Monash University, Clayton, Vic., Australia.

Shuard, H. (1986). The relative attainment of girls and boys in mathematics in the primary years. In L. Burton (Ed.), *Girls into maths can go* (pp. 23–37). London: Holt, Rinehart and Winston.

Smith, S. (1986). *Separate tables? An investigation into single-sex setting in mathematics.* London: HMSO.

Smith, S. E., & Walker, W. J. (1988). Sex differences in New York State Regents Examinations: Support for the differential course-taking hypothesis. *Journal for Research in Mathematics Education, 19,* 81–85.

Spender, D., & Sarah, E. (Eds). (1980). *Learning to lose.* London: Women's Press.

Stage, E., Kreinberg, N., Eccles, J., & Becker, J. (1985). Increasing participation and achievement of girls and women in mathematics, science, and engineering. In S. S. Klein (Ed.), *Handbook for achieving sex equity through education* (pp. 237–269). Baltimore: Johns Hopkins University Press.

State Board of Education. (1986, December). *Curriculum policy: A comprehensive statement.* Melbourne, Vic., Australia: Author.

Steedman, J. (1983). *Examination results in mixed or single sex schools: Findings from the National Child Development Study.* London: Equal Opportunities Commission.

Stein, A. H., & Bailey, M. M. (1973). The socialization of achievement orientation in females. *Psychological Bulletin, 80,* 345–366.

Walden, R., & Walkerdine, V. (1985). *Girls and mathematics: From primary to secondary schooling* (Bedford Way Papers, No. 24). London: Institute of Education, London University.

Webb, N. M., & Kenderski, C. M. (1985). Gender differences in small-group interaction and achievement in high- and low-achieving classes. In L. C. Wilkinson & C. B. Marrett (Eds.), *Gender influences in classroom interaction* (pp. 209–236). New York: Academic Press.

Weiner, B. (1972). *Theories of motivation.* Chicago: Rand McNally.

Weiner, B. (1980). The order of affect in rational (attributions) approaches to human motivation. *Educational Research, 19,* 4–11.

Wilkinson, L. C., Lindow, J., & Chiang, C. P. (1985). Sex differences in sex segregation in students' small-group communication. In L. C. Wilkinson & C. B. Marrett (Eds.), *Gender influence in classroom interaction* (pp. 185–208). New York: Academic Press.

Wise, L. L. (1985). Project talent: Mathematics course participation in the 1960s and its career consequences. In S. F. Chipman, L. R. Brush, & D. M. Wilson (Eds.), *Women and mathematics: Balancing the equation* (pp. 25–58). Hillsdale, NJ: Lawrence Erlbaum.

Wolleat, P. L., Pedro, J. D., Becker, A. D., & Fennema, E. (1980). Sex differences in high school students' causal attributions of performance in mathematics. *Journal for Research in Mathematics Education, 11,* 356–366.

Yates, J., & Firkin, J. (1986). Student participation in mathematics: Gender differences in the last decade. In N. F. Ellerton (Ed.), *Mathematics: Who needs what?* (pp. 119–127). Melbourne, Vic.: Mathematical Association of Australia.

# Spatial Skills, Gender, and Mathematics

LINDSAY A. TARTRE

*The relationship between spatial skills and mathematics achievement has attracted a considerable amount of research attention, most recently by those concerned with gender differences. After discussing many of the commonly used definitions of spatial skills, the classification scheme developed by Tartre and underpinning her own research is outlined. Further direction for these studies is provided by the review of literature concerned with the nature and extent of gender differences in spatial skills. The effect of students' preferred mode of solution, ascertained from interview data, on mathematics achievement is explored by Tartre in both of her studies. Her careful classification of the important components of spatial orientation skills makes explicit the between- as well as within-group differences in reliance on such skills and helps to refine the hypothesis that gender differences in mathematics achievement can be explained by parallel differences in spatial orientation skills.*

For a long time, spatial skills have been hypothesized to be important variables affecting gender differences in mathematics. The purpose of this chapter is to explore the relationships among spatial skills, mathematics, and gender. Before these relationships can be discussed, however, it is necessary to understand what is meant by spatial skills.

Although research on spatial skills traces its beginnings to Galton's work on imagery in the 1880s, the first systematic work was done in the 1920s and 1930s, as psychologists began to identify facets of general intelligence. Using factor-analytic techniques, researchers often identified at least one spatial factor, separate from numerical and verbal factors, as a component of general intelligence. Researchers have also investigated various skills believed to contribute to mathematics learning and have found spatial skills to be related to mathematics achievement. Using various techniques, studies have demonstrated that many spatial skills are positively correlated with a wide variety of mathematics tasks. Yet the precise nature of spatial skills and the manner in which they contribute to or predict performance in mathematics, or might influence gender differences in mathematics, is largely unknown. There are many unresolved problems.

One such problem has been to find satisfactory definitions of spatial skills. Such diverse skills as mentally rotating a cube or reorienting oneself in relation to a fixed object are included in the broad area identified as spatial skills.

Researchers often assume that spatial skill is a single generalized attribute, and yet each argument about the relationship between mathematics and spatial skill is dependent upon the specific spatial skills tested or discussed. Often the specific spatial skills are only vaguely defined; moreover, when a clear definition is provided, it sometimes contradicts other definitions that use the same term (Clements, 1981). To confuse the issue further, several different terms have been used to describe the same skill. Each researcher appears to have his or her own definition of "spatial skill." When all of these problems are combined with the multifaceted nature of mathematics and the nuances of the English language, the relationship between spatial skills and mathematics becomes very difficult to delineate. As Clements (1981) stated, "In view of the fact that, at present, universally accepted definitions of spatial ability, visual imagery, or even mathematics, do not exist, it is hardly surprising that there is very little direct discussion in the existing literature on why spatial ability, mental imagery and mathematics performance might be expected to be related" (p. 43).

Because definitions of spatial skills have tended to be vague or lacking, some researchers have attempted to identify specific spatial tasks. For example, Wattanawaha (Clements & Wattanawaha, 1978) developed a classification scheme, called the DIPT system, to organize spatial tasks along four characteristics: "(i) the *D*imension of thinking required by the task . . . (ii) the degree of *I*nternalization required . . . (iii) the manner in which the task requires an answer to be *P*resented . . . and (iv) the *T*hought processes required by the task" (p. 432). While this scheme has provided some insight into the components of spatial tasks, it has not proved to be complete enough to explain fully the complexity of spatial skills.

## SPATIAL SKILLS CLASSIFICATION SCHEME

It is important to devise a scheme which attempts to classify a large variety of spatial skills. The following one was devised by categorizing the various tasks described in the literature as measuring spatial tasks, according to the mental process that was expected to be used in performing them. This scheme represents a synthesis of many ideas from several researchers as well as some new conceptualizations.

In his thorough review of spatial factors, McGee (1979) distinguished two broad categories of skills — *spatial visualization* and *spatial orientation*. Each is composed of several types of skills, differentiated on the basis of what is to be moved mentally, either an object (usually a pictorial representation) or the perspective of the person viewing the object. Thus, tests of spatial visualization expect that the viewer mentally move the representation of the indicated object, either turning it, as in mental rotation, or rearranging it, as in mental transformation. This movement of the object distinguishes spatial visualization from spatial orientation, in which nothing need move at all except the perspective of the person taking the test. Spatial orientation skill requires that the subject understand a visual representation or comprehend some change that has taken place between two representations.

Figure 3.1 shows the entire classification scheme, with the two major skill divisions broken down into types of skills. Let us take a look at definitions and examples of tasks that demonstrate the use of each skill.

### Spatial Visualization

Spatial visualization, as noted, is the skill of mentally manipulating all or part of an object (Werdelin, 1961). Rosser (1980) defined this skill as "performance involving the reproduction and/or combination of spatial information at the internal level" (p. 9). Fennema (1975) explained that "spatial visualization involves visual imagery of objects and movement or change in the objects themselves or change in their properties. In other words, objects or their properties must be manipulated in one's 'mind's eye' or mentally" (p. 34). Linn and Petersen (1985) stated that spatial visualization tasks "involve complicated, multi-step manipulations of spatially presented information" (p. 19). Kersh and Cook (1979) subdivided spatial visualization into two distinct categories — *mental rotation* and *mental transformation*. These are distinguished by whether all or only part of the object is to be mentally altered.

Figure 3.1   Spatial skills classification scheme

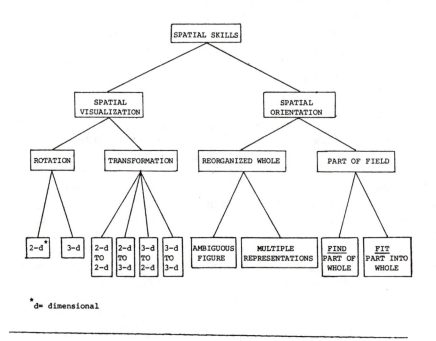

*d= dimensional

---

*Mental Rotation.*   This phrase describes the mental movement of an entire object to a different position and usually is characterized by mentally turning an object to determine if it agrees with a preset criterion. For example, one might be shown a picture of an object and then asked whether several others can be rotated to match it. Two types of items that measure mental rotation can be distinguished, depending on whether they suggest moving a 2-dimensional (2-d) or 3-dimensional (3-d) representation.

Some examples of 2-d rotation are shown in Figure 3.2. In each case, the subject is asked to rotate the figures to the right of the vertical line to determine whether or not each is identical to a reflection of the figure to the left of the line.

Examples of a test of 3-d rotation are included in Figure 3.3. The directions for this task suggest that the whole cube be turned and compared mentally.

Although some researchers include both 2-d and 3-d mental rotation as spatial relations or spatial orientation skills, they are included

Figure 3.2   2-d mental rotation

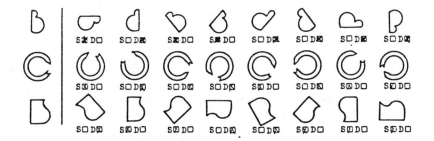

Each problem in this test consists of one card on the
left of a vertical line and eight cards on the right.
Check the box beside the S if it is the same as the
card at the beginning of the row (after you have moved
it mentally into the different positions).  Mark the D
if it is different from the one at the beginning of the
row (if the card would have to be flipped or made
differently).

here as spatial visualization skills because they involve the mental movement of the stimulus object.

*Mental Transformation.*   This category "involves different operations on separate parts of the mental image" (Kersh & Cook, 1979, p. 8).
At least four types of transformation skills can be distinguished, based
upon the number of dimensions of the initial state of the object presented and the number of dimensions of the goal state of the object. The task
could require starting with either a 2-d or 3-d representation and expecting either a 2-d or 3-d representation as an outcome. The possible
transformations are (1) 2-d to 2-d, (2) 2-d to 3-d, (3) 3-d to 2-d, and (4)
3-d to 3-d.
    A *2-d to 2-d transformation* is characterized by mentally moving
separate pieces to form a particular pictorial representation. An exam-

Figure 3.3    3-d mental rotation

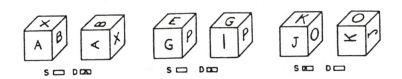

For each pair, must the one on the right be a different
cube or can they be the same cube?  No letters,
numbers, or symbols appear on more than one face of a
given cube.

From Ekstrom, R. B., French, J. W., & Harmon, H. H.
(1976).  Manual for kit of factor-referenced cognitive
tests (p. 152).  Princeton, NJ:  Educational Testing
Service.  Copyright (c) 1962, 1975 by Educational
Testing Service.  Reprinted by permission.

ple of an item from a test of this skill is shown in Figure 3.4. In this item, several two-dimensional shapes are moved to form another two-dimensional shape. Tangram activities can also be included in this category if the movement of the pieces is done mentally, that is, without physically moving the pieces.

A *2-d to 3-d transformation* has been tested by the presentation of a two-dimensional pattern that must be folded into its associated three-dimensional state (see Figure 3.5). Tests in this category have frequently been used as general measures of spatial skill, and test results have been used to compute correlations between spatial skill and mathematics performance. Consistent high correlations between spatial visualization and mathematics achievement tend to be found for tests in this category, particularly the Space Relations portion of the Differential Aptitude Test (Bennett, Seashore, & Wesman, 1973). Schonberger (1976), Connor and Serbin (1980), and Fennema and Sherman (1977) each found positive correlations $(r > .4)$ between this test and mathematics achievement.

A *3-d to 2-d transformation* skill can be used to accomplish such diverse tasks as imagining unfolding a piece of folded paper or mentally slicing a cross-section of a solid. The common thread between these tasks is that each presents a three-dimensional representation as the initial stimulus and, through some manner of transformation, expects a two-dimensional object as the outcome. Examples of test items of this skill are presented in Figure 3.6. Many concepts involved in analytic and

Figure 3.4    2-d to 2-d transformation

This is a test of your ability to tell what pieces can
be put together to make a certain figure.  Your task is
to decide which of the five shaded pieces will make the
complete figure when put together.

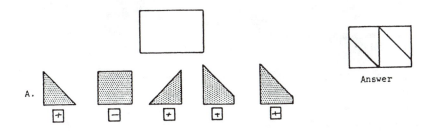

Answer

A.

From Ekstrom, R. B., French, J. W., & Harmon, H. H.
(1976).  Manual for kit of factor-referenced cognitive
tests (p. 175).  Princeton, NJ:  Educational Testing
Service.  Copyright (c) 1962, 1975 by Educational
Testing Service.  Reprinted by permission.

projective geometry, such as conic sections or projecting solids to a
plane, demonstrate applications of this skill.

A *3-d to 3-d transformation* skill requires the mental decomposition
of a three-dimensional object into parts. An example of such a test item
is shown in Figure 3.7. Mentally removing one piece from a whole pie is
another example of the use of this skill.

## Spatial Orientation

The other major division of spatial skills is spatial orientation. Tasks
of spatial orientation require that the subject understand a visual representation or comprehend some change that has taken place between two
representations. It "includes the comprehension of the arrangement of
elements within a visual stimulus pattern, the aptitude to remain un-
confused by the changing orientation in which a spatial configuration
may be presented, and an ability to determine spatial orientation with

Figure 3.5    2-d to 3-d transformation

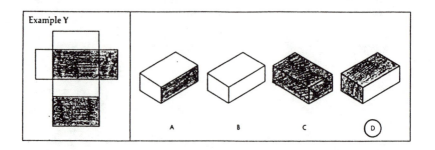

Instructions for this test are:   This test consists of
60 patterns which can be folded into figures.   To the
right of each pattern, there are four figures.   You are
to decide which <u>one</u> of these figures can be made from
the pattern shown.

---

respect to one's own body" (McGee, 1979, p. 909). Spatial orientation
requires that the subject mentally readjust her perspective to become
consistent with a representation of an object presented visually. It means
"re-seeing" it, seeing it from a different angle, recognizing it, or making
sense out of the object. The mental processing experienced with spatial
orientation tasks is often not as easy to analyze or articulate as with
spatial visualization tasks. Spatial orientation can be divided into two
categories — *reorganized whole* and *part of field*.

   *Reorganized Whole.*    These tasks involve the organization and
comprehension of an entire pictorial representation or a perceptual
change from one representation to another. There are two types of
reorganized-whole tasks, those involving *an ambiguous figure* and those
showing *multiple representations*.

   Figure 3.8 is an example of a pictorial representation that has more
than one object in one view, sometimes called *an ambiguous figure.*
Shepard (1978) stated that "such a figure demonstrates that not all of
what is perceived or imagined is contained in the concrete picture that is
externally presented or reconstructed" (p. 129). Wittrock (1974) agreed
that "the way in which one processes structurally organized information

Figure 3.6   3-d to 2-d transformation

Each hole is punched through all the thicknesses of
paper at that point.  Which one of the five figures at
the right of the vertical line shows where the holes
will be when the paper is completely unfolded?

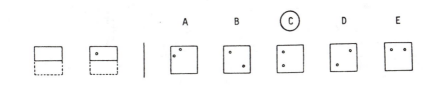

Each question shows a block of wood.  Imagine a cut
made where shown by the dotted lines.  Place a cross
(X) on one of the four drawings on the right which
shows the shape of the cut face.

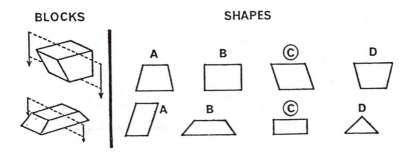

Top:   From Ekstrom, R. B., French, J. W., & Harmon, H.
H. (1976).  Manual for kit of factor-referenced
cognitive tests (p. 176).  Princeton, NJ:  Educational
Testing Service.  Copyright (c) 1962, 1975 by
Educational Testing Service.  Reprinted by permission.

Bottom:  Smith, I. M. (1964).  Spatial ability:  Its
educational and social significance (p. 369).  Kent,
England:  Hodder-Stoughton Company.  Copyright (c)
Hodder-Stoughton Company.

Figure 3.7   3-d to 3-d transformation

How many of the smaller blocks in the row below are
needed to build the larger one of the left?   Write the
number on each block.

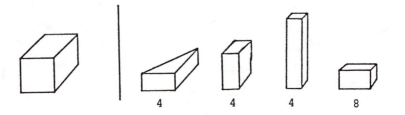

From Smith, I. M. (1964).   Spatial ability:   Its
educational and social significance (p. 369).   Kent,
England:   Hodder-Stoughton Company.   Copyright (c)
Hodder-Stoughton Company.

Figure 3.8   An ambiguous figure, reorganized whole

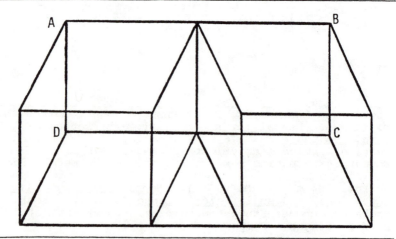

is crucial to the meaning derived from it" (p. 183). In this case, some structure or organization must be placed on the lines to determine whether one "sees" the trapezoidalpiped or the two adjacent cubes. All of the same lines are involved in both figures, but the role each line plays and the relationships among the lines are different. For example, rectangle ABCD, in Figure 3.8, can be either the top of the trapezoidalpiped or the backs of the two cubes.

One question that might be asked at this point is, As one switches back and forth between the two perceptions of the figure, what is moving? Clearly the "motion" is mental and does not require moving the lines on the page. What is changing, however, is the subject's perception and way of organizing the information on the page. The mere recognition of a two-dimensional representation as a depiction of a three-dimensional object, such as understanding three-dimensional drawings in textbooks, requires the use of this type of spatial orientation skill. None of the lines in Figure 3.8 stand up from the page to create a three-dimensional object. However, experience with two-dimensional representations of three-dimensional figures allows one to "see" the figure in a three-dimensional way.

Reorganized-whole tasks that include *multiple representations* require that the subject apprehend the change that has occurred between two representations. An example of a task that shows more than one view of an object is included in Figure 3.9. In his review of early research on spatial skills, McGee (1979) stated that by 1950 Thurstone had isolated this skill and had "asserted that it represented the ability to recognize the identity of an object when it was seen from different angles" (p. 892).

*Part of Field.* This class of spatial orientation skills is concerned with the relationship of part of a representation to the whole field, either presented visually or imagined. The two kinds of tasks within this category are to *find part of a whole* and to *fit part into the whole*. Although they seem to be opposites of one another, these skills operate together in some problems.

In *find part of a whole* tasks, the entire representation is given visually and the subject is asked to locate a particular part of it, such as a line or simpler figure. Many children's magazines include puzzles requiring that the child find the hidden animals or faces in the picture. An example of this type is shown in Figure 3.10. Asking students to identify or work with part of a complex drawing in geometry also requires use of this skill. In the Hidden Figures Test (Ekstrom, French, & Harmon, 1976; see example in Figure 3.11), a series of complex abstract

Figure 3.9   Multiple-representation

Two sample items from a spatial-orientation test.  As
the position of the boat changes with respect to the
background when we go from the upper to the lower
picture in each item, which alternative symbol should
show what the change is like?  The dot in each
alternative answer indicates the position of the prow of
the boat in the upper picture, and the rectangle
indicates the position of the boat in the lower picture.

From the Guilford-Zimmerman Aptitude Survey, Part V,
Spatial Orientation.  Copyright (c) 1947.  Sheridan
Psychological Services, Inc., Orange, California.  Used
by permission.

diagrams is presented. The subject must locate and identify which one
of five simpler shapes is embedded in each diagram.

The ability to complete the Hidden Figures Test has generated
controversy in the literature. This test was originally designed as a flexi-
bility of closure test in the Educational Testing Service's kit of factor-
referenced cognitive tests. It has been associated with personality traits
and success in other areas and has been considered an indication of a
consistent pervasive cognitive style called field independence. Witkin,
Moore, Goodenough, and Cox (1975) felt that success on this task represents "the extent to which the person perceives part of a field as discrete
from the surrounding field or the extent to which organization of the
prevailing field determines perception of its components; or to put it in
everyday terminology, the extent to which the person perceives analyti-
cally" (p. 18). Other researchers, however, have indicated that the test

Figure 3.10   Task for finding parts of a whole in a drawing

In this picture, find the heads of a goose, a rabbit, and a cat.  Also, a frog, teacup, flashlight, toothbrush, key, light bulb, horse, scissors, shoe, fish, bell, spool of thread, an ax, apple, ant, and a slice of bread.

Bell, A. (1980).  The hidden picture "The ten o'clock scholar."  Highlights for Children, 35(5), 10. Columbus, Ohio.  Copyright (c) 1980.  Used by permission.

Figure 3.11   Diagram for finding parts of a whole in
the Hidden Figures Test
_____

This is a test of your ability to tell which one of
five simple figures can be found in a more complex
pattern.

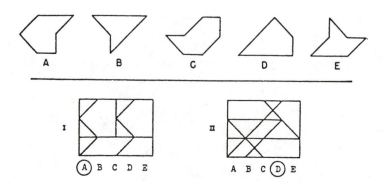

From Ekstrom, R. B., French, J. W., & Harmon, H. H.
(1976).   Manual for kit of factor-referenced cognitive
tests (p. 21).   Princeton, NJ:   Educational Testing
Service.   Copyright (c) 1862, 1975 by Educational
Testing Service.   Reprinted by permission.

should be classified among the spatial skill tasks (McGee, 1979; Sherman, 1967, 1974). Sherman (1967) argued that the "key measures of
. . . [the field-independence] construct do not appear differentiable
from the spatial factors . . . [and] the term analytical consequently implies unwarranted generality, especially since the construct appears unrelated to the verbal area" (pp. 297–298).

 *Fit part into the whole* requires that the subject recognize how a
part of a visual representation fits into the whole picture. The subject
might be shown part of a picture and be asked to identify what the
complete picture would be, such as in the puzzle task presented in
Figure 3.12, which shows part of a pair of eggbeaters. Structure is put
on the lines only when the whole picture is "understood" as part of a
pair of eggbeaters. Until that moment of understanding occurs, the
picture appears to be random lines. Maps of parts of cities, states, and
the like also require that the person reading them comprehend how the

Figure 3.12   Puzzle test for fitting a part into the whole

Answer:   egg beaters

map, which is a pictorial representation of only part of a region, fits into the entire surrounding area.

The Gestalt Completion Test (Ekstrom et al., 1976) is an example of a test of this skill (see Figure 3.13). It was originally designed as a speed of closure test in the Educational Testing Service's kit of factor-referenced cognitive tests. Ekstrom et al. indicate that one strategy for solving this test required "restructuring the stimulus perception" (p. 25). In the test, part of the representation of the object is shown to the subject, who is to "see" or mentally organize the information in order to understand what the completed representation would be.

One strategy for completing jigsaw puzzles demonstrates how these two part of field skills work together. A piece of the puzzle is first selected and examined. This step suggests the use of the *fit part into the whole* skill, since the picture on the individual piece needs to be recognized and understood as being, say, the front paw of a dog. Then the task becomes one of finding where the piece fits. This suggests using the

Figure 3.13  Problems for fitting a part into the whole
in the Gestalt Completion Test

This is a test of your ability to see a whole picture
even though it is not completely drawn.  You are to use
your imagination to fill in the missing parts.

Look at each incomplete picture and try to see what it
is.  On the line under each picture, write a word or
two to describe it.

Try the sample pictures below:

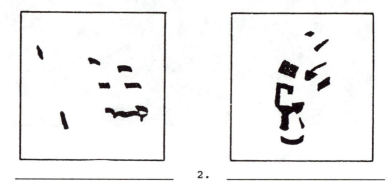

1.  _____    2.  _____

Picture 1 is a flag and picture 2 is a hammer head.

From Ekstrom, R. B., French, J. W., & Harmon, H. H.
(1976).  Manual for kit of factor-referenced cognitive
tests (p. 27).  Princeton, NJ:  Educational Testing
Service.  Copyright (c) 1962, 1975 by Educational
Testing Service.  Reprinted by permission.

*find part of a whole* skill, since examination of the completed picture
determines where in the puzzle the piece should be placed.

McGee (1979) also attempted to classify the spatial factors identified by other researchers. He found that some authors distinguished a
third spatial factor, other than spatial visualization or orientation,
which was often referred to as spatial relations. Some scholars did not
distinguish spatial relations from spatial orientation because the only
criterion they used for classification was the perception of the object as a
whole. Often spatial relations has been measured using 2-d or 3-d rotation tasks. It appears reasonable to classify the spatial relations tasks
among the visualization skills, however, since the instructions for rotation tasks suggest mentally moving the objects rather than "re-seeing"
them.

Connor and Serbin (1980) also attempted to classify spatial skills. Through factor analysis, they found that

> the visual-spatial tests divided into two factors . . . The Cube Comparison Test, Paper Folding Test, Card Rotations Test, and DAT Space Relations Test had high loadings on . . . [one factor]. This factor represents what ETS [Educational Testing Service] has referred to as the "spatial visualization" subdivision of visual-spatial ability. . . . [The second spatial factor] had high loadings on Hidden Patterns, Gestalt Completion, and Card Rotations. This factor represents what ETS has referred to as the "closure" subdivision of visual-spatial ability. [p. 27]

This description of two spatial factors agrees in principle with the classification of visualization and orientation presented in this chapter, except for the Card Rotation Test (refer to Figure 3.2), which appeared in both factors. This is consistent with the possibility that some items on this 2-d rotation test are solved using spatial visualization skills while other items are solved using spatial orientation skills. Cooper and Shepard (1973) found that the greater the angle of rotation of the object, the longer it took for subjects to determine if it agreed with the criterion representation, particularly if the angle of rotation was more than 90° from vertical. One hypothesis is that, if the object is not turned very far (less than 90° in either direction), one can "see" whether it is the same as the criterion without moving it; in that case, using spatial orientation skills. But if the object is turned more than 90° from vertical, then it must be rotated mentally to determine if it agrees with the criterion; in that case, using spatial visualization skills.

Although details of the classification scheme presented here (refer to Figure 3.1) differ substantially from some of the literature concerning spatial skills, it does appear to capture the distinctions between the two major skill divisions — spatial visualization and spatial orientation.

## GENDER DIFFERENCES IN SPATIAL SKILLS AND MATHEMATICS PERFORMANCE

One of the major reasons spatial skills have become important to researchers in recent years is their possible relationship to gender differences in mathematics achievement. Werdelin (1961) stated that gender differences in mathematics achievement are to be found in situations where the organization and reorganization aspect of the particular task is exaggerated. Sherman (1967) stated that "space perception . . . appears to be a relevant variable to control in studies of sex differences in geometric and mathematical problem solving" (p. 290).

Researchers have repeatedly observed that, beginning at or before puberty, males tend to score higher than females on measures of spatial skills. "The question of sex-related differences pervades much of the spatial ability literature, with reports of sex-related differences in favour of males being widespread" (Rowe, 1982, p. 55). "It has been found with some consistency that boys on the average excel girls on spatial tasks [and] that the spatial functions mature between the ages of eleven and fifteen" (Fruchter, 1954, p. 392).

In the 1920s, Cameron (1925) found the greatest discrepancy between secondary-level males and females on a test in which students had to sketch surfaces obtained by cutting geometric solids in various ways. Only 28% of the females were above the median for the males on this task, although no gender differences existed in overall mathematics achievement. One of the reports of the National Longitudinal Study of Mathematics Achievement (NLSMA) (McLeod & Kilpatrick, 1971) indicated gender differences in favor of tenth-grade males on several space-related tasks. The national norms of the Space Relations portion of the Differential Aptitude Test (Bennett et al., 1973) show gender differences in favor of males starting in Grade 8 and continuing through Grade 12. Sherman (1974) tested college psychology students and found significant differences between females and males on a test of spatial visualization, with males scoring higher. However, Linn and Petersen (1985), in a recent meta-analysis of studies of spatial skills, found gender differences for "tasks requiring skill in using kinesthetic cues and in speed of mental rotation, but not on spatial visualization tasks which require analytic processes to select and apply strategies to complex problems" (p. 2).

It may be, as Fennema (1980) has hypothesized, that the relationship between mathematics achievement and spatial skills, particularly spatial visualization, is quite indirect. This relationship also may tend to be different for females and males. In addition, the spatial component may play a different role in the intellectual functioning for each gender. Schonberger (1976) found that the correlation between problem solving and spatial visualization was higher for females than for males in her study of Grade 7 students. She concluded that "if girls, as a group, are less able to visualize the transformations involved in spatial tasks and more often resort to reasoning about the figures, then the cognitive processes used in solving spatial items would be more like those used in solving mathematics problems for girls than for boys" (p. 189).

It is possible that other factors that influence the development of gender differences in mathematics achievement also may be related to spatial skill. For example, Hilton and Berglund (1974) hypothesized that gender differences in mathematics achievement were due, at least in part, to gender-typed interests. As Schonberger (1976) put it, "According to Mitchelmore's (1975) survey of cross-cultural research, groups who hunt and wander have more highly developed spatial skills than those who farm. If boys in our [United States] culture wander more in their play than girls, this could be a cause of the sex differences in spatial ability" (p. 43).

Much research has been done to establish that gender differences exist in spatial skill, beginning in adolescence. In addition, many studies have shown that gender differences exist in many mathematics tasks. These two bodies of literature, along with the positive correlations often found between mathematics and spatial skills, have led many to speculate that the gender differences found in mathematics achievement may be due at least in part to differences in spatial skill.

The relationship of spatial skills to gender differences in mathematics and mathematics-related fields is, in fact, often assumed. For example, results from a study, originally reported in a popular science magazine, were reprinted in the *New York Times* and the *San Diego Union*. The study was described as follows:

> The 58 Harvard students began by taking a test that measured their "spatial skills." The women did worse than the men, as expected. Beyond puberty, women consistently score lower than men on this sort of test, which involves tasks such as imagining how an object would appear if it were rotated 90 degrees. Then some of the male and female students spent 5 hours apiece playing two shoot-'em-up video games, Targ and Battle Zone.
>
> Afterward, everyone took another spatial skills test. The men's scores didn't change significantly; neither did the scores of the women in the control group. But the women who played video games improved dramatically. They scored as well as the men.
>
> Are video games, then, the answer to that long-sought educational goal–improving women's spatial skills to ready them for careers in science and engineering? ["Gameswomanship," 1984, p. 7, 10]

The popular notion that spatial skills, presumably of all kinds, should be taught to females, in an attempt to narrow the gap in mathematics performance, needs to be examined. Actual data establishing that link are scarce. Do spatial skills contribute to performance? Do spatial skills help males, more than females, to learn mathematics? Do differences in spatial skill levels account for some of the gender differences in mathematics? Many aspects of the role that spatial skills might play in mathematics performance for males and females still need to be explored. The fundamental question is, If spatial skills do relate to mathematics, *how* and *why* do they contribute to performance in mathematics; further, if there is such a contribution, is it different for males and females?

To date, much of the gender-difference research has attempted to identify only overall differences between genders. Fennema (1982), offering direction for future research, stated, "We should quit generalizing about females [or males], but become more specific in our work. We know that all females do not have trouble with mathematics. Can we identify characteristics of females [and males] who do have trouble?" (p. 3). She suggested that researchers identify characteristics that may relate to mathematics achievement.

Because the range of achievement is so broad, for both females and males, research into possible gender differences related to spatial skills needs to be expanded. Research needs to continue to identify possible *overall* differences in mathematics performance between females and males which are related to spatial skill. However, research also needs to examine possible differences in mathematics performance within each gender related to level of spatial skill. For example, do females with highly developed spatial skills perform the same in mathematics as females with poor spatial skills? In addition, research needs to examine the mathematics performance of females and males with comparable spatial skills. For example, do females and males with poor spatial skills solve mathematics problems similarly? It is also important to examine whether or not the mathematics performance pattern for each gender, related to level of spatial skill, is the same for both genders. In other words, interactions between gender and spatial skill level need to be explored as well.

## SPATIAL SKILLS AND MATHEMATICS

Many hypotheses have been suggested to explain how and why spatial skills relate to mathematics performance. Smith (1964) proposed that "spatial abilities may be involved in the perception and assimilation of patterns, either in the structure of geometric figures or in the more general structure of mathematical symbolism. Conceptual thinking may involve abstraction and generalization in terms of configurations or gestalt-qualitäten rather than in terms of words" (p. 125). Schonberger (1980) stated that "the use of charts, diagrams, and graphs in all branches of mathematics argues for the logic of this connection between 'spatial ability' and mathematics" (p. 189).

Although there is ample speculation about how spatial skills and mathematics are related, and problem-solving processes in mathematics have been investigated from many perspectives, few researchers have attempted to identify processes used to solve mathematics problems that might be related to spatial skills. Two research studies will be discussed, however, that have attempted to examine the role of spatial skills in mathematics and to identify any gender-related differences.

## Middle School Study of Spatial Visualization Skill

The first study was a three-year longitudinal study of middle school students, Grades 6 through 8 (see Fennema & Tartre, 1985). The purpose of this study was to examine how students with discrepant spatial visualization and verbal skills translated mathematics problems into pictures and used those pictures to solve the problems.

Students were given the Space Relations portion of the Differential Aptitude Test, described earlier as a 2-d to 3-d transformation, spatial visualization (SV) test (refer to Figure 3.5); and a vocabulary test to measure verbal skill. Subjects were chosen who were high in one skill and low in the other. This process yielded four groups: high-SV/low-verbal females, high-SV/low-verbal males, low-SV/high-verbal females, and low-SV/high-verbal males. These students were interviewed during each of the three years; each time, they were given mathematics problems and asked to draw pictures that they could use to solve the problems. Examples of problems used in this study are included in Figure 3.14.

Although no overall difference between the two spatial skill level groups was found for the number of problems solved correctly, differences in patterns of behavior were detected. When asked to tell about the problem before solving it, students who were low in spatial visualization and high in verbal skills (low SV/high verbal) tended to demonstrate their higher verbal skill by responding with more detailed descriptions of the relevant information in the problems. Students high in spatial visualization and low in verbal skills (high SV/low verbal) tended to do a more complete job of translating the problem into a picture and also tended to have more detailed information on the picture if they got the correct answer.

It was discovered that, although the low-SV/high-verbal females tended to give more relevant verbal information when asked to explain what the problem was, they consistently put less information into their

Figure 3.14    Sample problems from the middle school
study

PROBLEM FROM YEAR II

PR1.    A baby came to a staircase; climbed up five
steps, climbed down three steps, and then climbed up six
steps and was at the top.    How many steps were in the
staircase?

Answer:    <u>8</u>

PROBLEM USED YEAR II AND III AND ITS ACCOMPANYING HINTS

PR9.    Four people ordered a pizza.    One person ate 1/3
of the pizza and left before anyone else had a piece.
The rest of the pizza was divided equally among the
other three people.    How much of the whole pizza did
each of these three get?

Answer:    <u>2/9</u>

HINTS

H1                        H2                            H3

pictures and tended to have the lowest mean of the four groups for
number of correct solutions. However, the low-SV/high-verbal males
tended to have the highest mean of the four groups for number of
correct solutions across all three years of the study.

   To begin the solution of each problem, the students were asked to
translate the information in the problem into a useful picture, on their
own. Those whose pictures were insufficient to solve the problem were
given assistance in the form of progressively more detailed hints for each
problem. An examination of the difference between the initial transla-
tion picture that they drew and the amount of information they had
when they finally solved the problem correctly (perhaps the result of a

more detailed hint) gave an estimate of how much help was needed to draw a picture complete enough to solve the problem. The two female groups were much more discrepant than the male groups on this variable. The low-SV/high-verbal females appeared to need the most help, while the high-SV/low-verbal females needed the least amount of help of the four groups.

The students in this study were also given mathematics achievement tests in Grades 6 and 8. In order to see how these groups scored in relation to the population of students in their respective grades, $z$-scores for the groups were computed, based on the entire sixth-grade population in those schools and a random sampling of their eighth-grade populations. The two female groups' scores were approximately the same as the sixth-grade population, with both means very close to $-.05$. By eighth grade, the high-SV/low-verbal females' mean had not changed much (.08), but the low-SV/high-verbal females' mean had dropped in relation to the rest of the population ($-.56$). The two male groups' means remained relatively stable during this time. The low-SV/high-verbal males scored the highest both years (.33 and .21, respectively), while the high-SV/low-verbal males scored among the lowest both times ($-.19$ and $-.23$).

## High School Study of Spatial Orientation Skill

The purpose of this second study was to explore the role of spatial orientation (SO) skill in the solution of mathematics problems and to identify possible associated gender differences. SO skill was measured for this study by using the Gestalt Completion Test (Ekstrom et al., 1976), described earlier as a part-of-field SO task (refer to Figure 3.13). From a random sample of tenth graders tested, students were selected to be interviewed based upon scores on the SO test. This interview sample included males and females who scored in the upper or lower third of the distribution on the test. This created four groups: high-SO males ($N=14$), high-SO females ($N=13$), low-SO males ($N=13$), and low-SO females ($N=17$).

The 57 students in this sample were then given a mathematics achievement test, and the means and standard deviations in scores for the four groups are shown in Table 3.1. What is striking about these data is that the low-SO females appeared to have a substantially lower achievement mean than did the other three groups.

The students were asked to solve 10 mathematics problems and to explain their solutions, during individual interviews. Their solution processes were coded and analyzed according to behaviors that were hy-

Table 3.1    Means and Standard Deviations for
             Mathematics Achievement

| SEX | SO GROUP | MEAN[a] | SD |
|-----|----------|---------|-----|
| FEMALES | High | 23.08 | 8.41 |
|         | Low  | 16.12 | 6.47 |
| MALES | High | 23.00 | 8.49 |
|       | Low  | 23.23 | 10.72 |

[a]Total possible=48.

pothesized as being manifestations of SO skill. Several of the behavior
categories were chosen for their obvious spatial component, such as
drawing a picture (drew picture), adding marks to a figure (added
marks), or indicating that objects were moved mentally (mental movement). Other behavior categories appeared to have a verbal component,
such as keeping track by writing verbal information (wrote).

Some of the categories were related to the problem-solving process,
such as getting the correct answer or indicating that they had done a
similar problem (done like). Other categories indicated that the student
had encountered some difficulty in the solution process, such as not
understanding what the problem was asking (misunderstood problem),
demonstrating an inability to analyze the problem or picture, or not
changing a mind-set that would provide an incomplete or inaccurate
solution (failure to break set). For one of the problems, a hint was given
to students who could not reach a solution. Whether or not it was
necessary to give the hint for that problem was coded. For some of the
problems, students were asked to estimate their answers before comput-
ing them. The estimate error category indicated the proportion of the
difference between the correct answer and the estimate given by the
student, a figure calculated by using the following formula:

$$\left| \ 1 \ - \ \frac{\text{(student response)}}{\text{(correct answer)}} \ \right|$$

Both geometric and nongeometric problems were included in this
study. In addition, the problems were presented visually (using a concrete or pictorial representation), nonvisually (exclusively with written
words), and also with just a visual framework (a grid) from which to
work (see Figure 3.15 for this framework presented problem and its
accompanying hint).

Figure 3.15   Problem presented using a framework origin

6. Draw a square that has area equal to 2 square inches
   using four of the points below as vertices (corners).

|←1 inch →|

Explain how you know that the area of your figure is
2 square inches.

(Hint:   You have used horizontal and vertical lines.
Is there any other alternative?)

Answer:

*Overall Between-Gender Differences.* No significant difference was found overall between males and females in SO skill or in mathematics achievement. No overall gender difference was found in the number of correct answers. Two significant differences were found in how females and males solved the problems.

First, males, more than females, focused on the use of a complement to help solve problems involving representations of three-dimensional objects. An everyday example of use of the complement would be to figure out how much pie is left in a pan by judging how much has been removed and then subtracting that amount from the whole pie. Research has suggested that males tend to perform better than females on spatial tasks involving three-dimensional figures (Clements, 1981). In this case, however, the use of complement category described the solution strategy used, not one that was necessary or even sufficient for successful problem solution.

The other overall gender difference found was for the use of writing. For some problems, one appropriate solution strategy was to keep a written record of information and/or answers. For those problems, females, more than males, tended to write the information down. As was the case for the other significant difference, however, writing information down was not necessary or sufficient for correct problem solution.

Both of these differences are consistent with other gender-difference research, but constructing a value judgment concerning the benefit or detriment of using these strategies is unwarranted.

*Within-Group Differences.* As was stated before, examining gender differences overall does not tell the whole story and can be misleading. It is as important to look for within-group differences, both within each gender by spatial group and within each spatial group by gender. For the spatial orientation study, that meant addressing the following questions:

1. Do high-SO males solve the problems differently than low-SO males?
2. Do high-SO females solve the problems differently than low-SO females?
3. Do low-SO females solve the problems differently than low-SO males?
4. Do high-SO females solve the problems differently than high-SO males?

Table 3.2 summarizes the significant differences found between spatial groups within each gender, after mathematics achievement had

**Table 3.2** Summary of Significant[a] Spatial Orientation Group Differences Within Each Gender

| BEHAVIOR CATEGORY | SO GROUP WITH HIGHER MEAN |
|---|---|
| FEMALES | |
| *Correct answer* | |
| Visually presented | High |
| Non-Geometric | High |
| *Correct partial process* | |
| Geometric | High |
| *Done line* | |
| Non-Geometric | High |
| *Drew picture* | |
| Combined | High |
| *Failure to break set* | |
| Visually presented | Low |
| *Mental movement* | |
| Geometric | High |
| Combined | High |
| MALES | |
| *Hint given* | |
| Framework presented | Low |

[a]$p < .05$.

been covaried out. Only one significant difference was found between the two male SO groups, namely, the low-SO males received the hint for the framework presented problem (refer to Figure 3.15) more often than the high-SO males. For females, however, several significant differences were found between the high-SO and low-SO groups. Most notable among them were that the high-SO females were more likely than the low-SO females to get the correct answer, for visually presented and nongeometric problems. High-SO females were also more likely to be able to construct at least part of a mathematically sound solution to the geometric problems (correct partial process). These differences along with differences in mental movement (geometric and combined) and drew picture suggest, thus, that the SO group differences were more pronounced between the female groups than between male groups.

No significant gender differences between the two low-SO groups were found; however, there were two found within the high-SO groups: estimate error (analytic) and correct answer (visually presented). The high-SO males had a higher mean than the high-SO females for esti-mate errors, which meant that the estimates of the answer given by the high-SO males before working analytic problems were less accurate than those given by high-SO females (see Figure 3.16 for a problem of this type). In fact, the high-SO males had the highest mean of the four groups, while the high-SO females had the lowest. Could this mean that spatial and analytic or language skills tend to be more separate for high-SO males than for high-SO females? It is possible that a tendency to-ward specialization of skills might actually interfere with the necessary integration of many problem-solving skills. For example, this separation of skills could be manifested by students relying exclusively on analytic or algorithmic processes to solve a problem rather than also checking that the solution is intuitively reasonable.

The other significant gender difference between the high-SO groups was for getting correct answers. The high-SO females correctly solved the visually presented problems more often than the high-SO males (see Figure 3.17 for an example of this type of problem). It is possible that this difference is related to the skill separation issue as well. It may be argued that successful problem solution for these visually presented problems is linked to the ability to integrate spatial and ana-lytic or language skills. If these skills tend to be more separate for males than females, then high-SO males might have more trouble integrating the skills needed to solve the problems.

*Profiles of the Four Groups.*   As the high school study progressed, it became apparent that there were behaviors that were more pronounced for one group than for any of the others. The profiles that follow sum-marize each group's characteristics.

Figure 3.16   Estimate-error (analytic) problem from high
              school study
_____

7.a. Without calculating, how many different groups of
     fruit do you think can be made using one or more of
     the following fruit:  an apple, a pear, an orange,
     a lemon, and a grapefruit?

  b. Find how many groups there are.

Answer:   31
_____

Figure 3.17   Visually presented problem from high school
study

2. Without counting, do you think there are more
   squares, or more rectangles that are not squares, in
   the figure?

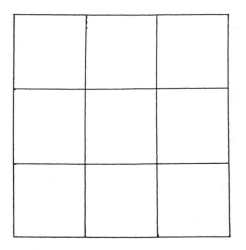

How many of each can you find?

Answer:   14 squares, 22 rectangles

The *low-SO male group* had a higher mean for correct answers to visually presented problems than the high-SO male group. The low-SO male group also had the highest mean for mathematics achievement, although this difference was not statistically significant. This group did not seem to be handicapped by its low level of spatial orientation skill.

The framework presented problem (refer to Figure 3.15) was the only problem for which the low-SO males had the lowest mean of the four groups for getting the correct answer without a hint. However, for this problem a hint was sometimes given. To examine the value of the hint in ultimately getting a correct solution, a new category was created. Based upon this new variable, it was learned that 80% of the low-SO males who received the hint were successful in getting a correct answer. Their ability to benefit from help in solving mathematics problems, as demonstrated by their effective use of the hint, may explain in part their good performance in mathematics achievement.

The *high-SO male group* was neither the highest- nor lowest-scoring group for most of the behavior categories. Both low-SO males and high-SO females scored as high or higher than the high-SO males on the mathematics achievement test as well as on the number of correct answers for all of the problems combined. Only 20% of those high-SO males who were given the hint for the framework presented problem were able to use it to solve the problem. Therefore, the results presented here do not support the hypothesis that spatial skill is involved in helping males, more than females, achieve well in mathematics.

The *high-SO female group* scored as well as any other group on mathematics achievement, and it had the highest mean of the four groups for number of correct answers for all of the problems combined. Fifty percent of the high-SO females were able to use the framework-problem hint when it was given to them. They also had the lowest mean for the estimate errors. They appeared to demonstrate an integration of spatial and analytic skills that may have contributed to their performance in solving mathematics problems.

The *low-SO female group* scored lower than the other groups on mathematics achievement. This group also had the lowest means of the four groups for many behavior categories, including getting correct answers (for every problem type and every problem, except the framework problem), using a correct partial process (for nonvisually presented and geometric problems), mental movement (geometric), and use of algorithms. They had the highest means for failure to break set (visually and nonvisually presented, geometric and nongeometric problems), and misunderstanding the problem (visually and nonvisually presented and nongeometric problems). In addition, over 75% of the low-SO females needed the hint for the framework problem, but only 23% who received the hint got the correct answer. Although not all of these differences were statistically significant, the pattern was clear; the low-SO female group experienced more trouble doing the mathematics problems than any other group. (See Tartre, 1985, for a more complete description of this study.)

## Conclusions

Both the middle school and high school studies were concerned with exploring the role of a particular spatial skill and identifying any associated gender differences. The findings suggest a reexamination of the hypothesis, mentioned frequently in the literature, that males do better than females in mathematics because of a higher level of spatial skill. It appears clear from both of these studies that examining differences overall between genders does not tell the whole story.

The conjecture that higher spatial skill level (either spatial visualization or spatial orientation) for males has contributed to their better achievement in mathematics was not supported by these studies. High-spatial and low-spatial males in both studies either performed equally well or the low-spatial males scored higher than the high-spatial males on mathematics achievement and on most performance-related variables. Low-spatial males in both studies did not seem to be hampered by their low level of spatial skill. They were able to make use of other skills, such as use of help given to them, to solve mathematics problems.

Spatial skill level does seem to be more related to mathematics performance for females than for males. In both of these studies, females who scored high on a test of spatial skill achieved as well as, and in some cases much better than, the male groups on mathematics achievement and measures of many other strategic variables. However, females who scored low on a test of spatial skill experienced difficulty in accomplishing many tasks involved in solving mathematics problems. They needed help more often than others and yet, when they received assistance, were not very successful in making use of it. They did not appear to be as able to draw upon other skills to compensate as were low-spatial males.

Perhaps what has appeared to be a fundamental difference between males and females in spatial skill level as it relates to doing mathematics has instead been a wide-ranging problem for a specific group of people who tended to be female. If a small group of females do substantially poorer than the rest of the population, this would have the effect of pulling down the mean of females overall and would cloud the issue of the existence of overall gender differences.

Spatial skills can be used in specific ways for many mathematics tasks. In the case of gender differences in mathematics, however, spatial skill level may only be an indicator that could be used to identify people, more often female than male, who may lack many skills or other characteristics important to being successful in doing mathematics.

## REFERENCES

Bennett, G. K., Seashore, H. G., & Wesman, A. G. (1973). *Differential aptitude tests: Administrator's handbook.* New York: Psychological Corporation.

Cameron, A. E. (1925). A comparative study of the mathematical ability of boys and girls in secondary schools. *British Journal of Psychology, 16*(1), 29–49.

Clements, M. A. (1981, April). *Spatial ability, visual imagery, and mathemati-*

*cal learning.* Paper presented at the annual meeting of the American Educational Research Association, Los Angeles.

Clements, M. A., & Wattanawaha, N. (1978). The classification of spatial tasks suitable for the classroom. In D. Williams (Ed.), *Learning and applying mathematics* (pp. 432–447). Melbourne, Victoria: Australian Association of Mathematics Teachers.

Connor, J. M., & Serbin, L. A. (1980). *Mathematics, visual-spatial ability, and sex roles* (Final Report). Washington, D.C.: National Institute of Education (DHEW). (ERIC Document Reproduction Service No. ED 205 305)

Cooper, L. A., & Shepard, R. N. (1973). Chronometric studies of the rotation of mental images. In W. G. Chase (Ed.), *Visual information processing* (pp. 75–176). New York: Academic Press.

Ekstrom, R. B., French, J. W., & Harmon, H. H. (1976). *Manual for kit of factor-referenced cognitive tests.* Princeton, NJ: Educational Testing Service.

Fennema, E. (1975). Spatial ability, mathematics, and the sexes. In E. Fennema (Ed.), *Mathematics learning: What research says about sex differences* (pp. 33–44). Columbus, OH: ERIC Clearinghouse for Science, Mathematics, and Environmental Education.

Fennema, E. (1980). Sex-related differences in mathematics achievement: Where and why. In L. H. Fox, L. Brody, & D. Tobin (Eds.), *Women and the mathematical mystique* (pp. 73–93). Baltimore: Johns Hopkins University Press.

Fennema, E. (1982, March). *Women and mathematics: New directions for future research.* Paper presented at the annual meeting of the American Educational Research Association, New York.

Fennema, E., & Sherman, J. (1977). Sex-related differences in mathematics achievement, spatial visualization, and affective factors. *American Educational Research Journal, 14*(1), 51–71.

Fennema, E., & Tartre, L. A. (1985). The use of spatial visualization in mathematics by girls and boys. *Journal for Research in Mathematics Education, 16*(3), 184–106.

Fruchter, B. (1954). Measurement of spatial abilities: History and background. *Education and Psychological Measurement, 14,* 387–395.

Gameswomanship. (1984, Jan/Feb). *Science,* 84, 7, 10.

Hilton, T. L., & Berglund, G. W. (1974). Sex differences in mathematics achievement: A longitudinal study. *Journal of Educational Research, 67*(50), 231–236.

Kersh, M. E., & Cook, K. H. (1979). *Improving mathematics ability and attitude: A manual.* Seattle: University of Washington, Mathematics Learning Institute.

Linn, M. C., & Petersen, A. C. (1985). Emergence and characterization of gender differences in spatial ability: A meta-analysis. *Child Development, 56,* 1479–1498.

McGee, M. G. (1979). Human spatial abilities: Psychometric studies and environmental, genetic, hormonal, and neurological influences. *Psychological Bulletin, 86*(5), 889–918.

McLeod, G. K., & Kilpatrick, J. (1971). Patterns of mathematics achievement in grade 10: Y-population. In J. W. Wilson, L. S. Cahen, & E. G. Begle (Eds.), *NLSMA Report #14*. Stanford, CA: Stanford University Press.

Mitchelmore, M. C. (1975, May). *Cross-cultural research on concepts of space and geometry*. Paper presented at the Research Workshop on Space and Geometry, Georgia.

Rosser, R. A. (1980). *Acquisition of spatial concepts in relation to age and sex*. Tucson: University of Arizona, Department of Educational Psychology.

Rowe, M. I. (1982). *Training in spatial skill requiring two- and three-dimensional thinking and different levels of internalization, and the retention and transfer of these skills*. Unpublished doctoral dissertation, Monash University, Melbourne, Victoria, Australia.

Schonberger, A. K. (1976). *The interrelationship of sex, visual-spatial abilities, and mathematical problem-solving ability in grade seven*. Unpublished doctoral dissertation, University of Wisconsin–Madison.

Schonberger, A. K. (1980). Sex-related issues in mathematics education. In M. M. Lindquist (Ed.), *Selected issues in mathematics education* (pp. 185–198). Berkeley: McCutchan.

Shepard, R. N. (1978, February). The mental image. *American Psychologist, 33*(2), 125–137.

Sherman, J. A. (1967). Problems of sex differences in space perception and aspects of intellectual functioning. *Psychological Review, 74*, 290–299.

Sherman, J. A. (1974). Field articulation, sex, spatial visualization, dependence, practice, laterality of the brain, and birth order. *Perceptual and Motor Skills, 38*, 1223–1235.

Smith, I. M. (1964). *Spatial ability: Its educational and social significance*. London: University of London Press.

Tartre, L. A. (1985). The role of spatial orientation skill in the solution of mathematics problems and associated sex-related differences (Doctoral dissertation, University of Wisconsin–Madison, 1984). *Dissertation Abstracts International, 46*: 94–95.

Werdelin, I. (1961). *Geometrical ability and the space factors in boys and girls*. Lund, Sweden: C. W. K. Cleerup.

Witkin, H. A., Moore, C. A., Goodenough, D. R., & Cox, P. W. (1975). *Field-dependent and field-independent cognitive styles and their educational implications* (Research Bulletin 75-24). Princeton, NJ: Educational Testing Service.

Wittrock, M. C. (1974). A generative model of mathematics learning. *Journal for Research in Mathematics Education, 5*(4), 181–196.

# 4 Internal Influences on Gender Differences in Mathematics

MARGARET R. MEYER
MARY SCHATZ KOEHLER

*In this chapter, Meyer and Koehler provide an extensive review of studies that have examined the link between psychosocial variables and achievement in mathematics. Two different models are discussed: the Autonomous Learning Behaviors model and the Model of Academic Choice. Two widely used measures of affective variables (the Fennema-Sherman Mathematics Attitude Scales and the Mathematics Attribution Scale) are described in some detail. Finally, the results of two longitudinal studies, whose conclusions are based on both quantitative and descriptive data, are presented. Each attempts to specify the relationships between affective variables and cognitive outcomes.*

Students bring more to the mathematics classroom than just their books and pencils. They also bring a wide assortment of skills, prior knowledge, work habits, attitudes, and beliefs. These variables interact with what goes on in the classroom and influence students' learning of mathematics. This chapter will examine certain attitudes and beliefs that are part of students' internal belief system. Along with definitions of the components of this belief system, ways of measuring these components will be considered. Two studies involving internal beliefs will be summarized to see what gender differences exist on these variables and to see how they relate to mathematics achievement and participation for females and males.

## THE INTERNAL BELIEF SYSTEM

There are many attitudes and beliefs that have been studied in relation to gender differences in mathematics achievement and participation for females and males. The ones that will be discussed here are those that have shown the most consistent links: confidence, perception of the usefulness of mathematics, the sex-role congruency of mathematics, fear of success, and attributional style. Because these variables interact with and influence each other, in combination they form an internal belief system. An examination of these components and their interaction helps in understanding why gender differences in mathematics occur.

### Confidence

In a review of affective variables, Reyes (1984) identified confidence as one of the most important affective variables. It is one part of self-concept and has to do with how sure a student is of his or her ability to learn new mathematics and to do well on mathematical tasks. Confidence influences a student's willingness to approach new material and to persist when the material becomes difficult. Despite the immediate difficulty of the task, the student persists when she is confident that a solution will be found or that the material will be understood. Confidence in mathematics is also reflected by continued participation in mathematics course taking and career aspirations in quantitative fields.

Some extensive research on the variable of confidence as it relates to mathematics is found in the Fennema-Sherman studies (Fennema & Sherman, 1977, 1978; Sherman & Fennema, 1977). One purpose of these studies was to collect information about the relationship between affective variables, including confidence, and mathematics achievement and to document gender differences in these relationships. Student confidence was measured by the confidence subscale of the Fennema-Sherman Mathematics Attitude Scales (Fennema & Sherman, 1976). (A detailed discussion of these scales will follow in a later section.) Students were also given a test of mathematics achievement. Results showed that, when a gender difference in mathematics achievement in favor of males was found, it was accompanied by a gender difference in confidence, also in favor of males. Gender differences in confidence were also found even when there were no differences in achievement. At both the middle school and high school levels, females reported lower levels of confidence in their ability to learn mathematics than did males. In addition, confidence was more strongly correlated with achievement ($r = .40$) than was any other affective variable measured in the study.

A follow-up study by Sherman (1979) collected longitudinal data on students from the original Fennema-Sherman sample. Cognitive and affective data from Grade 9 were used to predict mathematics perfor-mance in each of the next three years. While cognitive variables were the strongest predictors overall, confidence in learning mathematics was the strongest affective predictor for females in geometry. In addition, confidence was significantly related to achievement in Grade 11 for females.

Researchers have also investigated the relationship of confidence to gender difference in mathematics participation. Armstrong and Price (1982) surveyed a sample of high school seniors in an attempt to identify the most important variables affecting students' participation in mathe-matics. For the females, confidence in learning mathematics was the second most important variable, after perceived usefulness of mathe-matics; it was the third variable listed by males. Sherman (1982) found that the highest confidence was found in those females who took the most mathematics, and that confidence was stable from Grades 9 to 12.

Lantz and Smith (1981) examined variables contributing to the decision of high school students to enroll in optional mathematics courses. They found that confidence was a factor that differentiated students who intended to elect such courses and later did enroll, from those students who intended to but did not enroll. They also found that, despite the evidence of their good grades, the females in their study gave lower estimates of their future chances of achieving a satisfactory grade in mathematics than did the males. In a longitudinal study, Eccles (1983) found that perceived math ability was correlated more highly with the intention to take more mathematics than was an objective measure of math ability. One of the few gender differences found in that study indicated that females had a less positive self-concept of their mathematics ability than did males.

## Usefulness

Students' perceptions of the usefulness of mathematics, both imme-diately and in their future, is a variable that has been shown to be strongly associated with mathematics participation and achievement. As mathematics becomes optional and increasingly difficult for some students, it is unlikely that they will continue to engage in its study if they fail to see that it will be useful to them. The effect of a perception of usefulness on mathematics achievement is less obvious.

Usefulness may, in fact, influence participation on a short-term basis by increasing persistence when the material gets harder. This can be understood within the framework of the Expectancy X Value model of achievement motivation (Atkinson, 1964). In this model, motivation to engage in a given task is the product of the student's expectancy of success and his perception of the value of the task. The student's confidence, and therefore his expectancy of success, can be low, but a strong perception that mathematics is useful, and therefore valuable, will result in the motivation to continue, despite the difficulty.

A few studies have examined perceptions of usefulness relative to mathematics participation and achievement. Fennema and Sherman (1977, 1978) found that gender differences in achievement in favor of males were accompanied by a greater perception of the usefulness of mathematics on the part of males. Studies related to participation have found similar results. Pedro, Wolleat, Fennema, and Becker (1981) considered usefulness and other affective variables as predictors of plans to study high school mathematics. It was found that, after prior achievement, usefulness was the strongest single predictor for both sexes. Armstrong and Price (1982) reported that students ranked usefulness of mathematics as the most important reason in deciding to take more mathematics, while Eccles (1983) concluded that females felt that mathematics was of less value to them than did males. Lantz and Smith (1981) found that the subjective value placed on mathematics was the attitudinal variable most highly correlated with mathematics participation.

## Sex-Role Congruency

Sex-role congruency is an important influence on females' valuation of mathematics. It, too, can be interpreted within the framework of the Expectancy X Value model of achievement motivation (Atkinson, 1964). The value of mathematics to a female can be affected by whether or not she thinks studying mathematics is a sex-role–appropriate activity. If she believes mathematics is inappropriate for females, then her achievement in mathematics could result in a perception that she has not adequately fulfilled her sex role. She might also perceive that teachers and peers have lower expectations for her mathematical success because she is a female. Another possible outcome is a perception that others see her as somewhat less than feminine when she achieves in mathematics. For a school-age female, all of these perceptions can result in a belief that to participate and succeed in mathematics, she will have to pay a price. The price may well be much higher in the high school years when sex roles are salient and the judgments of peers most critical.

Sex-role congruency is not likely to be as important for males, since the prevailing stereotype is that mathematics is a male domain and therefore a very appropriate subject for male study and achievement. This stereotype has diminished somewhat in recent years, but it shows no signs of disappearing in our society.

The effects of stereotyping math as a male domain have been considered in a number of studies with varying results. Fennema and Sherman (1977, 1978) found that, on the subscale of the Fennema-Sherman Mathematics Attitude Scales (Fennema & Sherman, 1976) measuring math as a male domain, male and female responses differed significantly, with males stereotyping math more strongly than did females. More recently this result was replicated in the U.S. data from the Second International Mathematics Study (International Association for the Evaluation of Educational Achievement, 1984). Students in Grades 8 and 12 were assessed in various affective areas, including the extent to which they viewed mathematics as a male domain. Both groups held a positive view of females and mathematics, but, when the responses were separated by sex, males were much more likely to stereotype mathematics. The least stereotypic belief was held by twelfth-grade females.

Armstrong and Price (1982) reported that, for twelfth-grade females, mathematics participation was significantly correlated with a nonstereotypic perception of mathematics. Brush (1980) reported that stereotyping mathematics as a male domain was not a major predictor of either course preferences or course enrollment plans. Contrary to the usual hypothesis, Sherman (1979) found that when in the ninth grade, females who subsequently enrolled in a fourth year of theoretical mathematics were more stereotypic in their views of mathematics than were females who took less than four years of math.

These mixed results suggest that, in spite of the theoretical relevance of this variable to gender differences, it has not been useful in predicting either participation or achievement in mathematics. Perhaps it is the interaction of this belief with other variables that makes it more or less important. For example, we can hypothesize that the belief might become more or less potent as a function of age and maturity. An adolescent female might be more influenced by stereotypic beliefs than would a college-age female whose overall self-concept was more firmly established.

## Fear of Success

Fear of success was first postulated by Horner (1968) as a variable useful in explaining gender differences in the research on achievement motivation. It describes the conflict, resulting fear, and decreased performance that many women experience because of the clash they perceive between attaining success and fulfilling the female role in our society. Fear of success is the fear of the negative consequences that accompany success. Horner identified two sources for these negative consequences: (1) the individual's loss of her sense of femininity and self-esteem and (2) social rejection because of the success.

Leder (1982) investigated the relationship between fear of success (FS), mathematics performance, and course-taking intentions for males and females. She found that, for high-achieving males, high FS was associated with the intention of leaving school or taking no further mathematics. In contrast, high-achieving females who were high in FS expressed intentions to take two additional mathematics courses. In terms of performance, no relationship was found between high FS and high mathematical performance for the males. However, it appeared that the females who performed well in mathematics were also likely to be high in FS, while for others, being high in FS was incompatible with continued high performance in mathematics. Leder suggested that the females in this latter group resolved their conflict either by lowering their performance in an attempt not to appear so successful or by opting out of continued mathematics study.

As with sex-role congruency, fear of success does not seem to provide clear explanations for gender differences in mathematics. Its interaction with other beliefs could again be the key to understanding its role. Fear of success would seem to be related to sex-role congruency as described earlier. For some females, these two variables might interact to decrease the value of participation and achievement in mathematics.

### Attributional Style

The way in which a student attributes causation for success and failure is another affective variable prominent in the literature on gender differences in mathematics. According to Weiner (1974), the reasons people give for their successes and failures fall into four categories: ability, effort, task difficulty, and luck. These four causes can be classified along the dimensions of stability and locus of control, as illustrated in Figure 4.1.

Stability and locus of control of causal attributions are important because they relate to an individual's expectation for performance on similar tasks in the future. For example, if a student attributes her failure to lack of ability, then she will have little reason to expect success in the future, since ability is a stable characteristic. On the other hand, an attribution of failure to lack of effort does not preclude success in the future, since effort is within an individual's control and can be adjusted

Figure 4.1   Weiner classification of causal attributions

Locus of Control

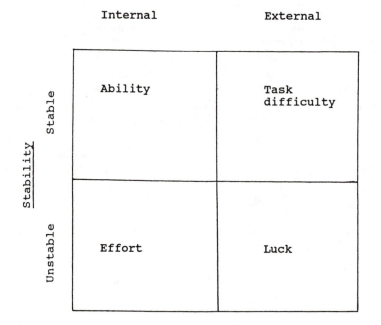

Adapted from Weiner, B. (1975).   Achievement motivation
and attribution theory.   Morristown, NJ:   General
Learning Press.

to make success possible. A student who attributes success to her ability
has every reason to expect success in the future, because ability will
remain relatively constant. An attribution of success to luck, however,
carries no such assurance, since luck by its very nature is outside of one's
control. The luck category is sometimes expanded to include other external, unstable influences. For example, an attribution to unusual help
from the teacher or other students would come under this category as
well as unusual circumstances in the environment. This expanded definition is reflected in alternate namings of the category: others or environment.

Several studies have investigated attribution patterns for males and females in mathematics. A study by Wolleat, Pedro, Becker, and Fennema (1980) compared attribution patterns with achievement scores for 647 female and 577 male secondary school students enrolled in college preparatory algebra and geometry classes in 10 high schools. Attributions for success and failure were measured by the Mathematics Attribution Scale (MAS) (Fennema, Wolleat, & Pedro, 1979). (A detailed discussion of this scale will follow in a later section.) In terms of attribution patterns, several gender differences were found. The males attributed their success experiences to ability more strongly than did the females, whereas the females attributed their success to effort more strongly than did the males. The females attributed failure experiences in mathematics, more strongly than did the males, to a lack of ability or to the difficulty of the task.

Comparisons of the subscales with sex and achievement scores yielded other gender differences. At all levels of achievement, females were more likely than were the males to attribute their success to effort. As the achievement level of the females increased, however, the extent to which they attributed success to effort decreased. For both males and females, the attribution of success to ability increased as achievement increased and the attribution of failure to low ability decreased as achievement increased.

Data from this same study were used to predict students' plans to take high school mathematics. Pedro et al. (1981) used achievement data, attribution scores from the MAS, and other attitudinal data as predictors. Achievement was included, since past mathematics achievement is one of the most important determinants of future mathematics achievement; it was entered as a control variable in the first step of a stepwise multiple regression. It was found that, for both males and females enrolled in algebra, the score for attributing success to ability was significantly related to plans to take more mathematics (females, $r = .31$; males, $r = .41$) and added significantly to regression equations predicting math plans. For females enrolled in geometry, the score for attributing failure to ability was significantly related to plans to take more mathematics ($r = .37$), and it, along with the score for attributing success to the environment ($r = .04$), added significantly to an equation predicting plans to take more mathematics courses.

Leder (1984) used a modified version of the MAS to determine whether attribution of success and failure in mathematics would be affected by the sex of the stimulus figure. That is, it was hypothesized that, if subjects read statements describing a person's performance, replacing the neutral *you* in the statement with gender-specific names like John or Anne would elicit different attributions, depending on the sex of the stimulus figure and the sex of the respondent. Maximum differences were expected when the sex of the respondent matched the sex of the stimulus figure. These hypotheses were generally not supported by the data. The sex of the stimulus figure did not affect the students' attributions of success and failure. One interesting result, however, was that, irrespective of the sex of the students and the stimulus figure, students perceived effort as the most important determinant of both success and failure in mathematics.

Fennema & Peterson (1984a, 1984b) developed an attribution scale for a study involving fourth-grade students, which tested some of the theories of the Autonomous Learning Behavior model. The ALB Mathematics Attribution Scale contains a series of questions about how important ability, effort, difficulty of task, and others (an expanded luck category) are as factors determining success and failure on high-cognitive-level mathematics problems. The scale contains five items for each of eight subscales and five choices in a Likert format for each item. In preliminary results (1984a) from this study, significant differences were found in the means for fourth-grade males and females on four of the subscales. Males were more likely than females to attribute their success to their ability and their failure to lack of effort. Females were more likely than males to attribute their success to effort and to help from others.

Attributions of success and failure in mathematics are variables that have a strong intuitive appeal, because they are both descriptive of students' understanding of past events and predictive of their future academic choices and achievement-related behaviors. However, this appeal is tempered by the complexity of the theory, which results in difficulties in measurement and interpretation of results. As these obstacles are overcome, these beliefs are likely to be of great help in understanding gender differences in mathematics.

### Summary

Several affective variables related to gender differences in mathematics have been identified. These variables are components of students' internal belief system. The foregoing discussion suggests several important questions:

> How do the components of the internal belief system interact with each other?
> What is the effect of the internal belief system?
> How does it interact with a student's cognitive abilities in mathematics?

What observable behaviors can be predicted from differences in the internal beliefs?

Are the answers to these questions the same for females and males?

Does the internal belief system help in understanding gender differences in mathematics?

Having examined the components of the internal belief system, we can begin to speculate on the answers to these questions.

## MODELS RELATING THE INTERNAL BELIEF SYSTEM TO GENDER DIFFERENCES IN MATH

Two different models have been proposed to explain the relationship between affective variables in the internal belief system and gender differences in mathematics achievement and participation: the Autonomous Learning Behaviors model (Fennema & Peterson, 1985) and the Model of Academic Choice (Eccles et al., 1985). These two differ in their focus and degree of specificity, but they are similar in their inclusion of most of the affective variables discussed earlier.

### Autonomous Learning Behaviors Model

The Autonomous Learning Behaviors (ALB) model, shown in Figure 4.2, attempts to explain causation of gender differences in achievement on mathematical tasks of high cognitive complexity. High-level tasks were chosen as the focus for two reasons: (1) because the gender differences are most apparent at this level and (2) because skill on high-level tasks is associated with problem solving, which is a major goal of mathematics learning. The model hypothesizes that gender differences on these tasks are caused by differential participation by females and males in autonomous learning behaviors (ALBs). These behaviors act as mediators among the internal belief system, external/societal influences, and the development of high-level cognitive skills.

Autonomous learning behaviors are those that characterize the autonomous learner. A student who is autonomous is one who increasingly assumes control of the learning process. That student *chooses* to engage in high-level mathematical tasks and prefers to *work independently* on them. When a task proves to be difficult, the autonomous learner *persists* with the task. A result of choosing, working independently, and persisting with high-level tasks is that the learner experiences *success* on those tasks. This success strengthens the internal belief system and, in

Figure 4.2  Autonomous Learning Behavior Model

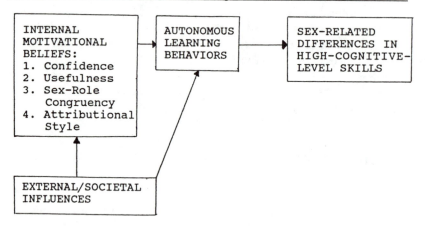

From Fennema, E., & Peterson, P. L. (1985). Autonomous
learning behavior: A possible explanation of gender-
related differences in mathematics. In L. C. Wilkinson,
& C. B. Marrett (Eds.), Gender-related differences in
classroom interactions (pp. 17-35). New York: Academic
Press. Reprinted with permission.

turn, engenders more success. Greater participation in ALBs leads to
greater autonomy and to greater performance on high-level tasks.

The internal belief system that influences the development of ALBs
consists of *confidence*, a perception of the *usefulness* of mathematics, a
facilitative *attributional style*, and a perception of *sex-role congruency*.
Confidence is essential to the autonomous learner because there is little
certainty when engaging in high-level tasks. Confidence is an important
prerequisite for choosing to do and persisting on high-level tasks. A sense
of confidence also supports the learner in working independently. Initially the perception that mathematics is useful is important in motivating the behavior of choosing high-level tasks. It also contributes to persistence by ascribing value to the task. A facilitative attributional style,
in which (1) success is attributed to the internal factors of ability and
effort and (2) failure is attributed to unstable factors, also contributes to
motivation to choose high-level tasks and persistence. These patterns of
attributions exhibited by autonomous learners are reflective of a sense of
control in academic situations. Finally, autonomous learners are enabled in the study of mathematics by a sense that this involvement is
congruent with their sex role. A lack of congruence would lead to an

attachment of negative value to mathematics and consequently to the ALBs themselves.

The final component of the ALB model is external/societal influences. There are many variables that could come under this heading, but the one considered most important by the model's authors is the classroom. What goes on in the classroom influences both the internal belief system and the development of learner autonomy. This variable will be considered in detail in Chapters 6 and 7.

## Model of Academic Choice

Figure 4.3 shows the Model of Academic Choice (Eccles et al., 1985). This is a general model used to explain the factors involved in student academic choices; however, it can be applied to gender differences in mathematics course election (participation). The model proposes two strands that together explain academic choices: expectation of success on a task and the subjective value of the task for the individual. The components are based on the Expectancy X Value model of achievement motivation (Atkinson, 1964). "Task" can be understood either as a specific short-term task such as a mathematics problem, or a longer-duration task such as enrollment in an elective math course.

A significant factor in this model is the individual's interpretation of past achievement and socialization experiences in determining the value of the task and the expectation for success on that task. As in the ALB model, factors internal to the individual act as mediators among past events and future expectancies. An examination of several of these beliefs will make this clear.

The Model of Academic Choice proposes that attributions of past events are instrumental in the formulation of the individual's self-concept of ability and perception of task difficulty. Self-concept of ability is an assessment of one's own competence to perform a given task. This construct is analogous to confidence in the ALB model. It should be noted that, while the ALB model acknowledges an interconnection between attributions and confidence, the Model of Academic Choice makes this connection explicit: Attributions, especially failure attributions, influence self-concept of ability, which in turn influences the individual's expectation of success.

The Model of Academic Choice also includes the variable of utility. It is a component of the construct labeled "child's perception of task value" (refer to Figure 4.3) and is synonymous with perceived usefulness.

Sex-role congruency is also incorporated into the Model of Academ-

Figure 4.3 Model of Academic Choice

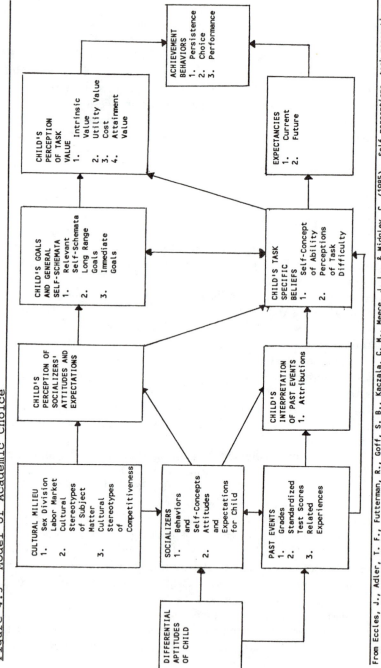

From Eccles, J., Adler, T. F., Futterman, R., Goff, S. B., Kaczala, C. M., Meece, J. L., & Midgley, C. (1985). Self perceptions, task perceptions, socializing influences, and the decision to enroll in mathematics. In S. F. Chipman, L. R. Brush, & D. M. Wilson (Eds.), *Women and mathematics: Balancing the equation* (pp. 95-121). Hillsdale, NJ: Lawrence Erlbaum Associates. Reprinted with permission.

ic Choice, under the construct labeled "child's goals and general self-schemata." A part of the self-schemata is a "need to act according to socially prescribed expectations for how each sex should behave" (Meece, Parsons, Kaczala, Goff, & Futterman, 1982, p. 340). This need most directly affects perceived task value. When a specific task is seen as being incongruent with one's sex-role identity, then the value or attractiveness of that task is diminished and the individual's focus might shift to the "cost" of engaging in the task. This argument is especially pertinent when the task is as sex-typed as doing mathematics is. Perception of the negative consequences of task involvement is related to the fear-of-success variable.

Also of importance in this model is the role of other people in students' lives. Individual differences in students' attitudes toward the value of mathematics and toward themselves as learners of mathematics are assumed to result from their perceptions of the beliefs and expectancies of major socializers. Parents and teachers are the socializers who have the most potential influence.

The two models just presented are important for a number of reasons:

1. They attempt to specify the interaction of variables related to gender differences in mathematics.
2. They focus on observable behaviors that can result from beliefs.
3. They suggest specific testable hypotheses which lead to further refinement of the models.

## MEASUREMENT

Models that relate internal beliefs to outcomes are important because they provide the theoretical basis for studies. However, the best of theories cannot take the place of carefully constructed instruments for measuring the components of the internal belief system. Various instruments have been used to measure affective variables, and the ones that will be discussed here are representative of those available.

### Fennema-Sherman Mathematics Attitude Scales

The Fennema-Sherman Mathematics Attitude Scales (Fennema & Sherman, 1976) are some of the most frequently used for measuring

affective variables in mathematics and are referenced often in the literature. These paper-and-pencil tests were developed by the authors in an
attempt to assess various dimensions of attitude toward mathematics.
Until that time, attitude had been viewed as unidimensional. Problems
of interpretation resulted from the use of scales that contained such
diverse items as "I like mathematics" and "I get nervous when I can't get
the answer to a math problem."

There are nine different scales in the Fennema-Sherman Mathematics Attitude Scales: confidence in learning mathematics; father,
mother, and teacher scales measuring the perceptions of attitudes toward one as a learner of mathematics; effectance motivation in mathematics; attitude toward success in mathematics; mathematics as a male
domain; usefulness of mathematics; and mathematics anxiety. Each of
the scales contains 12 Likert-type items with five possible responses
ranging from strongly disagree to strongly agree. Six of the items are
positive statements, and six are negative. The following four are representative of items from the confidence, usefulness, teacher, and math as
a male domain scales, respectively:

1. I am sure of myself when I do mathematics.
2. I don't expect to use much math when I get out of school.
3. My teachers think taking advanced math would be a waste of
   time for me.
4. Studying math is just as good for women as for men.

When the scales are administered, items from several of the scales
are randomly mixed to form a single instrument. Scores on each scale
can range from 12 to 60, with higher scores being indicative of positive
attitudes. For example, high scores on the confidence and usefulness
scales indicate more confidence and a greater appreciation for the usefulness of mathematics. High scores on the math as a male domain scale
indicate a less stereotypic view of mathematics. (For more information
on the scales, including items and reliabilities, see Fennema & Sherman,
1976).

The Fennema-Sherman scales were investigated for construct validity in a study involving 1,541 junior high school students (Broadbooks,
Elmore, Pedersen, & Bleyer, 1981). Results of the factor analysis showed
support for the theoretical structure of the scales. Items from the scales
separated into eight different factors, indicating that eight different
dimensions of mathematics were being measured by the scales.

## Mathematics Attribution Scales

There are several instruments that measure causal attributions in general academic situations, but in mathematics only two scales have been used with any frequency. The first, the Mathematics Attribution Scale (MAS) (Fennema et al., 1979), was designed to measure high school students' perceptions of the causes of their performance in mathematics. It contains eight subscales, based on success and failure for the four attribution categories (refer to Figure 4.1). The subscales thus are success due to ability, success due to effort, success due to task, success due to others, failure due to ability, failure due to effort, failure due to task, and failure due to others. The others category is actually called "environment" in the MAS, and it is an extension of the category called "luck" in the Weiner (1974) model. It was intended to include a range of unstable, external attributions made by high school students, such as help from others, the effectiveness of the teacher, or luck.

The MAS consists of eight stem items, each presenting a success or failure situation. The stem is followed by four attribution statements that reflect the four categories. The following is an example of a success stem and its four attribution statements, which reflect task, effort, others, and ability, respectively:

Event: You got a good grade in math for the semester.
1) The content included things you already knew.
2) You spend hours of extra time studying math.
3) The way the teacher presented the material helped.
4) You are a very good math student.

Students indicate their degree of agreement with each attribution as an explanation of the event. Responses are on a five-point Likert-type scale ranging from "strongly disagree" to "strongly agree."

A review of the MAS (Marsh, Cairns, Relich, Barnes, & Debus, 1984) noted several aspects of the scale that contribute to its importance as an attribution research instrument. The MAS is "(a) based upon individual difference data; (b) it looks at the generality of self-attributions across situations (i.e., different scenarios) and outcomes (i.e., success and failure); (c) it calls for separate ratings of each cause (as opposed to a forced-choice or ipsative-type format); and (d) it is specific to academic situations" (p. 9).

The MAS was written for use by high school students. Another, the

ALB Math Attribution Scale (Fennema & Peterson, 1984b) was used in the autonomous learning behaviors study with students in Grade 4. The items were again based upon success and failure for the four Weiner (1974) categories. However, in this scale, each item contains its own event. The following items reflect success attributions to ability and effort and failure attributions to others and task, in that order.

1) When you figure out how to do a thought problem, is it because you are smart?
2) If you understand how to do a thought problem, is it because you tried hard?
3) If you can't learn how to do a thought problem, is it because no one helped you?
4) When you have trouble with a thought problem, is it because the problem is hard?

There are 5 items for each of the eight subscales, making a total of 40 items. For each item, the student responds on a five-point Likert-type scale with the response choices being "YES!" "yes," "?," "no," and "NO!" These choices were intended to be easier for younger children to understand than the usual "strongly agree" to "strongly disagree" responses. In the administration of the scale, the items are read aloud, so that the reading ability of the student is not a factor.

Notice that each of the example items just given is centered around a type of mathematics problem called a thought problem. The intention with this wording was to have students consider noncomputational, nonroutine mathematical situations that required thought. Students were given examples of thought problems and their opposites, which were called plain problems, in order to be able to make the distinction.

## Interview Techniques

The instruments discussed so far are paper-and-pencil instruments, so named because they can be administered to groups of individuals and require little more than a pencil and a sheet of paper to record the responses. The ease of administration constitutes an advantage, and it is one of the reasons they have been so widely used. However, one disadvantage of this type of instrument is that important information is sometimes not elicited by the items in a group setting. Each individual has different experiences and perceptions, and these can go undetected by predetermined items in a scale.

An alternative methodology is the individual interview, where trained interviewers ask questions of the individual student. These questions are usually planned, but often variations in the interview result as a function of the student's responses. Interviews are usually audiotaped, but videotaping might also be used. Analyses are done on the transcribed interviews. Clearly this technique has a higher cost, in terms of time and effort to train the interviewers, interview the students individually, transcribe and analyze the interviews, and finally interpret the results. However, the rich nature of the resulting data makes it worthwhile.

One example of this technique that has been used in research on affective variables is the projective interview. It is called projective because the individuals being interviewed are not asked questions about themselves directly. Instead, they are asked questions about other people with whom they can identify. The assumption is that they will be able to respond more freely to questions that are asked indirectly.

Projective interviews were used by Fennema (1983b). In one example from that study, students were shown a photograph of two females and two males working at a table. The script the interviewer used included this text.

> Here are two girls and two boys looking over a math test. One did poorly, two did pretty well, and one did *very* well.
>
> 1. Which one did *very* well?
> 2. (Point to the student who did best.) How does the one who did well feel about her/himself?
> 3. How do the others feel about the one who did well?
> 4. Who did most poorly?
> 5. How does the one who did most poorly feel about him/herself?
> 6. How do the others feel about the one who did poorest?

## DO AFFECTIVE VARIABLES MAKE A DIFFERENCE?

Most research on affective variables as they relate to gender differences in mathematics has been of a single type. Students at some given time are assessed using some outcome variable, usually achievement or participation. At the same time, measures of the affective variables of interest are also made. The analyses of the data typically include tests for gender differences on the measures and correlations between the variables. While these results give us valuable information about students, they fail to answer the question of how student beliefs develop over time or how beliefs influence students in their study of mathematics. In order to examine questions of this type, studies are needed that collect data on students over a longer period of time. This section will consider a major longitudinal study that examined the development and influence of student beliefs as they relate to gender differences in mathematics.

This two-part longitudinal study, directed by Fennema (1983b), followed the same students over six years from Grade 6 to Grade 12. Part of the study looked at confidence and expectations over a two-year period, and the other part was a six-year study focused on the influence of internal beliefs. Each part began with testing of the entire sixth-grade population of four middle schools in Madison, Wisconsin. The SRA Mathematics Concepts test (Naslund, Thorpe, & LeFever, 1971) was used as a measure of achievement, and selected subscales from the Fennema-Sherman Mathematics Attitude Scales (Fennema & Sherman, 1976) were given. From this testing, subsamples were selected for the two studies.

## Confidence and Expectations

Subjects for the confidence and expectations portion of the study were in two subsamples: the "interview" sample and the "random" sample. The interview sample consisted of students who had scores above the mean of the population in achievement, but whose scores on the confidence subscale were either above the 75th percentile or below the 25th percentile. This sample was then arranged into four groups: high-confidence females ($n=15$), low-confidence females ($n=17$), high-confidence males ($n=16$), and low-confidence males ($n=15$).

The random sample ($n=108$) was selected from the original population and included some of the students from the interview sample.

Both samples were tested in Grades 6 and 8, using the confidence, math as a male domain, and teacher subscales of the Fennema-Sherman Mathematics Attitude Scales (Fennema & Sherman, 1976). In Grade 8, the STEP Mathematics Basic Concepts test (Educational Testing Service, 1979) was used as an achievement test. The projective interview described earlier was used with all students in the interview sample, during the spring as they progressed through Grades 6, 7 and 8. The interview pictures were changed each year so that the ages of the students pictured would be close to the age of the students being interviewed.

The purpose of the confidence portion of the study was to assess how males and females in Grades 6 through 8 changed with respect to (1) mathematics achievement, (2) confidence, (3) their perception of mathematics as a male domain, and (4) their perceived expectations of their teachers. The expectations portion of the study also focused on how males and females changed from Grades 6 through 8, with respect to (1) their expectations of success or failure in mathematics for females and males and (2) their view as to whether success is a positive or negative event for females and males. Results from these two parts of the study will be summarized in turn, and quotes from the interviews will be given to illustrate these results.

*Confidence Results.*    Analysis for the confidence measures were done using analysis of variance (ANOVA), with sex and confidence group as sources of variance. In terms of achievement on the SRA Mathematics Concepts test (Naslund, et al., 1971), there were no significant differences between the females and males in these groups. However, there was a significant difference in achievement between the confidence groups in both grades, with the high-confidence groups having higher achievement scores than the low-confidence groups. Table 4.1 summarizes these results.

Figure 4.4 shows another interesting result having to do with the relative positioning of the four groups in terms of confidence and achievement, from Grade 6 to 8. Within both the high-confidence and low-confidence groups, the difference between the confidence means for the males and females remained almost constant, with the females

**Table 4.1**    Mean Scores for Mathematics Achievement and Confidence, by Group

| SEX | GROUP | n | MATHEMATICS ACHIEVEMENT[a] | | CONFIDENCE | |
|---|---|---|---|---|---|---|
| | | | *6th-grade mean* | *8th-grade mean* | *6th-grade mean* | *8th-grade mean* |
| FEMALE | High | 15 | 30.7 | 42.8 | 56.6 | 52.5 |
| | Low | 17 | 26.7 | 39.5 | 38.1 | 45.5 |
| MALE | High | 16 | 29.1 | 43.6 | 56.4 | 51.8 |
| | Low | 15 | 26.9 | 40.0 | 37.6 | 44.8 |

[a]Grade 6: SRA Mathematics Concepts subtest (Naslund, Thorpe, & LeFever, 1971). Grade 8: STEP Mathematics Basic Concepts (Level I, Form X) subtest of the Sequential Test of Educational Progress (Educational Testing Service, 1979).

**Figure 4.4**  Z-scores of interview groups computed with population data

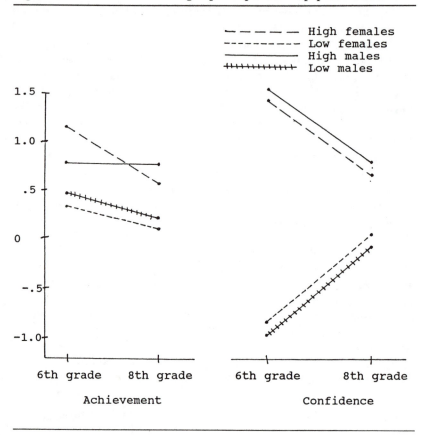

maintaining a slightly higher position in each group. Three of these groups also maintained their relative positions in mathematics achievement from Grade 6 to Grade 8. Only the high-confidence females lost position: In Grade 6, they had been the highest achieving of the four groups, but in Grade 8 they dropped in position and the high-confidence males were achieving at the highest level for the four groups.

*Expectations and Feelings Results.*   Within the interview, both expectations questions and feelings questions were asked. In one example of an expectations question, the student was shown a picture of a boy and girl working a problem alone and was asked, "Who will succeed?"

In this type of expectations question (type I), the student was forced to select either a female or a male as the one who succeeded. A type II question required the student to select either success or failure for a given person. For example, in showing a picture of a boy and girl working, the interviewer pointed to either the boy or the girl and asked, "How will this (girl, boy) do?" The percentage of time that a male was selected in response to a type I question, or success was selected for a male in response to a type II question, was calculated for each group in each grade.

Using the data for the expectations questions, 27 ANOVAs were calculated to examine the question as to whether there were differences in expectations of success of males and females by the various groups. The eight ANOVAs that were significant are summarized in Table 4.2. They show that there were few differences in expectations of success of males or females. The only consistent finding appears to be in the sixth grade, when the male groups chose males to succeed more than the female groups chose males to succeed. Because there were so few differences found by confidence group, data were combined across confidence groups and the remainder of the analyses were done using sex as the single source of variance.

**Table 4.2** Analyses of Variance of Responses to Expectations Questions

| | GRADE | SOURCE | $F$-RATIO | $p <$ | $d.f.$ | GROUP |
|---|---|---|---|---|---|---|
| *Who will succeed?* | | | | | | |
| Anyone[a] | 6 | Sex | 8.28 | .01 | 1,59 | Boys[b] |
| Teacher | 6 | Sex | 7.75 | .01 | 1,59 | Boys[b] |
| Individual | 8 | Sex×Confidence | 4.20 | .05 | 1,59 | |
| High-level mathematics | 6 | Sex | 5.02 | .03 | 1,59 | Boys[b] |
| *How will male do?* | | | | | | |
| Peers | 7 | Sex×Confidence | 5.00 | .03 | 1,59 | |
| Teacher | 8 | Sex | 6.12 | .02 | 1,58 | Girls[c] |
| *How will female do?* | | | | | | |
| Teacher | 8 | Sex×Confidence | 3.91 | .05 | 1,57 | |
| Low-level mathematics | 8 | Confidence | 10.21 | .00 | 1,48 | High[c] |

[a]Refers to the perceived respondent (individual, group of students, or teacher).
[b]Group with higher choice of male success.
[c]Group with higher choice of success.

Another question of interest relative to expectations was whether there were differences in expectations for females and males and whether the relative level of expectations changed over time. Analyses of the responses to type I expectations questions, as summarized in Table 4.3, showed that sixth-grade females selected a male to succeed rather than a female only 27% of the time. However, by Grade 8, these females selected a male to succeed 55% of the time, which is a strong indication of their rising expectations for males and falling expectations for females. The responses of the male subjects were more consistent over time, but they, too, indicated rising expectations for males. They selected a male to succeed over a female 43% of the time in Grade 6 and 53% of the time in Grade 8.

Analyses of the responses to type II expectations questions showed a similar trend of diminishing expectations for the females. In Grade 6, females said that females would succeed 74% of the time and males 52% of the time. By Grade 8, the expected success rate for the females dropped to 69% and that for the males increased to 80%, as reported by female subjects. The male subjects' responses were remarkably constant across the years, and in each of the three interviews their expectations for females were higher than their expectations for males.

Questions were also asked to assess students' feelings about success and failure. The analyses tried to determine whether the various groups had different feelings about success and failure for females and males. Few differences were found. Generally, all groups felt positive about both females' and males' success and negative about all failure.

*Discussion.* Perhaps the most surprising result of this extensive data collection and analysis is that so little was revealed about males and females with above-average achievement who differ in confidence level. One looks for reasons to explain this and questions the sampling process, the interview technique, the analyses, and interpretations. Little explanation is revealed, except some insight concerning the nature of the factors that influence the learning of mathematics for females and males. These factors seem to be much more subtle and complexly interwoven than we have suspected before. Or, it could be that the quantification of the interview data is masking important information. An examination of some of the individual student responses might show additional data not tapped by analyses of variance.

Several of the transcripts (Fennema, 1983a) contained indications that some of the students believed that there was scientific evidence that

**Table 4.3** Mean Success Expectations, by Grade and Sex

| | TYPE I | | | TYPE II | | | | | |
| | Who will succeed?[a] | | | How will female do?[a,b] | | | How will male do?[a,b] | | |
| PERCEIVED RESPONDENT | Grade 6 | Grade 7 | Grade 8 | Grade 6 | Grade 7 | Grade 8 | Grade 6 | Grade 7 | Grade 8 |
|---|---|---|---|---|---|---|---|---|---|
| *Females' Responses* | | | | | | | | | |
| Anyone | 27 | 34 | 55 | 74 | 72 | 69 | 52 | 64 | 80 |
| *Males' Responses* | | | | | | | | | |
| Anyone | 43 | 33 | 53 | 70 | 74 | 78 | 60 | 73 | 69 |

[a]Percentage of time male was chosen in each grade.
[b]Percentage of time success was chosen in each grade.

males are genetically superior to females in mathematics. An interview with a male subject contained the following interchange:

I:   Why did he get the right answer?

S:   I read somewhere, this is probably the study you're doing that, um, boys are, it's some kind of scientific thing that boys are better in math than girls are. Well, I read that somewhere.

A female subject opined that males did better in math than did females, so the interviewer questioned her further:

I:   Why do you think that boys are better?

S:   Cuz, I've seen like studies and they say boys are better.

Other transcripts contained responses that were also stereotypic, but they did not always point so clearly to male superiority in mathematics. A real ambivalence was found in the following exchange with a female subject who chose the female to succeed:

I:   How would this boy feel about her getting the right answer?

S:   He might . . . sort of be a little mad because maybe she was a girl and girls usually aren't really supposed to . . . I don't know, boys, they're supposed to be smarter or something.

There were other indications that some students held views about the roles of females and males that were stereotypic. The following excerpts were from the summary interview with a female subject:

I:   Do you think that teachers tend to call on boys more or on girls more in math class?

S:   Probably on boys more.

I:   Why do you think this is?

S:   Well, they'll probably think that, um, since the guy is, um, you know, supposed to be the man in the house and stuff, he should know how to do a lot of stuff too and learn a lot of math and stuff . . . understand it better.

This excerpt also points out a problem with the projective interview methodology: It is not clear whether this subject believed what she was saying or if she was only conjecturing about what teachers believe and how they act. The following is a continuation of the previous interview, and we can see that her response to the next question was not stereotypic:

I:    Some people say that girls are better in math than boys, and some say the opposite, that boys are better than girls. What do you think?

S:    I don't think . . . It's not like they're boys or girls, like, if they want to do stuff, then they can do it. But if they don't, you know, it's just, they don't, then they just don't really try.

Some students also had difficulty with the fact that they were being forced to choose between males and females on some of the questions. Take, for example, this portion of an interview with a female:

I:    (Showing a picture) And here we have a boy and a girl. . . . I want you to tell me who would probably have the right answer.

S:    Um . . . Well, I don't think it makes any difference. It doesn't have any influence whether they're male or female, but let's just say that he has the right answer this time.

The interview continued with the next picture, with a similar question being asked:

I:    Again, who would probably have the right answer this time?

S:    Well, you probably want me to say that *she* got it right this time . . .

I:    No, I don't want you to say anything, this is up to you . . . I don't want you to say anything in particular.

S:    It doesn't make any difference, I don't think. I don't think boys are any smarter at math than girls, but, for a change, we'll say that *she* got it right this time.

This student's responses make one wonder how many other students, without saying so, tried to equalize the number of times they referred to a male or female.

The interview transcripts also contained passages that apply to other beliefs that have been discussed. For example, there were comments that concerned the students' perceptions of the usefulness of mathematics. One male clearly saw that mathematics was associated with future jobs:

The boys have been trying harder so they don't have to worry about getting good jobs in four years.

Later in the same interview he said,

> The boys just end up working harder and they try to get the jobs
> that sort of pay more and so they end up having to use their math.

Another male expressed similar thoughts about the importance of math
for future careers and gave reasons for the differences between males
and females in math:

> The guys, I mean, they want good grades and everything, but . . .
> they don't really [care]. I mean, if they get a good grade, they'll be
> happy, but the girls I think always want the better grade. But then
> you know, as life goes on, I think the guys think more seriously
> about careers and then really try in math.

One female saw math skills as important for both males and females,
despite her stereotypic view of what their work would be:

> With girls, they're expected to grow up and become housewives and
> everything, and this way, when they go shopping, they have to
> compare prices and they have to know how to do that. And they
> have to learn how to do the arithmetic in their head, you know, or
> on a piece of paper, really fast. Unless they have a pocket calculator
> (chuckle). But, as a housewife, you're doing things with math all
> the time, and you'll need your skills in math.

Later in the same interview, she expressed her views on why males use
math more in their careers:

> Well, because men grow up and they're expected, you know, they
> work in offices and as mechanics and things like that and they
> always have to do things with numbers and . . . it's just kind of
> natural to find a man working with numbers or a calculator or
> something like that.

Many of the questions in the interview were designed to investigate
students' feelings of confidence in doing mathematics. From the comments, it is clear that confidence was a reflection of perceived ability.
One male subject identified a female in the picture as getting the problem right, and he was asked why the student would think that she could
get the right answer. He replied,

She knows that she's a good math student, and she catches on to things easily, and she can figure out how to do it.

He later contrasted this with the male, whom he did not believe would get the right answer:

Well, he probably doesn't have as much confidence in math as the girl. He probably struggles and doesn't know how to do it.

A girl being interviewed drew similar contrasts. When asked why a male would think he could get the right answer, she said,

Whenever there is anything new, he catches on really fast. . . . He knows he's smart and that he can do it.

When later asked the same question about a female who did not think she could do the problem correctly, this subject gave this response:

Well, because it's too hard. She needs it explained step by step.

Notice the lack of autonomy implied in that response. Another female student gave the following very thorough description of a confident, able student. The excerpts come from responses to questions on a single picture in the interview.

She's confident of herself, and she really understands and knows what she's doing. . . . She probably listens in class really well and she probably studies, and she's probably just a good student overall in school. . . . She's the type that thinks things through and that understands what words mean, and she can understand and comprehend a sentence. . . . She listens to the teacher a lot and tries to get along with everybody.

Another interesting comment about confidence came from a female who was asked to speculate as to why females are sometimes not so confident.

Maybe girls are not so confident sometimes, because they maybe feel that they have to prove that they are just as good as boys, and so they have to really worry about it and work harder.

Because many of the interview questions concerned situations where students got correct or incorrect answers, the responses of the students contained many comments that distinguished between good and not-so-good students. The following phrases were taken from the interviews of several different subjects. It is interesting to note that the subjects did not often characterize students in terms of ability alone, but rather in terms of behaviors associated with good students and not-so-good students. Statements made by subjects about good math students include the following phrases:

> Tries hard . . . listens carefully . . . does the assignments . . . follows the directions . . . does his work . . . really concentrates on the problem . . . pays attention . . . has been listening . . . studies pretty good . . . takes the time to learn how to do the problems right and listens carefully . . . listens good when the teacher explains it . . . doesn't daydream a lot in class . . . takes notes . . . doesn't goof off a lot . . . always gets her assignments in on time . . . practices the problems . . . follows along.

The descriptions associated with students who were not so good in mathematics were similar in that they also focused on behaviors rather than on ability:

> Doesn't really care . . . not listening . . . wasn't concentrating on the problem . . . off in another world . . . just doesn't think . . . daydreaming . . . never took the time to understand it . . . not listening to directions . . . doesn't really try that much and doesn't worry about math . . . not a good worker . . . doesn't study his work at home . . . messing around when they were learning new math . . . skips class or is always getting into trouble . . . goes home and plays with the guys and doesn't do his school work . . . always thinking about something else . . . always talking to someone behind him . . . staring out the window . . . not concentrating on what the teacher is saying . . . doesn't get into it and really try.

The focus of these comments seemed to be on effort as the key to success, rather than a reliance on ability alone. As one student put it,

> Well, if you don't study, you're not going to get it right.

A focus on effort is, of course, desirable, since ability alone is seldom enough to insure success in mathematics.

Students will reveal many things about their internal belief systems. The challenge for researchers is to structure situations that will elicit honest responses.

## Internal Beliefs

Previous research has given us reason to think that internal beliefs have a long-term influence on achievement-related choices and behaviors. Longitudinal data allow us to test some of these hypotheses. By extending the data from the two-year examination of confidence and expectations, to cover a six-year span, we could see if affective variables measured in the middle school years were predictive of mathematics achievement and participation for females and males in high school (Meyer, 1986). The affective variables considered were confidence, mathematics as a male domain, usefulness, teacher attitude, and causal attributions. Gender differences in these variables, their predictive ability, and their stability over time were investigated.

The sample consisted of 151 students (84 females; 67 males) with data from Grades 6, 8, and 12. Affective data for independent variables consisted of scores on the confidence, math as a male domain, usefulness, and teacher scales from the Fennema-Sherman Mathematics Attitude Scales (Fennema & Sherman, 1976), for Grades 6, 8 and 12; and scores on the Mathematics Attribution Scale (Fennema et al., 1979) subscales of success due to ability, success due to effort, failure due to ability, and failure due to effort, for Grades 8 and 12. Other independent variables were prior achievement from Grades 6 and 8. The dependent measures were twelfth-grade achievement and participation. No interview data were used in this portion of the study.

*Gender Differences.*    The achievement results in the three grades, as summarized in Table 4.4, show a typical progression for females and males. In Grade 6, there were no significant differences between female and male achievement means. In Grade 8, the males scored significantly higher than did the females on each of two achievement measures. There were no significant differences for females and males on two Grade-12 low-cognitive-level achievement measures (computation and low-level concepts), but on a measure of high-level concepts, the males scored significantly higher than did the females. In terms of math

**Table 4.4**   Mean Scores and *t*-Tests for Achievement and Participation, by Sex

|  |  | MEAN SCORE | | |
| --- | --- | --- | --- | --- |
| VARIABLE | GRADE | *Females* | *Males* | *t*-TEST |
| Concepts | 6 | 25.30 | 26.28 | −1.04 |
| Computation | 8 | 43.38 | 46.58 | −2.38[a] |
| Concepts | 8 | 37.80 | 42.10 | −3.69[a] |
| Computation | 12 | 49.52 | 50.03 | −.60 |
| Concepts, high | 12 | 17.90 | 19.87 | −2.90[a] |
| Concepts, low | 12 | 21.03 | 21.85 | −1.83 |
| Math GPA | 12 | 2.84 | 2.67 | 1.38 |
| Participation[b] | 12 | 6.70 | 6.88 | −.65 |

[a]Significance level: $p < .05$.
[b]Number of semesters of mathematics completed.

grade-point average (GPA) and participation through Grade 12, there were no significant differences.

The only affective variable for which there was a gender-related difference was math as a male domain. Higher scores on this scale represent a less stereotypic view of mathematics. In each of the three grades, males reported significantly more stereotyping than did females. It should be noted that both males and females reported less stereotyping in Grade 12 than they did in Grade 6. Even with this improvement, however, the mean for the males in Grade 12 (49.09, $s.d. = 9.41$) was less than that for the females in Grade 6 (52.89, $s.d. = 5.19$).

*Stability.*   There are two different ways to approach the question of stability of affective variables over time. One way would be to consider changes in the variables from one measurement to another. A second way is to consider the relationships (correlations) of these variables to achievement and to look at changes in these relationships over time. It is this latter approach that was taken, based upon the assumption that it is not an isolated level of an affective variable that is important, but rather the potential influence of that variable on achievement.

For the males, none of the correlations between the affective variables and achievement were significantly different between any of the years. For the females, three of the relationships were unstable: math as a male domain from Grade 6 ($r = .49$) to Grade 12 ($r = .09$), teacher attitude from Grade 8 ($r = .02$) to Grade 12 ($r = .37$), and failure due to ability from Grade 8 ($r = .01$) to Grade 12 ($r = -.57$). This pattern is similar to that found in the confidence and expectations portion of the study (refer to Figure 4.4).

*Prediction of Achievement and Participation.*   In order to test the ability of the affective variables to predict achievement and participation in Grade 12, a series of 15 regression analyses were carried out for each sex. The Grade-12 measures of achievement and participation were used as dependent variables, and the affective variables and prior achievement of each of Grades 6, 8, and 12 were used as independent variables. Prior achievement was included as a control variable, to see if the affective variables had predictive ability beyond that of prior achievement.

The results of the regression analyses showed that the affective variables had more predictive ability for the females than they did for the males. For the males, in only 5 of the 15 analyses was an affective variable predictive beyond prior achievement; for the females, affective variables were predictive in 12 of the 15 analyses. For both females and males, the variable that most frequently predicted the dependent variable was confidence. It is interesting to note that the attribution variables of failure and success due to ability were also predictive, especially for the females, and that these variables are closely related to the variable of confidence. Yet, additional analyses of the relationship between confidence and achievement, carried out using analysis of linear structural relationships, revealed that confidence for both females and males, is more appropriately understood as an outcome of achievement, rather than achievement being an outcome of confidence (Meyer, 1986).

*Discussion.*   This longitudinal portion of the study invites the continued inclusion of affective variables in studies of gender differences in mathematics. The results show that, even when gender differences in the affective variables are not present, the variables have differential effects on mathematics achievement and participation for females and males. For example, in Grade 6, there was not a significant difference in confidence between the females and males, and yet the variable was predictive of achievement for females six years later. This difference in predictive ability, along with the differing stability of the relationships of the affective variables with achievement, leads to the tentative conclusion that the affective variables have a more important influence on the achievement and participation of females than they do for males. Why this might be true and what exactly the influence of the affect is on behaviors is not illuminated by the data.

The importance of confidence and the attribution of success and failure to ability suggest the existence of a larger, more comprehensive belief, of which these three variables are a part. An argument can be made that a variable called self-concept of ability would encompass these and other components of the internal belief system. This construct is one's understanding of one's mathematics ability. This understanding includes not only confidence in ability, but also belief in the role that ability has in successes and failures. The other attribution variables — success and failure due to effort — are also part of self-concept of ability; they reflect one's understanding of the relationship between ability and effort. The degree to which mathematics is seen as being sex-role appropriate is also a part of this construct, in the sense that this belief can either enable or hinder the individual's underlying ability. Fear of success, although not included in this longitudinal study, might also be classified as a component of self-concept of ability. Part of understanding one's ability is being aware of the possible consequences of success due to that ability. If the consequences are seen as negative, then the ability might be restrained or denied.

Thus it appears that more understanding can be gained by thinking of affective variables as parts of larger constructs (such as self-concept of ability) rather than viewing them as separate entities. (Kloosterman does this with a set of attribution variables in Chapter 5, in an attempt to explain differences in achievement-related behaviors.)

## FUTURE DIRECTIONS FOR RESEARCH ON BELIEFS

This chapter has explored the effect of the internal belief system on gender differences in mathematics. What has emerged is a recognition that the relationship between the affective components of this belief system and the cognitive outcomes of mathematics achievement and participation is complex and largely unknown. However, there is evidence to support some tentative conclusions and to suggest directions for future research. We know that affective variables are related to achievement and participation and that these variables might have differing influence for females and males. In addition, there is reason to suspect that the role of affective variables might vary over time, with some variables being more important at certain critical times in a student's development, and others, like confidence, being more constant over time.

Future research will challenge and test these conclusions. It should also test models, such as those presented here, that attempt to specify the relationships between the affective variables and cognitive outcomes. These models will need to include a focus on achievement-related behaviors. Another challenge is to learn how the internal belief system is developed and whether or not it can be changed, once it is formed. Along these lines, Chapters 6 and 7 explore the possible influences of the mathematics classroom on students' belief systems.

## REFERENCES

Armstrong, J. M., & Price, R. A. (1982). Correlates and predictors of women's mathematics participation. *Journal for Research in Mathematics Education, 13*(2), 99–109.

Atkinson, J. W. (1964). *An introduction to motivation.* Princeton, NJ: Van Nostrand.

Broadbooks, W. J., Elmore, P. B., Pedersen, K., & Bleyer, D. R. (1981). A construct validation of the Fennema-Sherman Mathematics Attitude Scales. *Educational and Psychological Measurement, 41*, 551–557.

Brush, L. (1980). *Encouraging girls in mathematics: The problem and the solution.* Cambridge, MA: ABT Books.

Eccles, J. (1983). Expectancies, values, and academic behaviors. In J. T. Spence (Ed.), *Achievement and achievement motives* (pp. 75–146). San Francisco: Freeman.

Eccles, J., Adler, T. F., Futterman, R., Goff, S. B., Kaczala, C. M., Meece, J. L., & Midgley, C. (1985). Self-perceptions, task perceptions, socializing influences, and the decision to enroll in mathematics. In S. F. Chipman, L. R. Brush, & D. M. Wilson (Eds.), *Women and mathematics: Balancing the equation* (pp. 95–121). Hillsdale, NJ: Lawrence Erlbaum.

Educational Testing Service. (1979). *Sequential test of educational progress: Mathematics basic concepts.* Monterey, CA: CTB/McGraw-Hill.

Fennema, E. (1983a). [Research on relationship of spatial visualization and confidence to male/female mathematics achievement in grades 6–8: Expectations interview transcripts]. Unpublished raw data.

Fennema, E. (1983b). *Research on relationship of spatial visualization and confidence to male/female mathematics achievement in grades 6–8.* (Final report of National Science Foundation grant SED78-17300, A01). Madison: University of Wisconsin–Madison.

Fennema, E., & Peterson, P. (1984a). [Classroom processes, sex differences, and autonomous learning behaviors in mathematics: Attribution scale scores]. Unpublished raw data.

Fennema, E., & Peterson, P. (1984b). *Classroom processes, sex differences, and autonomous learning behaviors in mathematics* (Final report of National Science Foundation grant SED 8109077). Madison: University of Wisconsin–Madison.

Fennema, E., & Peterson, P. (1985). Autonomous learning behavior: A possible explanation of gender-related differences in mathematics. In L. C.

Wilkinson & C. B. Marrett (Eds.), *Gender-related differences in classroom interaction* (pp. 17–35). New York: Academic Press.

Fennema, E., & Sherman, J. (1976). Fennema-Sherman Mathematics Attitude Scales. *JSAS: Catalog of Selected Documents in Psychology, 6*(1), 31. (Ms. No. 1225)

Fennema, E., & Sherman, J. (1977). Sex-related differences in mathematics achievement, spatial visualization and affective factors. *American Educational Research Journal, 14*(1), 51–71.

Fennema, E., & Sherman, J. (1978). Sex-related differences in mathematics achievement and related factors: A further study. *Journal for Research in Mathematics Education, 9,* 189–203.

Fennema, E., Wolleat, P., & Pedro, J. D. (1979). Mathematics Attribution Scale. *JSAS: Catalog of Selected Documents in Psychology, 9*(5), 26. (Ms. No. 1837)

Horner, M. S. (1968). *Sex differences in achievement motivation and performance in competitive and non-competitive situations.* Unpublished doctoral dissertation, University of Michigan, Ann Arbor.

International Association for the Evaluation of Educational Achievement. (1984). *Second International Mathematics Study summary report for the United States.* Champaign, IL: U.S. National Coordinating Center.

Lantz, A. E., & Smith, G. P. (1981). Factors influencing the choice of nonrequired mathematics courses. *Journal of Educational Psychology, 73*(6), 825–837.

Leder, G. C. (1982). Mathematics achievement and fear of success. *Journal for Research in Mathematics Education, 13*(2), 124–135.

Leder, G. C. (1984). Sex differences in attributions of success and failure. *Psychological Reports, 54*(1), 57–58.

Marsh, H. W., Cairns, L., Relich, J., Barnes, J., & Debus, R. L. (1984). The relationship between dimensions of self-attribution and dimensions of self-concept. *Journal of Educational Psychology, 76*(1), 3–32.

Meece, J. L., Parsons, J. E., Kaczala, C., Goff, S. B., & Futterman, R. (1982). Sex differences in math achievement: Toward a model of academic choice. *Psychological Bulletin, 91,* 324–348.

Meyer, M. R. (1986). The prediction of mathematics achievement and participation for females and males: A longitudinal study of affective variables (Doctoral dissertation, University of Wisconsin–Madison, 1985). *Dissertation Abstracts International, 47,* 819A.

Naslund, R. A., Thorpe, L. P., & LeFever, D. W. (1971). *Mathematics concepts test.* Chicago: Science Research Associates.

Pedro, J. D., Wolleat, P., Fennema, E., & Becker, A. D. (1981). Election of high school mathematics by females and males: Attributions and attitudes. *American Educational Research Journal, 18*(2), 207–218.

Reyes, L. H. (1984). Affective variables and mathematics education. *Elementary School Journal, 18*(2), 207–218.

Sherman, J. (1979). Predicting mathematics performance in high school boys and girls. *Journal of Educational Psychology, 71*(2), 242–249.

Sherman, J. (1982). Continuing in mathematics: A longitudinal study of the attitudes of high school girls. *Psychology of Women Quarterly, 7*(2), 132–140.

Sherman, J., & Fennema, E. (1977). The study of mathematics by girls and boys: Related variables. *American Educational Research Journal, 14*, 159–168.

Weiner, B. (1974). *Achievement motivation and attribution theory.* Morristown, NJ: General Learning Press.

Wolleat, P. L., Pedro, J. D., Becker, A. D., & Fennema, E. (1980). Sex differences in high school students' causal attributions of performance in mathematics. *Journal for Research in Mathematics Education, 11*(5), 356–366.

# 5

# Attributions, Performance Following Failure, and Motivation in Mathematics

PETER KLOOSTERMAN

*In this chapter, Kloosterman examines the relationship between attributions, performance following failure, and mathematics achievement. Two studies of particular interest are set in context through an extensive review of the relevant literature. Beginning with Murray's pioneering efforts, the development of motivation research is traced through its latest refinements in attribution theories, achievement motivation theories, learned helplessness and mastery orientation. The relevance of this body of work to gender differences in performance is explained and further refined by consideration of the construct, "performance following failure." Two studies relating the contribution of performance following failure to gender differences in mathematics achievement are described in detail. The chapter concludes with a discussion of the theoretical and practical implications of the research data.*

In the previous chapter, an internal belief system about mathematics was defined and explained. Mere knowledge of the existence of such a belief system does not, however, suggest what effect beliefs might have on motivation or why beliefs should be related to achievement in mathematics for females and males. In this chapter, an attributional theory of motivation will be presented and explained in terms of beliefs. While it is clearly just a theory, some of the implications for achievement in mathematics are interesting, particularly with respect to gender differences. After looking at some of the theoretical implications of attribution theory, data from two studies designed to test applicability of the theory to mathematics teaching will be presented.

The chapter will cover three main areas. The first is a historical review of motivation research. This review has been included as an aid in understanding the development of the concept of an internal belief system. Included in the review will be the evolution of the construct of academic learned helplessness. As will be shown, this is a variable on which gender differences have at times been found. The idea behind academic learned helplessness is that some students have failed to succeed so often that they have come to feel that they can never really prosper in school. In a sense, they have "learned" that they are helpless in their struggle to achieve success in school. This phenomenon will be explained first from a behaviorist perspective and then along more recent lines of thought which explain it in terms of attribution.

Next this chapter will deal with two studies involving learned helplessness in mathematics. A unique method for measuring learned helplessness will be discussed. Called "performance following failure" (PFF), this method requires presenting students with exceptionally difficult mathematical word problems. After the difficult word problems, students are presented with easier problems to see what effect, if any, being subjected to failure on the hard problems has on ability to do easier problems. While PFF is essentially a behaviorist methodology for measuring motivation, it can be related to, and in some sense explained by, more cognitively oriented attribution theories. After explaining the concept and measurement of PFF, data concerning the construct will be reported. Gender differences in PFF, by itself and in relation to achievement in mathematics, will also be discussed.

Finally, in this chapter, the relationships among attributions (internal belief variables), PFF, and mathematics achievement will be summarized and clarified. Gender differences in mathematics beliefs, achievement, and in relationships between beliefs and achievement will be discussed throughout the chapter. As will be seen, the findings with respect to gender differences are intriguing but not always consistent.

## HISTORICAL VIEWS OF MOTIVATION

For centuries it has been common knowledge that individuals vary in the extent to which they put forth effort on school or job-related tasks; some people are considered lazy while others are seen as hard workers. In an early definition of achievement motivation, Murray (1938) wrote about it in terms of a stable, dispositional tendency to strive toward performance excellence. Following the thinking of the time, Murray maintained that the strength of such dispositional tendencies varies among individuals. While Murray advanced knowledge about motivation by considering it as a unique construct, there was little explanation in his work for the manner in which a person's thoughts and beliefs might influence or direct motivation. In essence, Murray considered motivation a trait that could be used to explain other behaviors.

Following Murray's initial work on motivation, Rotter's (1954) text on social learning theory explained an individual's motivation in terms of (1) the expectancy of reinforcement for completing a given task and (2) the value to the individual of that reinforcement. Set firmly in the behaviorist tradition, Rotter claimed that motivation would be increased by making the rewards for completing a task greater. Similarly, motivation would be decreased by removing rewards for task completion. The question of how an individual processed information about rewards was never asked. An individual's past history of reward or punishment was the primary criterion for determining whether that individual expected a sufficient reward to attempt to complete a new task. The more consistently a person had received valuable rewards for completing previous similar tasks, the more likely that the individual would attempt the new task.

### Early Attribution Theory

While Rotter's (1954) model helped to explain the level of motivation displayed by an individual, the specific mechanisms by which past experience mediate expectancy of success were not addressed. In 1958, Heider began a theoretical break from behaviorism when he proposed that individuals were aware of the reasons they were rewarded or punished (Heider, 1958) and that these reasons affected behavior. The perceived reasons, or attributions, for the rewards and punishments were classified by Heider as personal (internal) or environmental (external). Personal forces were subdivided into power (perceived ability) or motivation (intent or effort). For example, when an individual felt that he had failed on a task on which success was expected, the failure could be blamed on either internal or external factors. If the person blamed failure on personal lack of effort, he would try harder on the next attempt. If failure was blamed on environmental forces, effort on future attempts to accomplish the task would not necessarily increase because there would be no reason to expect the environmental causes for failure would be altered by effort. Thus, with Heider's scheme, attribution of success or failure to internal forces would result in greater changes in motivation than attributions of success or failure to external forces.

While Rotter's (1954) and Heider's (1958) works dealt specifically with success and failure or completion/noncompletion of a task, it should be noted that success and failure were often spoken of as if they were a single dichotomous variable rather than end points on a continuum (Rotter, 1975). Throughout the literature on motivation, it is common to find reference to success *or* failure on a task, when in fact one does not always clearly succeed or clearly fail on most tasks. This is particularly true of many of the tasks students are asked to complete in school. For example, if the average score on an exam is 75% and a student gets 75% correct, she has not failed, nor has she been as successful as was possible, either. Thus, one must keep in mind that attributional theories of motivation are based on the assumption that students feel either success or failure on school-related tasks.

In 1966, Rotter published another paper concerning motivation, in which he categorized control of expected reinforcements as external or internal, explaining the difference as follows:

> When a reinforcement is perceived by the subject as following some action of his own, but not entirely contingent upon his action, then in our culture, it is typically perceived as the result of luck, chance, fate, under the control of powerful others, or as unpredictable because of the great complexity of the forces surrounding him. When the event is interpreted in this way by an individual, we have labeled this a belief in external control. If the person perceives that the event is contingent upon his own behavior or his own relatively stable characteristics, we have termed this a belief in internal control. [p. 1]

Rotter (1966) postulated that individuals differ on perceived locus of control (internal/external) and that motivation to achieve is higher when the individual perceives the locus of control as being internal. This latter postulate is similar to Heider's (1958) and employs the same rationale, except that it deals more specifically with reasons for reinforcement upon completion of a task. Rotter (1966) summarized internal versus external locus of control by asserting that individuals with a greater internal locus of control would see themselves as being responsible for rewards following success or nonrewards following failure on a task. On the other hand, individuals with an external locus of control would not be greatly affected by success or failure because, for them, rewards tend to be less contingent upon their actions.

Kelley (1967) further refined and applied the motivational concepts set forth by Rotter and Heider by defining attribution as "the process of inferring or perceiving the dispositional properties of entities in the environment" (p. 193). In other words, when individuals infer a cause for something happening, they are making an attribution for the cause of the event. According to Kelley, covariation is the general method people use to determine causation. That is, if two phenomena occur together, one can be presumed to affect (be the cause of) the other. For example, if a student failed on an exam after not studying, she might blame the failure on lack of effort, as lack of study was accompanied by (covaried with) failure on the exam. It is entirely possible, however, that the exam was so difficult that even intense study would not have allowed the student to pass. While difficulty of the exam was the "true" reason for failure, according to Kelley the perceived reason of lack of study would be the only one that would influence the student's motivation. In short, Kelley clarified the importance of perception when making attributions, explaining that inaccurate perceptions were the result of the improper assumption that covariation of two events meant that one was the cause of the other.

In addition to covariation, Kelley (1973) discussed other factors that influence attributions. For example, he claimed that a discounting principle applies when several possible causes of an event are present. Under such circumstances, one cannot be sure about the importance of any one of them; however, past experience often dictates which cause is likely to be most important, making the others less likely to be considered, even though they may be just as relevant. According to Kelley, the covariation and discounting principles are both examples of causal schemata. A causal schema can be viewed as "an assumed pattern of data in a complete analysis of variance framework" (p. 115). In simple terms, it is a system for making judgments based on incomplete information. As attributions are nothing more than judgments or beliefs about the cause of an event, the concept of causal schema is potentially very useful to the attribution theorist.

A reasonable question to consider is whether or not Murray, Heider, Rotter, and Kelley felt their theories were more applicable to males than to females. Their writings indicate that potential gender differences in the applicability of their theories were not generally considered. As will be shown later in this chapter, it was not until their theories were applied to motivational ideas and to the classroom that the potential for attributional theories to explain gender differences in achievement became apparent.

## Achievement Motivation

In contrast to the work of Rotter, Heider, and Kelley, who could all be considered attributional researchers, McClelland and Atkinson worked in the area of achievement motivation. The overlap between these areas is most obvious when attribution theory is used to explain motivation and achievement in school. While some attributional theories are intended to be broad enough to explain why people react as they do to any event, a student's motivation in school is a subset of attribution theory which ties in with achievement motivation concepts. Similarly, achievement motivation theory encompasses achievement in business, politics, and so forth, but again ties in closely with attribution theory when we look at achievement in school. Thus, the work of McClelland and Atkinson will be briefly reviewed with emphasis placed on the overlap between their theories and those of the attribution theorists.

McClelland, Atkinson, Clark, and Lowell (1953) postulated and investigated the motive to achieve success. Also known as achievement motivation, this motive involved the amount an individual would persist to gain what he believed to be success. The *Thematic Apperception Test* (TAT) (Murray, 1938), on which subjects wrote stories about abstract pictures they were shown, was used to measure a person's motive to achieve success. The stories were then scored on a variety of achievement subcategories. It was assumed that subjects' stories would be a projection of their own personalities, so that, by looking at the achievement desires shown in the stories, one would have a reasonable estimate of the underlying need to achieve success of the individual who produced the stories.

Subsequently, Atkinson (1957) refined this theory to include a motive to avoid failure, which was measured by the *Test Anxiety Questionnaire* (TAQ) (Saranson & Mandler, 1952). Some individuals, he claimed, are achievement oriented in that they are motivated chiefly by a wish to succeed (Atkinson, 1964); others are more failure oriented, predominantly motivated by a strong need to avoid failure (Atkinson, 1964). While achievement-oriented people work to fulfill high aspirations, failure-avoiding individuals settle for mediocrity in order to avoid the failure that often occurs when one is attempting to reach a challenging goal. As was the case with success and failure, the categories of achievement orientation and failure avoidance should be viewed as end points on a continuum, rather than as dichotomous variables, even though they are often referred to in that fashion.

Atkinson (1957) also presented a formula for individual motivation. He postulated that a person's tendency or willingness to attempt an achievement-oriented activity was a multiplicative function of that person's motive to succeed, motive to avoid failure, expectancy of success, and incentive value of success. Atkinson's expectancy of success involved the perceived probability of succeeding under the assumption that a low chance of success would weaken one's desire to continue. This is similar to Rotter's (1954) expectancy of reinforcement, in that both depend on past history to determine present expectancy. The two expectancies differ, however, in that Atkinson (1957) was talking about whether or not a person expected to succeed, while Rotter (1954) was speaking of whether or not the person expected certain rewards for succeeding. Nevertheless, the inclusion of either Atkinson's incentive value of success or Rotter's value of reinforcement in a formula for motivation implies that people will not put forth effort without expecting some sort of reward. Atkinson's (1957) third parameter, motive to succeed, is defined as a "disposition to strive for a certain kind of satisfaction" (p. 360). This motive is not perceived as a drive in the Freudian sense, but rather as a developed pattern or trait. In some ways, this variable is related to Rotter's (1954) expectancy of reinforcement, because it is developed in part by the reinforcement given for exhibiting achievement-oriented behaviors.

Further study of Atkinson's (1957) work reveals some interesting similarities to the work of Rotter (1954, 1966) and Heider (1958) with regard to attempted tasks and the attribution of success or failure when a task is or is not completed. According to Atkinson (1957), achievement-oriented people choose to do challenging yet reasonable tasks. Failure-avoiding people, however, either choose very easy tasks on which there is negligible chance of failure, or very difficult tasks on which there is little chance of success. The advantage of choosing difficult tasks is that failure can be blamed on the difficulty of the task rather than on lack of ability by the individual. The idea that task difficulty can be a factor for failure requires the assignment of attributions as defined by Rotter and Heider; thus, achievement motivation theory again interweaves with attribution theory in the explanation of motivation.

One final point concerning achievement motivation needs consideration. As has been mentioned, Atkinson (1957, 1964) spoke of a motive to achieve success and a motive to avoid failure. Horner (1968) extended this notion by postulating that, early in life, individuals develop a motive to avoid success in addition to their motive to succeed. This motive to avoid success may be stronger in females than in males because sex-role conditioning for females does not emphasize the importance of success in the way that it does for men. Leder (1982) found that males with a high motive to avoid success, which she called fear of success, did not intend to continue in optional secondary school mathematics classes. In contrast, females with high fear of success did intend to continue taking mathematics. Thus, while the stability of motive to avoid success has been questioned (Leder, 1979), it is a useful construct when considering the attributions that individuals, especially females, make about their successes and failures in mathematics.

## CAUSAL ATTRIBUTIONS AND MOTIVATION

The literature reviewed thus far builds a framework for the explanation of motivation in terms of causal attributions. While Murray (1938) viewed motivation as an underlying trait that could be measured but not necessarily explained, later researchers (Heider, 1958; Kelley, 1967) began to explain motivation in terms of individuals' beliefs about the reasons for their successes and failures. Attributional theories of motivation, often considered a branch of study in themselves, deal with the reasons or attributions individuals make and how those attributions translate into actions (Weiner, 1984). In the same way that most people reflect on success and failure in their lives, many students think about their successes and failures in school (Weiner, 1979). Because the correctness of a problem is usually clearly determined in school mathematics, it is easy for students to know when they succeed and when they fail; thus, attribution theory should be valid in this subject area (Dweck & Licht, 1980; Kloosterman, 1988a).

Weiner (1972, 1974), building on the work of Heider (1958), Rotter (1966), and Kelley (1967), proposed a theoretical framework for the attribution of causation of successes and failures that has been useful in noncontent-specific studies. According to his 1974 model, attributions vary on at least two dimensions, locus of control and stability. When the dimensions of external and internal control are crossed with the dimensions of stability and instability, a $2 \times 2$ matrix results (refer to Figure 4.1). Events that are both internally controlled and stable are perceived to be the result of a person's inner capabilities, which Weiner (1972, 1974) called *ability*. Internally controlled but unstable outcomes are seen to be the result of the *effort* a person puts out. Externally controlled, stable outcomes are attributed to *task difficulty*, while externally controlled, unstable events are simply the result of *luck*. The terms *ability*, *effort*, and *task difficulty* have been used in many studies, while the term *luck* has often been changed to *environment* or *help from*

*others* (Fennema & Peterson, 1984; Fennema, Wolleat, & Pedro, 1979).
(Chapter 4 in this volume contains more detail on Weiner's classification
system for attributions.)

## Academic Learned Helplessness, Mastery Orientation, Motivation, and Achievement

Overmier and Seligman (1967) and Seligman and Maier (1967) first
used the term *learned helplessness* to refer to the condition of laboratory
dogs subjected to periodic electric shocks. At first, the dogs attempted to
escape from their cages each time they received a shock, but they were
prevented from doing so. After a period of time, the cages were changed
so that it was possible for the dogs to escape, but they were so used to
being unable to escape that they did not attempt it when the shocks
came. The dogs had learned that they were helpless to control their own
destiny. It should be noted that this conception of learned helplessness is
based on a behaviorist framework for motivation. As in earlier motivation research (*cf.* Murray, 1938), the only critical question was whether
or not the dogs gave up their attempts to escape shock. No one asked
what the dogs were "thinking." What caused them to give up?

Over the years, researchers have begun to question the thought
processes individuals entertain when placed in situations they are helpless to control. Specifically, attribution theory predicts that the attributions individuals make for their successes and failures will have a direct
bearing on their motivation to attempt difficult tasks. Thus, the term
*learned helplessness* is now used to describe the behaviors of students
who believe they are unable to succeed in school (Covington & Beery,
1976; Dweck & Reppucci, 1973; Kloosterman, 1988b). In terms of
Weiner's (1974) model of attribution, students with learned helplessness
attribute their successes, infrequent as they may be, to external factors
such as the task being easy or their being given help from others. Failures, on the other hand, are usually attributed to the internal and
unstable factor of low effort or the internal and stable factor of low
ability (Covington & Beery, 1976).

In contrast to the self-defeating attributional tendencies of those
with learned helplessness, the term *mastery orientation* has been used to
categorize the disposition of persons who are confident of their ability
and thus are not worried about failure (Covington & Beery, 1976;
Dweck & Goetz, 1978). Feeling that they are responsible for their own
successes, mastery-oriented individuals usually attribute success to
possessing sufficient ability and effort to accomplish the task at hand,
while attributing failure to the difficulty of the task or to lack of help
from others.

To connect mastery orientation and learned helplessness with achievement, one must look to the connection between attributions and motivation to succeed in school, and then assume that increasing students' motivation to succeed will lead to increases in their achievement. Figure 5.1 diagrams the theorized causal relationships among attributions, expectations of success, and effort, for students with learned helplessness and with mastery orientation. Note that Figure 5.1 deals with hypothesized *thought processes* of students rather than just their actions. Thus Figure 5.1 is an extension of the early notions of learned helplessness (e.g., Seligman & Maier, 1967), which focused solely on the actions of learned-helpless individuals.

To understand the thought processes implicit in Figure 5.1, it is useful to understand how students, particularly those with learned helplessness, determine expectation of success. Covington and Omelich (1967) state that students differentiate between effort and ability as determinants of success or failure in school. Theoretically, if failure is attributed to low ability, the student has no reason to expect to succeed at a later time, because ability is perceived to be a stable cause of failure. Effort, on the other hand, is an unstable cause of failure. By attributing failure to lack of effort, a student might expect success if more effort were expended. The problem is that students with learned helplessness do not try harder. Although this may seem surprising, it is quite reasonable if one considers the potential reasons for failure when consistent effort is applied. While it is plausible that assigned school tasks are always too difficult or that the teacher never gives sufficient help, these possibilities are unlikely to occur in school on a consistent basis. Following the logic of Kelley's (1973) discounting principle, learned-helpless students believe the realistic alternative for failure in school learning is lack of ability. Because lack of ability is a stable cause of failure that cannot be overcome, learned-helpless students *withhold effort* rather than risk failure and "confirmation" of low ability.

Students with mastery orientation vary from students with learned helplessness in their thinking about the importance of effort. Mastery-oriented students have usually experienced some success in school but, more importantly, they interpret the causes of their successes differently. In terms of Kelley's (1967) principle of covariation, mastery-oriented students believe that ability is no obstacle to success and thus it is effort that covaries with achievement in school. If mastery-oriented individuals fail, their belief in effort as the cause of success often gets them to try harder in school. This is in direct contrast to students with learned helplessness in that they fear that increased effort will have little if any effect on their chances of success.

Figure 5.1 Attributions, expectations, and effort for learned-helpless and mastery-oriented students.

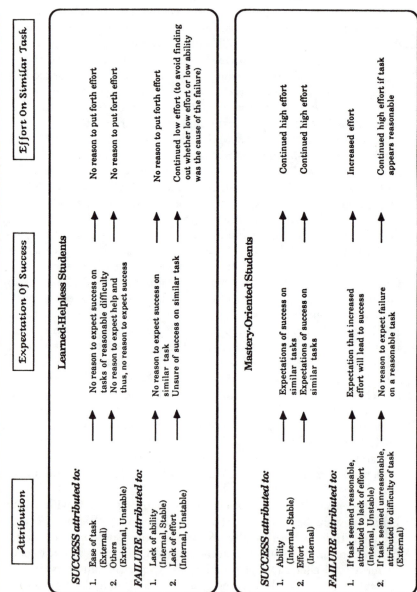

While lack of effort is one way of identifying learned helplessness in students, the type of tasks they choose to do is another. When such individuals have a choice of tasks to work on, they are motivated to choose tasks they perceive to be either very easy or very difficult (Covington & Beery, 1976). On easy tasks, success is assured. When failure occurs on a very difficult task, it can be attributed to the unreasonableness of the task, thus avoiding the feared conclusion that failure resulted from low ability. When mastery-oriented students have a choice of problems to work on, they choose challenging yet reasonable ones, not worrying about occasional failure. Thus, while task choice is not a thought process that fits into the attribution/expectancy/effort schema in Figure 5.1, it is a characteristic which differentiates learned helplessness from mastery orientation.

Atkinson's (1957) work on motivation can be tied to attribution theory when task choice is considered. The task choices of individuals with learned helplessness (Dweck & Goetz, 1978) are very similar to those of failure-avoiding individuals (Atkinson, 1957); that is, both choose tasks on which failure is unlikely or can be blamed on external factors, so their sense of self-worth can be preserved. Individuals with a high fear of success (Leder, 1982) avoid tasks that would make them appear successful to others. Task choices of mastery-oriented individuals (Dweck & Goetz, 1978) and success-oriented individuals (Atkinson, 1957) are also quite similar; that is, both choose challenging but realistic tasks, since they feel they have the ability to succeed on such challenges.

In short, causal attribution theory attempts to predict motivation and achievement in school, based on students' perceptions of the reasons for their successes and failures on school tasks. Attribution theory is an outgrowth of pioneering works such as those of Heider, Rotter, and Kelley, which attempted to explain rather than just measure human motivation. In school, students with learned helplessness tend to see academic success as beyond their control and thus have little reason to be motivated. Mastery-oriented individuals feel academic success is the result of sufficient effort and thus are willing to try hard to succeed in school.

## Gender Differences in Attributional Style

In the study of attributions of success and failure, the topic of gender differences has often been addressed. A number of noncontent-specific studies of the 1970s concluded that, when gender differences were found, females tended to display more of a learned-helpless orientation than males. Specifically, males tended to attribute their successes to internal causes and their failures to external causes. Females tended to show the reverse of this pattern, taking personal responsibility for their failures while attributing their successes to external factors (Bar-Tal, 1978; Dweck & Bush, 1976; Parsons, Ruble, Hodges, & Small, 1976). Such conclusions were made mostly on the basis of laboratory studies such as those of Dweck and Gilliard (1975), Dweck and Reppucci (1973), and Nicholls (1975). Dweck and Reppucci (1973), for example, administered solvable and unsolvable puzzles to 40 randomly selected fifth-grade males and females. The *Intellectual Achievement Responsibility* (IAR) scale (Crandall, Katkovsky, & Crandall, 1965) was also administered, to see whether the students attributed their successes and failures internally or externally. Findings included the fact that males were significantly more likely than females to attribute failure to the internal cause of lack of effort. No statistically significant gender differences were found on the subscales that measured success or failure due to ability.

Nicholls (1975) presented 96 fourth-grade students with an angle-matching task, telling them that most children got about 13 correct out of 20. He manipulated success so that the subjects correctly solved either 7 items (the failure group) or 19 items (the success group). Results indicated that males were more likely than females to cite the external factor of luck as a reason for failing. Females, on the other hand, were more likely than males to attribute failure to lack of ability. While both the Dweck and Gilliard (1975) and Nicholls (1975) findings did show females exhibiting more learned helplessness than males, it should be emphasized that the mean differences between the groups were small.

Dweck and Gilliard (1975) studied the effects of asking fifth-grade students how well they expected to do on four puzzles requiring construction of geometric forms. Twenty students were asked only before the last puzzle, 20 were asked before the first and last, and 20 were asked before each of the four puzzles. The first three puzzles were not solvable, but all students succeeded on the fourth. Dweck and Gilliard found that asking the males how well they would do on the first puzzle significantly increased their persistence (time spent attempting the next puzzle), while, for females, the same question resulted in a decrease in persistence. Because the first three puzzles were not solvable, students' expectancies of success were predicted to decline between the first and fourth trials. For the 10 females in the group where expectancy was measured before the first and last trials, expectancy of success did decline significantly. For the 10 males in that group, however, the decline was not significant.

One explanation given for this involved attributions. Dweck and Gilliard (1975) suggested that the larger decreases in persistence and expectancy of success by females could be interpreted as evidence supporting the hypothesis that females had a greater tendency to attribute failure to lack of ability than did males. According to their line of reasoning, by asking the students about their expectations of success, the experimenter made them more conscious of their attributions and the possibility of failure. If females attributed failure more to low ability than did males, they would be less likely to think that effort would help them solve the puzzles and thus they would persist less. As females in this study did persist less, one could conclude that the data supported this theory and that females displayed more of a learned-helpless pattern than males.

Recent research on gender differences has attempted to apply findings such as those of Dweck and Gilliard (1975), Dweck and Reppucci (1973), and Nicholls (1975) to the mathematics classroom. Parsons, Meece, Adler, and Kaczala (1982) studied attributions for success and failure among mathematics students in Grades 5 through 11 by having them report attributions on open-ended and rank-ordered questionnaires. On the open-ended questions, there were no gender differences in the mention of internal versus external attributions for either success or failure. In other words, females and males were equally likely to exhibit a learned-helpless orientation. On the rank-ordered questions, males ranked ability as a more important cause of success and effort as less important than did females. A reverse pattern was found for failure, as males ranked lack of ability as a less important cause for failure and effort as more important than did females. Rank-order gender differences on six other attributions were not significant. In short, females tended to view effort as more important than did males when asked to contrast ability and effort as reasons for success, although females did not spontaneously mention ability or effort more frequently than males on the open-ended questions.

On questions referring to attributions for task difficulty and help from others, Parsons et al. (1982) found no gender differences and thus concluded that "sex differences in attributions depended on the type of methodology used (open-ended or rank-ordered questions)" and that, "taken together, these results provide little support for the hypothesis that girls are generally more learned helpless in mathematics than boys" (p. 421). Citing data from Parsons et al. (1982) and other studies, McHugh, Frieze, and Hanusa (1982) reached the similar conclusion that "the literature on sex differences in attributions is characterized by inconsistencies and has not yet fulfilled its promise as the key to understanding differential achievement in men and women" (p. 467). Additional data on this issue will be presented later in this chapter.


## PERFORMANCE FOLLOWING FAILURE: TWO STUDIES

In various places in the literature, high persistence in the face of potential failure has been mentioned as a distinguishing feature of mastery-oriented students. The following statement by Dweck and Licht (1980) is typical of the connection that has been made between attributions and effort in academic settings.

> Failure has dramatic effects on performance. For some children, these effects are positive ones: Effort is escalated, concentration is intensified, persistence is increased, strategy use becomes more sophisticated, and performance is enhanced. For other children, the effects are quite the reverse: Efforts are curtailed, strategies deteriorate, and performance is often severely disrupted. Indeed, these children often become incapable of solving the same problems they solved easily only shortly before. Although the behavior of these two groups of children differs markedly following failure, it looks remarkably similar before failure occurs. In all of our research on failure effects in achievement situations, we find that the two groups start out with virtually identical performance — that is, equivalent speed, accuracy, and sophistication of problem-solving strategies. They are also indistinguishable on standardized measures of intelligence. What distinguishes them are their cognitions about their successes and failures. [p. 197]

The last sentence of this quote points out the key difference between academically mastery-oriented children and those with academic learned helplessness: the difference in their thoughts and feelings. In Seligman and Maier's (1967) early work with learned helplessness, it was helpless behaviors rather than thoughts about the behaviors that were the salient feature of the definition of the phenomenon. In 1973, Dweck and Reppucci began to associate learned-helplessness behaviors with certain thought patterns, when they found that "the subjects who showed the largest performance decrements were those who took less personal responsibility for the outcomes of their actions and who, when they did accept responsibility, attributed success and failure to presence or absence of ability rather than to expenditure of effort" (p. 109).

Dweck and Reppucci (1973) arrived at this conclusion by performing an experiment in which 40 fifth-grade children were asked to complete some block puzzles. Prior to the beginning of the experiment, all children were given the Intellectual Achievement Responsibility (IAR) scale (Crandall et al., 1965), which was used to indicate the extent to which children felt that they themselves were responsible for their successes and failures (internal control), as opposed to feeling that others were responsible (external control).

Two experimenters then worked separately with each child, one always giving easily solvable puzzles (the "success" experimenter) and the other always giving unsolvable puzzles (the "failure" experimenter). After administering a number of puzzles in this fashion, both experimenters finished by giving several solvable puzzles.

In analyzing their results, Dweck and Reppucci (1973) divided the children into two groups. The first consisted of those students who failed to solve the final solvable problems from the failure experimenter (the "helpless" group), while the second consisted of students who did solve the final solvable problems from the failure experimenter (the "persistent" group). Analysis of variance was used to show that the persistent group had significantly higher internal-control scores on the IAR than the helpless group and that the persistent group attributed their successes more to effort than did the helpless group.

When considering the results of the Dweck and Reppucci (1973) study, one must keep in mind that it was not typical of a school learning situation. Like the Dweck and Gilliard (1975) and Nicholls (1975) studies noted earlier, the testing was done in a psychological laboratory where there was no fear of a poor grade or reprimand from the teacher if performance was unsatisfactory. The block puzzles students were asked to complete were not something they would normally be asked to do in school, particularly in a mathematics class. Thus, while one must use caution in assuming the Dweck and Reppucci (1973) findings would be similar for school-related settings and tasks, it can be said that, in some situations, there is a connection between children's feelings of control of success on a task and the effort they will give to that task.

While the Dweck and Reppucci (1973) study provided evidence that, after a failure experience, students who were able to solve puzzles had more internal-control attributions than those who were not able to solve puzzles, evidence more specific to mathematics was needed. To assess the extent to which failure in mathematics would result in reduced performance on mathematical word problems, I designed the Performance Following Failure (PFF) instrument (Kloosterman, 1985). It was modeled, to some extent, on the Dweck and Reppucci (1973) experimental design, but included mathematical word problems instead of puzzles and integrated the solvable and unsolvable problems into a single paper-and-pencil test.

On the PFF scale, the procedure for inducing and measuring reactions to failure on word problems was

1. To measure skill in solving word problems by giving students several moderately difficult word problems, creating a "prefailure" score
2. To induce failure by giving the students several very difficult word problems
3. To measure performance following the failure experience by asking the students to complete several more word problems similar to those on the prefailure part of the instrument, creating a "postfailure" score.

Following the logic of Dweck and Licht (1980), students who had mastery-oriented attributional styles were expected to try harder after failing and thus to have higher postfailure than prefailure scores. In contrast, students with learned helplessness were expected to show diminished effort after failure and thus to have lower postfailure than prefailure scores. Given the mixed findings concerning gender differences in attributional style, the question of gender differences on this measure was also an important question for study. If females do, in fact, exhibit more learned helplessness than males in mathematics, it should be apparent by considering the prefailure-to-postfailure score ratio for females and males. To test these questions, I used the PFF instrument in two studies, one with secondary school algebra students and the other with somewhat younger seventh graders.

## PFF for Algebra Students

As described, performance following failure was measured by comparing a postfailure score to a prefailure score for each student. Items for the postfailure and prefailure sections of the instrument were word problems similar or identical to those used for the mathematics portion of the National Assessment of Educational Progress (NAEP) (Carpenter, Corbitt, Kepner, Lindquist, & Reys, 1981). Ten items were chosen that 13-year-old students correctly solved 50% to 75% of the time. For each subject, these items were randomly divided into groups of six prefailure and four postfailure problems. In addition, six items were chosen to induce failure. These were NAEP word problems that 17-year-old students correctly solved less than 13% of the time. After piloting, there was some instrument revision to insure that many but not all students could correctly answer the prefailure and postfailure word problems and to insure that few if any students could correctly solve the problems intended to induce failure. (Additional details on the PFF scale can be found in Kloosterman, 1985.)

The first study using the PFF scale had a sample of 63 males and 61 females enrolled in algebra courses (age range of 14 to 16 years). The prefailure items were given to entire classes at once, while the failure-inducing and postfailure items were administered as a single instrument to small groups of students. To insure that students knew that they had failed on the failure items, each time they finished one of these items, they were told whether the answer they gave was correct or incorrect. This was also done with the postfailure items, so the students would not be alerted to the fact that they differed from the failure items.

The highest possible score on the PFF instrument was +5, meaning that an individual did much better after as opposed to before the failure-inducing problems (indicating mastery orientation). The lowest possible score was −5, meaning that the individual performed very poorly on the postfailure as compared to the prefailure items (indicating learned helplessness). Results from the 124 students tested indicated that females were more susceptible than males to performance decrements following a failure experience in mathematics. The mean score for males was positive (0.44), indicating that males, on the average, achieved higher after the failure problems than they had before the failure problems. In contrast, the mean score for females was negative (−0.25), indicating that, on the average, they achieved lower after the failure problems than they had before the failure problems. A $t$-test showed that the differences between the males' and the females' scores was statistically significant ($t=2.23$, $p<.05$).

## PFF for Seventh-Grade Students

Results from the initial study of performance following failure in mathematics indicated clear gender differences in reaction to failure. To extend these findings, the instrument was rewritten and used again with a much larger sample of students. In the second study, 12- and 13-year-old students (seventh graders) were used, to see if initial results would be repeated with somewhat younger subjects. The second PFF instrument deviated from the original one in the problems used and the way in which problems were sequenced, although the overall design of measuring prefailure performance, inducing failure, and measuring postfailure performance was the same.

The prefailure measure of achievement on word problems for these seventh graders consisted of 10 of the 40 items of the applications subtest of the Stanford Mathematics Achievement Test, advanced form F (Gardner, Rudman, Karlsen, & Merwin, 1982). By using items from a standardized test, it was possible to insure that all problems were of appropriate difficulty for 13-year-old students. In addition to being mathematical word problems of moderate difficulty, prefailure items were chosen from the 40-item subtest because they required general problem-solving strategies rather than specialized knowledge. Note that because the students' teachers were interested in results of the entire applications subtest, all 40 items were administered one week before the failure-inducing and post-failure items. Only 10 of the test items were counted, however, in the prefailure score.

Potential failure-inducing items for the second PFF study were collected from a variety of sources. As in the first study, an effort was made to find items that looked reasonable but were, in fact, too difficult for 13-year-old students. Two examples of the failure-inducing problems follow.

> When I arrange the members of a marching band in rows of 2, 3, or 4, there is always 1 person left over. However, when I arrange them in rows of 5, all of the rows are even. There are more than 30 but less than 100 people in the band. How many people are in the band?

> A woman was 3/8 of the way across a railroad bridge when she heard a train coming. She knew the train always traveled at 50 miles per hour and that she could just save herself by running to either end of the bridge as fast as she could. How fast can she run? (Give her speed in miles per hour.)

A number of potential failure items were pilot tested and revised to make sure that students got them wrong, yet that they understood the problems well enough to realize that their answers were not correct. Comments from students who had completed the final version of the failure problems indicated that they felt they were failing on most, if not all, of the failure items.

Once failure had been induced, it was necessary to see how well the students would achieve on problems of the same difficulty as the prefailure items. Thus, postfailure items were written to be parallel to the 10 items chosen from the Stanford applications subtest as prefailure items. An example of a prefailure item and its postfailure parallel is the following:

*Prefailure*: Vicky is buying a used pair of skates for $7.49. If the sales tax is 30 cents, how much change should she get from $10?
*Postfailure*: Tom bought a record for $6.53. Tax on the record was 26 cents. How much change did he get from $20?

In this second PFF study, failure-inducing and postfailure items were arranged somewhat differently than in the first PFF study. Students were given five failure-inducing items, five postfailure items, three more failure-inducing items, five more postfailure items, and two very easy items to let all students feel some success on the instrument. The failure items were randomly ordered; postfailure items, however, were used in the order in which the items they were parallel to had appeared in the Stanford subtest. Placement of the three failure items in the middle of the instrument was intended to make sure that failure was still in the minds of the students when they got to the final five. Scores on the second PFF instrument had a possible range of $+10$ to $-10$. Like the first PFF instrument, a positive score meant that a student achieved higher after the failure items than before those items (indicating mastery orientation), while a negative score meant that the student did worse after the failure items than before them (indicating learned helplessness).

Subjects for the second PFF study were 233 female and 196 male students enrolled in seventh-grade mathematics at one of three schools in rural or small-city communities. Subjects were representative of all ability levels at the schools except for the top 10% and bottom 10% of the seventh-grade classes. *T*-tests were used to determine whether there was a significant gender difference on the performance-following-failure instrument. In contrast to the results of the first PFF study, where the mean score for males was positive, the mean score for males in the second study was negative ($-0.54$). As in the first PFF study, the females had lower mean scores than the males ($-0.90$). While this difference was not statistically significant ($t=1.82$, $p=.07$), the trend was for females to show more learned helplessness than males.

## PFF and Achievement

While performance following failure is an interesting concept in and of itself, the extent to which student scores on PFF are related to their scores on mathematics achievement tests is important when considering PFF as a measure of motivation. As part of the first PFF study, the algebra students were asked to complete Level I, Form X of the STEP Mathematics Basic Concepts Test (Educational Testing Service,

1979). This 50-item multiple-choice test was designed to measure mastery of mathematical concepts, as opposed to arithmetic computation. To assess the relationship between PFF and achievement, correlations between PFF scores and STEP scores were computed for females and males. For females, the correlation was 0.24, statistically significant at the $p < .05$ level. For males, the correlation was $-0.10$, which was not statistically significant. In other words, those females who had the greatest adverse reaction to failure also had the lowest achievement scores. For males, however, there was no relationship between reaction to failure and mathematical achievement.

The relationship between PFF and achievement was also measured during the second study. The seventh-grade students were asked to complete two subtests of the Stanford Mathematics Achievement Test, advanced form F (Gardner et al., 1982). The two subtests were concepts of mathematics and applications of mathematics. For both of these subtests, *negative* correlations between the achievement test scores and PFF were found. The correlations were relatively small for the concepts subtest ($r = -0.19$ for females; $r = -0.09$ for males), although the correlation for females was statistically significant at the $p < .05$ level. Correlations between PFF and the applications subtest were stronger and statistically significant for both females ($r = -0.28$) and for males ($r = -0.30$). In other words, those females and males who gave up most easily on the postfailure items were the highest achievers. More will be said on this intriguing finding later in this chapter.

### PFF and Attributional Style

A few pages back, a quote from Dweck and Licht (1980) was used to emphasize a hypothesized relationship between students' thoughts or attributions and their reaction to failure. Specifically, Dweck and Licht made the claim that, rather than ability differences, "cognitions about successes and failures" (p. 197) distinguish the learned-helpless pattern from mastery orientation. Attributions are nothing more than beliefs or cognitions concerning the reasons for success and failure in school. PFF is an indicator of reaction to failure, in the behaviorist sense. Thus, if Dweck and Licht are correct, one would expect a significant, positive correlation between attributional style as measured by both an attribution scale and the PFF instrument. In addition to measuring the correlation between the two measures of attributional style, it is appropriate to ask if the correlation between the two measures varies by gender.

To assess attributional style from the perspective of attributions for success and failure, subjects in both the first and second PFF studies were asked to complete the eight subscales of the ALB Mathematics Attribution Scale (Fennema & Peterson, 1984). As noted in Chapter 4, the subscales ask respondents to indicate the extent to which their successes and failures are the result of ability, effort, task difficulty, and help from others. For example, one success-due-to-ability item was, "When you figure out how to do a thought problem, is it because you are smart?" Students responded to each item by checking "YES!" "yes," "?" "no," or "NO!" Note that the categories of ability, effort, task difficulty, and help from others correspond to Weiner's (1972) attribution categories as explained earlier in this chapter (see also Chapter 4).

While scores from the eight ALB Mathematics Attribution subscales are useful in determining individuals' perceptions of the reasons for their successes and failures in mathematics, they do not give an overall attributional style (AS) score. To overcome this problem, six of the subscale scores were combined using a formula suggested by Fennema and Peterson (1984). First of all, the subscale score for each individual was transformed into a standard ($z$) score. Subscale scores were then combined using this formula:

Attributional style (AS) =

Success due to ability (SA)
+ Success due to effort (SE)
+ Failure due to lack of effort (FE)
− Failure due to lack of ability (FA)
− Success due to ease of the task (ST)
− Success due to help from others (SO)

or, in short,

$$AS = (SA + SE + FE) - (FA + ST + SO).$$

This formula was based on the hypothesis that mastery-oriented students attribute success to ability and effort and attribute failure to lack of effort. Students with learned helplessness, on the other hand, attribute failure to lack of ability and success to ease of the task or help from others. Note that the mastery-oriented and learned-helpless attributions are exactly those outlined in Figure 5.1. The other two ALB subscales, testing failure due to the difficulty of the task and to the lack of help from others, were not included in the AS formula because there was not good reason to expect that they would differentiate mastery-oriented individuals from those with learned helplessness. Finally, it is important to note that obtaining a positive score from the AS formula is indicative of mastery orientation. The higher the score, the more mastery oriented the individual is expected to be. Similarly, a negative AS score is indicative of learned helplessness, and the more negative it is, the more extreme the pattern is expected to be.

Surprisingly, no relationship was found between the measure of attributional style based on performance decrements in the face of failure in mathematics (PFF) and attributional style calculated from the ALB Mathematics Attribution subscales (AS). In the first PFF study, the correlation between PFF and AS was −0.13 for females and −0.08 for males. In the second PFF study, it was −0.05 for females and −0.01 for males. There were no significant gender differences in the correlations.

### Attributional Style and Gender

In addition to the question of the relationship between PFF and attributions, it is also important to ask whether there are gender differences on AS alone. Such differences were considered in both the first and second PFF studies, although none were found. In the first PFF study, the mean AS score for females was −0.10, while the mean score for males was 0.10. This difference was not, however, statistically significant. This pattern was reversed in the second PFF study, as the mean score was 0.13 for females and −0.15 for males, again, not significant. Taken together, findings from the two studies indicate there is probably not a gender difference in attributional style as calculated from the ALB Mathematics Attribution subscale scores.

### Attributional Style and Achievement

A final issue relating to motivation and attributional style is that of the relationship between mathematics achievement and attributional style, as defined using the ALB Mathematics Attribution subscale scores. In both PFF studies, correlations between AS and achievement were calculated. In the first, the correlation was 0.29 for females and 0.06 for males. Only the correlation for females was statistically significant ($p < .05$). In the second PFF study, the correlation between the concepts score and AS was 0.27 for females and 0.28 for males. The correlation between the applications score and AS was 0.26 for both females and males. All correlations in the second PFF study were statistically significant ($p < .05$). In other words, a reasonably consistent positive relationship was found between achievement in mathematics and attributional style as calculated from self-reports of attributions.

## Summary and Conclusions

In reviewing the two performance-following-failure (PFF) studies, it is possible to summarize the findings as follows:

1. PFF is a variable on which gender differences are sometimes found. Females had significantly greater performance decrements following failure (indicating more learned helplessness) than males in the first PFF study. In the second, females also had greater performance decrements than males, although the difference failed to reach statistical significance.
2. The relationship between PFF and achievement in mathematics is not clear. In the first study, there was a significant positive correlation between PFF and achievement for females. The correlation for males was nonsignificant. In the second PFF study, however, a significant negative correlation was found between PFF and mathematical concepts for females and between PFF and mathematical applications for both females and males.
3. There appears to be no relationship between PFF and attributional style (AS), as measured by self-reports on attribution subscales.
4. There are no gender differences on AS.
5. There appears to be a significant positive correlation between AS and achievement in mathematics. Such a correlation was found for females in the first PFF study. In the second PFF study, significant positive correlations were found for both females and males on both mathematical concepts and mathematical applications.

These results will be considered individually.

*Gender Differences on PFF.* The finding of gender differences on PFF in the first PFF study is not surprising, considering other findings that females show more learned helplessness than males (e.g., Dweck & Bush, 1976; Parsons et al., 1976). While gender differences on PFF were expected in the second PFF study, the lack of such differences has precedent in the literature. Consider, for example, the Dweck and Reppucci (1973) study noted earlier. While that study has often been used as support for the existence of gender differences in learned helplessness, the differences found by Dweck and Reppucci were on the IAR attribution scale. They found no significant gender differences in the extent to which students persisted in the face of prolonged failure. Similarly, Dweck and Gilliard (1975) found that females' persistence deteriorated more than males' when subjects were asked to predict their performance after each failure puzzle in the experiment. For the group that was not asked to predict their performance until the final failure puzzle, females consistently persisted longer than males. In other words, performance following failure is a complex phenomenon, apparently varying with the type of task and frequency of reminders about success or failure. On mathematical tasks, when students are not asked to predict their performance, gender differences may be found. When they are, females show more learned helplessness than males.

*Correlation Between PFF and Achievement.*  The second major finding of the PFF studies was that of a positive correlation between PFF and achievement for females in the first study and a negative correlation for both females and males in the second study. These results were unexpected, although several explanations based on differences between the first and second PFF instruments could account for the negative correlation in the second study. First of all, two of the "failure" items on the second PFF instrument were puzzle problems on which trial and error was a feasible, although very slow, method of solution. The problems were included because it was easy for students to realize when they were not getting the correct answer on them. However, observation of students during administration of the instrument indicated that, in general, students spent more time on these two problems than on most of the others. When researchers returned to the schools to show students how to solve the problems on the instrument, these two items generated more interest and discussion than any of the others on this, or, for that matter, on the first PFF instrument. It is possible that mastery-oriented students put so much time and energy into these two problems that they did not have the enthusiasm needed to solve the postfailure items when they got to them.

A second possible explanation for the negative correlation between PFF and achievement in the second study involves the direct failure feedback given by an adult researcher during the first study but not during the second. Dweck, Davidson, Nelson, and Enna (1978) note that failure feedback is more debilitating when given by adults than by peers. Dweck and Gilliard (1975) demonstrated the impact on persistence of asking students whether they expected to succeed or fail. The fact that students were actually told that they were wrong on the failure problems on the first PFF instrument may have made the failure more salient and made the instrument a better indication of learned helplessness.

A third potential explanation for the negative correlations in the second study is that good problem solvers know when to quit. Recent research on metacognition (*cf.* Garofalo & Lester, 1985; Silver, 1985) has indicated the importance of control processes in problem-solving performance. Specifically, some students appear to be able to sit back and look at the solution process they are using on difficult mathematical problems. These students are often able to decide whether they should continue with that solution process or shift to a new process. It is possible that mastery-oriented students began to realize that the second PFF instrument was just too difficult and gave up intentionally. By the time they reached the postfailure items, they were putting forth very little effort and blamed their lack of success on the difficulty of the problems. Students with learned helplessness may have persisted without realizing the futility of many of their solutions on the failure items and so continued persisting on the postfailure items. This inability to see they were "set up" would have resulted in continued effort and thus success on the postfailure items.

*Lack of Correlation Between PFF and Attributional Style.* The third noteworthy finding of the PFF studies was the lack of a positive correlation between PFF (a behavioral measure of learned helplessness) and AS (an attributional measure of learned helplessness). This finding was not expected; it failed to support the Dweck and Licht (1980) claim that what distinguishes students who react positively as opposed to negatively to failure are "their cognitions about their successes and failures" (p. 179). Attribution theory predicts that motivation and achievement will be influenced by attributions (cognitions). Behavioral measures of learned helplessness, such as PFF, have been researched much less often than attributional measures and have never before been researched using mathematical word problems. Given the substantial evidence supporting attribution theory, the most reasonable explanation for a lack of correlation between PFF and AS is the type of instruments or the setting used to measure PFF. It is possible that a mathematics test that involves more word problems than students are used to seeing and that does not count for a grade just does not force students into attributional thinking the way regular classroom assignments do. Seventh-grade students do report making attributions for successes and failures in mathematics some of the time, but not after every problem or test (Kloosterman, 1988a). The lack of a class grade on the PFF test made it less threatening and thus less worrisome than a graded test. Since emotional situations are believed to result in more attributional thinking than nonemotional situations (Weiner, 1984), the lack of the pressure of grades may have kept students from worrying about the PFF exam and from making attributions, thereby resulting in nonsignificant correlations between PFF and AS.

A second possible explanation for the lack of a correlation between

PFF and AS is that attributions are made most often in situations where an outcome (success or failure) is not expected (Weiner, 1984). Students may have come to expect failure part way through the PFF; if so, then actually failing on the problems would have done little to trigger attributional thinking.

*Lack of Gender Difference on Attributional Style.*    The fourth significant finding of the PFF studies was the lack of a gender difference on attributional style (AS), as calculated from the ALB Mathematics Attribution subscales. Given the inconsistency of gender-difference findings on attributional style noted in the literature (e.g., McHugh et al., 1982; Parsons et al., 1982), this result was not surprising. If anything, it is in agreement with the Parsons et al. finding that gender differences in mathematics occurred when an open-ended attributional questionnaire was used but not when a closed-ended rank-order questionnaire was used. The Likert format of the ALB Mathematics Attribution Scale used in the PFF studies meant that the subjects were making closed-ended responses similar to those in the Parsons et al. study, where no gender differences were found.

*Consistency of Positive Correlations Between Attributional Style and Achievement.*    The final significant result of the PFF studies was the reasonable consistency with which significant positive correlations were found between AS and achievement. This finding supports an attributional explanation of motivation and achievement, as suggested by Weiner (1974, 1979, 1984), and will form the basis of the support for the attribution-motivation-achievement model presented in the next section.

## AN ATTRIBUTIONAL INTERPRETATION OF
## MOTIVATION AND ACHIEVEMENT IN MATHEMATICS

From an attributional perspective, achievement in school results from motivation which, in part, results from attributions for the causes of academic successes and failures. Specifically, attribution theory suggests the following sequence:

Attributional style  $\longrightarrow$  Motivation  $\longrightarrow$  Achievement

The positive correlations between attributional style and mathematics achievement found in the PFF studies indicate a relationship between the two, although the correlational nature of the data make causal inferences inappropriate. No data are available on motivation per se; thus, motivation is a theoretically rather than empirically based link between attributions and achievement.

The model just presented is similar to Atkinson's (1957) model in that he saw the tendency to achieve as a function of motive to succeed in combination with expectancy of success and incentive value of success. Atkinson's expectancy of success was the probability of success as perceived by the individual. Attributional thinking, as envisioned by Heider (1958), Kelley (1967), and Weiner (1974, 1979, 1984) clarifies expectancy of success by putting it in terms of attributions for past successes and failures. A person with a mastery-oriented attributional style expects effort on a reasonable academic assignment to yield a high probability of success. A person with a learned-helpless attributional style expects effort will have little if any bearing on success; thus, the probability of success is uncertain, making tendency to achieve low. This relationship was diagrammed in Figure 5.1, which, on inspection, is very similar to the sequence suggested in the foregoing model.

Performance following failure (PFF) has not been included in this attribution-motivation-achievement sequence. Theoretically, PFF is a behavioral measure of learned helplessness and thus could have been substituted for attributionally defined attributional style in the model. Lack of a significant correlation between PFF and AS, however, together with conflicting findings concerning PFF and achievement, have resulted in AS being used rather than PFF.

Since gender differences were found on PFF in the first study and suggested in the second, PFF does have merit for continued study. In addition, the theoretical link between attributions and effort is strong enough to expect some lack of effort — and thus deterioration in performance — in the face of failure. A possible although ethically questionable method of finding significant performance deterioration in reaction to failure might involve an experimental setting where failure was continuous over an extended period of time. Alternatively, it might be possible to identify and track students who exhibited low motivation in mathematics and question those individuals about their attributions when their motivation seemed the lowest. This method, while not a true experiment, has the advantage of not subjecting students to failure beyond that which they were already experiencing in the classroom.

A final issue for consideration is whether or not the attribution-motivation-achievement sequence differs for females and males. There were gender differences on the first PFF instrument. The conjecture concerning saliency of immediate negative feedback for females, noted as part of the discussion of the relationship between PFF and achievement, could account for the variation in correlations between the two variables for females and males in the first PFF study. This is a research area that should be addressed. Another point to note is the lack of gender differences found on achievement scores in either the first or the second PFF studies. Although this finding was not mentioned earlier in the chapter, it is consistent with NAEP findings, where gender differences for 13-year-old students were less than 2% across the four cognitive levels assessed (Fennema & Carpenter, 1981). The attribution-motivation-achievement sequence offers a possible explanation of this result: If the achievement instruments were not precise enough to find gender differences, it is not surprising that the attribution measures had the same failing, especially if such differences were relatively modest. An alternate explanation is that no gender differences exist in either PFF or achievement. It is also harder to predict which variables may lead to gender differences in achievement when no achievement differences have been uncovered. In short, the findings of the PFF studies tend to confirm the observation of McHugh et al. (1982) that, while attributions are important, they have not, at this time, been shown to be the key to understanding differential achievement in females and males.

In closing, it is important to caution that the PFF studies reported here should not be used as conclusive evidence that gender differences in attributional style do not exist. Rather, it will take additional data to determine the relevance of the gender differences in the attribution-motivation-achievement sequence and whether such differences could account for documented gender differences in achievement for high school students (Fennema & Carpenter, 1981). It is possible, if not probable, that attributional thinking differs for females and males in significant ways. For example, it appears that adolescent females make attributions for their failures in mathematics somewhat more often than males (Kloosterman, 1988a). This would suggest that the sequence could explain achievement more easily for females than for males, although more research is needed on this issue. It is also possible that it takes several years for the sequence to affect females and males differentially and that such a time lag is the reason no gender differences in AS were found in the PFF studies. Students are not capable of differentiating the implications of various attributions before the age of 9 or 10 (Nicholls, 1978, 1984) and thus may not have been using attributional reasoning long enough for gender differences in such reasoning to appear. Had the same studies been repeated with older individuals, the findings could have been different. In short, there may well be gender differences in the attribution-motivation-achievement sequence that account for gender differences in achievement in high school. Only additional studies will answer this question definitively.

## REFERENCES

Atkinson, J. W. (1957). Motivational determinants of risk-taking behavior. *Psychological Review, 64*, 359–372.

Atkinson, J. W. (1964). *An introduction to motivation*. Princeton, NJ: Van Nostrand.

Bar-Tal, D. (1978). Attributional analysis of achievement-related behavior. *Review of Educational Research, 48*, 259–271.

Carpenter, T. P., Corbitt, M. K., Kepner, H. S., Lindquist, M. M., & Reys, R. E. (1981). *Results from the second assessment of the National Assessment of Educational Progress*. Reston, VA: National Council of Teachers of Mathematics.

Covington, M. V., & Beery, R. (1976). *Self-worth and school learning*. New York: Holt, Rinehart, & Winston.

Covington, M. V., & Omelich, C. L. (1979). Effort: The double-edged sword in school achievement. *Journal of Educational Psychology, 71*, 169–182.

Crandall, V. C., Katkovsky, W., & Crandall, V. J. (1965). Children's belief in their own control of reinforcements in intellectual-academic achievement situations. *Child Development, 36*, 91–109.

Dweck, C. S., & Bush, E. (1976). Sex differences in learned helplessness. Part 1: Differential debilitation with peer and adult evaluations. *Developmental Psychology, 12*, 147–156.

Dweck, C. S., Davidson, W., Nelson, S., & Enna, B. (1978). Sex differences in learned helplessness. Part 2: The contingencies of evaluative feedback in the classroom; Part 3: An experimental analysis. *Developmental Psychology, 14*, 268–276.

Dweck, C. S., & Gilliard, D. (1975). Expectancy statements as determinants of reactions to failure: Sex differences in persistence and expectancy change. *Journal of Personality and Social Psychology, 32*, 1077–1084.

Dweck, C. S., & Goetz, T. E. (1978). Attributions and learned helplessness. In J. H. Harvey, W. Ickes, & R. F. Kidd (Eds.), *New directions in attribution research* (Vol. 2) (pp. 157–179). Hillsdale, NJ: Lawrence Erlbaum.

Dweck, C. S., & Licht, B. G. (1980). Learned helplessness and intellectual achievement. In J. Garber & M. E. P. Seligman (Eds.), *Human helplessness, theory, and applications* (pp. 197–221). New York: Academic Press.

Dweck, C. S., & Reppucci, N. D. (1973). Learned helplessness and reinforcement responsibility in children. *Journal of Personality and Social Psychology, 25*, 109–116.

Educational Testing Service. (1979). *Sequential test of educational progress: Mathematics basic concepts*. Monterey, CA: CTB/McGraw-Hill.

Fennema, E., & Carpenter, T. P. (1981). Sex-related differences in mathematics: Results from National Assessment. *Mathematics Teacher, 74,* 554–559.

Fennema, E., & Peterson, P. (1984). *Classroom processes, sex differences, and autonomous learning behaviors in mathematics.* Final Report to the National Science Foundation. Madison: University of Wisconsin. School of Education.

Fennema, E., Wolleat, P., & Pedro, J. D. (1979). Mathematics attribution scale. *JSAS: Catalog of Selected Documents in Psychology 9*(5), 26. (Ms. No. 1837).

Gardner, E. F., Rudman, H. C., Karlsen, B., & Merwin, J. C. (1982). *Stanford Achievement Test.* Cleveland, OH: Psychological Corporation/Harcourt Brace Jovanovich.

Garofalo, J., & Lester, F. K. (1985). Metacognition, cognitive monitoring, and mathematical performance. *Journal for Research in Mathematics Education, 16,* 163–176.

Heider, F. (1958). *The psychology of interpersonal relations.* New York: John Wiley.

Horner, M. S. (1968). Sex differences in achievement motivation and performance in competitive and non-competitive situations (Doctoral dissertation, University of Michigan, 1968). *Dissertation Abstracts International, 30,* 407B.

Kelley, H. H. (1967). Attribution theory in social psychology. *Nebraska Symposium on Motivation, 15,* 192–238.

Kelley, H. H. (1973). The process of causal attribution. *American Psychologist, 28,* 107–128.

Kloosterman, P. (1985, April). *Sex-related differences in students' reactions to failure on algebra word problems.* Paper presented at the annual meeting of the American Educational Research Association, Chicago. (ERIC Document Reproduction Service No. ED 258 829).

Kloosterman, P. (1988a). Self-confidence and motivation in mathematics. *Journal of Educational Psychology, 80,* 345–351.

Kloosterman, P. (1988b). Motivating students in the secondary school: The problem of learned helplessness. *American Secondary Education, 17*(1), 20–23.

Leder, G. C. (1979). *Fear of success and sex differences in participation and performance in mathematics.* Unpublished doctoral dissertation, Monash University, Clayton, Victoria, Australia.

Leder, G. C. (1982). Mathematics achievement and fear of success. *Journal for Research in Mathematics Education, 13,* 124–135.

McClelland, D. C., Atkinson, J. W., Clark, R. A., & Lowell, E. L. (1953). *The achievement motive.* New York: Appleton-Century-Crofts.

McHugh, M. C., Frieze, I. H., & Hanusa, B. H. (1982). Attributions and sex differences in achievement: Problems and new perspectives. *Sex Roles, 8,* 467–479.

Murray, H. A. (1938). *Explorations in personality.* New York: Oxford University Press.

Nicholls, J. G. (1975). Causal attributions and other achievement-related cognitions: Effects of task outcome, attainment value, and sex. *Journal of Personality and Social Psychology, 31,* 379–389.

Nicholls, J. G. (1978). The development of the concepts of effort and ability, perceptions of academic attainment, and the understanding that difficult tasks require more ability. *Child Development, 49,* 800–814.

Nicholls, J. G. (1984). Conceptions of ability and achievement motivation. In R. Ames & C. Ames (Eds.), *Research on motivation in education. Vol. 1: Student motivation* (pp. 38–73). Orlando, FL: Academic Press.

Overmier, J. B., & Seligman, M. E. P. (1967). Effects of inescapable shock upon subsequent escape and avoidance responding. *Journal of Comparative and Physiological Psychology, 63,* 28–33.

Parsons, J. E., Meece, J. L., Adler, T. F., & Kaczala, C. M. (1982). Sex differences in attributions and learned helplessness. *Sex Roles, 8,* 421–432.

Parsons, J. E., Ruble, D. N., Hodges, D. L., & Small, A. W. (1976). Cognitive-developmental factors in emerging sex differences in achievement-related expectancies. *Journal of Social Issues, 32,* 47–61.

Rotter, J. B. (1954). *Social learning and clinical psychology.* Englewood Cliffs, NJ: Prentice-Hall.

Rotter, J. B. (1966). Generalized expectancies for internal versus external control of reinforcement. *Psychological Monographs, 80,* 1–28.

Rotter, J. B. (1975). Some problems and misconceptions related to the construct of internal versus external control of reinforcement. *Journal of Counseling and Clinical Psychology, 43,* 56–67.

Saranson, S. B., & Mandler, G. (1952). Some correlates of text anxiety. *Journal of Abnormal and Social Psychology,* 561–565.

Seligman, M. E. P., & Maier, S. F. (1967). Failure to escape traumatic shock. *Journal of Experimental Psychology, 74,* 1–9.

Silver, E. (1985). Research on teaching mathematical problem solving: Some under-represented themes and needed directions. In E. Silver (Ed.), *Teaching and learning mathematical problem solving: Multiple research perspectives* (pp. 247–266). Hillsdale, NJ: Lawrence Erlbaum.

Weiner, B. (1972). Attribution theory, achievement motivation, and the educational process. *Review of Educational Research, 42,* 203–215.

Weiner, B. (1974). *Achievement motivation and attribution theory.* Morristown, NJ: General Learning Press.

Weiner, B. (1979). A theory of motivation for some classroom experiences. *Journal of Educational Psychology, 71,* 3–25.

Weiner, B. (1984). Principles of a theory of student motivation and their application within an attributional framework. In R. E. Ames & C. Ames (Eds.), *Motivation in education. Vol. 1: Student motivation* (pp. 15–38). Orlando, FL: Academic Press.

# 6 Classrooms, Teachers, and Gender Differences in Mathematics

### MARY SCHATZ KOEHLER

*Studies that investigate how teachers interact with the males and females in their classes are reviewed in this chapter. Koehler discusses ways in which females and males are treated differently in classrooms and explores the effects of differential treatment on students' achievement in mathematics. Her own study builds on earlier research and highlights how students' learning environments are affected by the subtle interaction of many different variables. The facilitative, as well as debilitative, effects of teacher assistance are explored.*

This chapter examines the influence of the educational environment on the learning of mathematics by males and females. The learning environment is complex and difficult to analyze, but it provides some important — and perhaps startling — insights into the differences between the mathematics performance of females and males.

The educational environment is composed of many factors, such as texts, materials, teachers, physical surroundings, and organization. The most important of these, however, is the teacher. All of the teacher's actions and words have a bearing, either directly or indirectly, on students' learning of mathematics. Because the teacher is so influential on a student's learning of mathematics, a good part of this chapter will focus on teachers' behaviors and their relationship to the mathematics performance of males and females.

This chapter will first discuss one of the earliest suspected influences on gender differences in mathematics, namely, sex-role stereotyping. It will then discuss the movement to a more sophisticated rationale and research paradigm, which attempted to explain gender differences in mathematics through an analysis of teacher/student interactions. This will be followed by a line of research that combined teacher/student interactions with broader classroom processes and achievement outcomes. The last section will focus on research on the effect of organizational variables.

## EARLY INVESTIGATIONS

When the investigation of gender differences in mathematics began, the teacher's role in portraying mathematics as a male domain was examined through such factors as stereotypic remarks of teachers, use of sex-biased texts, and the sex of the teacher. As discussed in Chapters 2 and 4, if, due to stereotyping in various forms, mathematics is perceived as an inappropriate domain for females, then achievement in mathematics is not congruent with a female's sex-role identity. That is, a female successful in mathematics might believe that others perceive her as less feminine, and this might make her uncomfortable with her success. If a female feels that her success is not valued and is, in fact, not even appropriate, she may decide not to put forth the effort necessary for continued success in mathematics.

While blatant stereotypic remarks by classroom teachers are sometimes made, they are probably not as widespread as once believed; however, comments need not be made frequently to be damaging. For example, when I was in high school, a teacher was discussing the Scholastic Aptitude Test (a college-entrance examination), since the students were awaiting their scores. In an all-knowing voice that some teachers seem to have, the teacher announced, "Now girls, your English score will be higher than your math score and the boys will have their math score higher than their English score. This is because boys are better in math and girls are better in English." What might be the feelings of a girl who got "boy" scores, that is, a girl who did better in math than in English? This teacher probably had no idea that her remarks could have been detrimental to some students.

Because of many types of equity intervention programs, most teachers are now more aware of how damaging stereotypic comments can be, and they are careful to avoid making them. The problem has not been totally eliminated, however. In an eleventh-grade advanced algebra class, in a somewhat progressive Midwestern city, a teacher recently chastised the boys in the class for "letting" a *girl* get the highest grade on an exam!

In the mid 1970s, the influence of sex-biased mathematics texts was questioned (Kepner & Koehn, 1977; Kuhnke, 1977; Rogers, 1975). When texts were examined critically, it was found that boys' names were used in most of the story problems, especially those involving more "action." When some texts showed applications of mathematics in certain careers, most often white males were portrayed as the engineers or scientists using mathematics. While this may seem like a minor point, it could have been sending the message to the females (and minorities) in the class that mathematics was not for them, so they need not expend much effort on it. Since then, texts have been improved and many of the blatantly stereotypic portrayals have been removed. Most texts, as Nibbelink, Stockdale, and Mangru (1986) point out, are now "safely nonsexist." That is, texts avoid references to people, use gender-free labels, and use neutral-role problems, which neither confirm nor deny the traditional sex-role stereotypes. Nibbelink, Stockdale and Mangru argue that the type of books needed are "openly anti-sexist" ones.

Another factor that was addressed early in the research on females' underachievement in mathematics was that of the influence of the sex of the teacher. Some believed that students would perform better when taught by a teacher of the same sex. Research has indicated that this is not necessarily the case. In a review of studies that examined the performance of females and males with same or opposite-sex teachers, Brophy (1985) reported that, although there were a few studies indicating that children achieve better with same-sex teachers, "most studies showed no difference, and the studies showing a slight advantage to same-sex teachers were balanced by other studies showing a slight advantage to opposite-sex teachers" (p. 119).

It soon became obvious that the problem of differential performance of females and males in mathematics was much more complex than could be understood by studying any of the single factors of stereotypic remarks, biased texts, or sex of the teacher. The next level of investigation focused on the interactions that teachers had with students: the types of questions that were asked, who the teacher called on to respond to questions, how incorrect answers were handled, whether praise or criticism was given, and how a request for help was handled. Studies that investigated the complex area of teacher/student interactions (Koehler, 1985; Reyes, 1981; Wilkinson & Marrett, 1985) revealed that indeed teachers were treating males and females differently within the mathematics classroom, and that usually this difference was in favor of males. Several studies of this type, which are referred to as *differential treatment* studies, will now be reviewed in some detail.

## DIFFERENTIAL TREATMENT STUDIES

When researchers entered the mathematics classroom to investigate the differential mathematics achievement of males and females, the basic question under consideration was, Are females and males treated differently within the classroom, and, if so, how? The underlying assumption in these studies was that differential treatment led to differential achievement.

Figure 6.1 shows a typical differential treatment model. Researchers observed the behavior of teachers and students and the interactions between them, indicated by the arrows. These interactions might be teacher initiated, such as the teacher asking a question and calling on a particular male or female, or they might be student initiated, such as a female or male student asking a question.

### Elementary Level

Good, Sikes, and Brophy (1973) observed 16 seventh- and eighth-grade mathematics and social studies classes. Interactions between the teacher and each student in the class were coded for 10 hours, using the Brophy-Good Dyadic Interaction Observation System (Brophy & Good, 1970). The researchers concluded that "male and female students are not treated the same way" (p. 83). More specifically, they found that, with one exception, males were involved in more of all types of interactions than females. Males were asked a greater percentage of "process" or higher-cognitive-level questions, while females received a higher per-

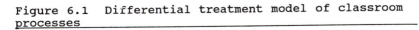

Figure 6.1   Differential treatment model of classroom processes

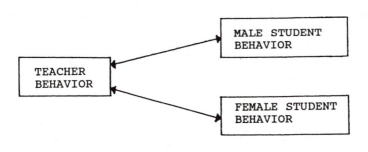

centage of "product" or lower-cognitive-level questions. Males also created more response opportunities for themselves by initiating more contacts with the teacher, calling out answers and guessing more frequently. Teachers directed more affect at boys, both positive and negative.

In addition, Good, Sikes, and Brophy (1973) examined the question of whether teachers interact with same-sex students differently from opposite-sex students. They concluded that teachers do not treat same-sex students differently nor more appropriately than opposite-sex students.

Leinhardt, Seewald, and Engel (1979) examined the hypothesis that "teachers teach girls . . . less mathematics than they teach boys" (p. 433). Their sample consisted of 33 second-grade classrooms. A videotape of each class was made, and then teacher and student behavior was coded from the videotape. The frequency, content, and length (in time) of each teacher/student interaction was coded. Their data showed that males received more academic and management contacts and more instructional time than did females. The authors concluded that "there are specific identifiable teacher behaviors that are differentially applied depending on the sex of the student" (p. 437).

Fennema and Reyes (1981) used a modification of the Brophy-Good Dyadic Observation System (Brophy & Good, 1970) to observe teacher/student interactions in sixth-, seventh-, and eighth-grade mathematics classes. Their sample was made up of students who were above the mean in mathematics achievement and were either high or low in confidence. Each class (8 classes in the sixth grade, 12 classes in the seventh grade, and 11 classes in the eighth grade) was observed for 15 to 20 days. Fennema and Reyes (1981) found that "teachers initiate more interactions with boys, ask boys more questions for discipline purposes, [and] ask boys more higher, lower, and non-mathematics questions" (p. 21). Males were also found to volunteer more and to call out more than females did. The researchers concluded that, "overall, girls are receiving less attention from teachers than are boys" (p. 34).

The next three studies dealt primarily with teacher/student interactions involving feedback given by the teacher to the students regarding their performance or behavior. Dweck, Davidson, Nelson, and Enna (1978) conducted a study in two fourth-grade classes and one fifth-grade class for about 10 days. The observations were made for the entire day, so the results pertain to all subjects, not just mathematics. All instances of evaluative feedback and attributions were noted and analyzed. It was found that more than 90% of the praise that males received for their academic work was praise of their intellectual capabilities, whereas only 80% of the praise that females received fell into this category. Almost 20% of the positive feedback that females received was for such things as neatness. When negative feedback was given for failure, 54% of the feedback the males received was critical of their intellectual capacities; the remaining criticism was for not following rules. For the females, however, 89% of the criticism they received following failure was aimed at their lack of intellectual prowess.

Heller and Parsons (1981) also focused specifically on teachers' use of evaluative feedback. Their study was conducted in eight seventh-grade and seven ninth-grade mathematics classes. Each class was observed for 10 hours, during which teacher/student interactions involving praise, criticism, and attributional statements were coded. Three categories of praise and criticism were coded, as they were directed to the quality of the work, to the form of the work, or to conduct. Four categories of attributional statements were coded as they pertained to task difficulty, effort, ability, and incorrect use of a mathematical operation. No significant gender differences were found, and the authors reported that "there was no evidence supporting the hypothesis that teachers use evaluative feedback or make differential attributions for boys and girls in junior high mathematics classes" (p. 1019).

In a related study, Parsons, Kaczala, and Meece (1982) observed 17 mathematics classes in Grades 5, 6, 7, and 9. Again teacher/student interactions were observed, including those involving praise, criticism, and attributional statements. In this study, females received less criticism overall and also less criticism regarding their work and conduct than did males. Females also asked more questions than males. However, the authors note that "boys and girls were treated similarly" and, "on the average, the boys and girls in this sample participated equally" (p. 333). (A more thorough discussion of attributions can be found in Chapters 4 and 5.)

## Secondary Level

Becker (1981) collected both quantitative data (in the form of teacher/student interactions) as well as qualitative data (using a participant-observer technique) in 10 geometry classes for 10 days. She found that teachers called on males who volunteered to respond more often than females who volunteered to respond, teachers asked males more process or higher-order questions, and teachers acknowledged males' call-outs more often than females'. From her qualitative observations, Becker found that males received 70% of the encouraging remarks made by the teachers, while females received 90% of the discouraging remarks. (These were remarks regarding students' academic abilities and/ or pursuits.) Teachers persisted in helping males longer and offered help to them more frequently than they did females. They interacted more informally with males than females and gave males both more positive and negative affect. Becker concluded that "there was differential treatment occurring in these geometry classes" (p. 50) and that this worked in a more positive way for males.

Stallings (1979) also conducted a study in tenth-grade geometry classes by observing 22 classes for three days each and recording classroom events and teacher/student interactions. The interactions were recorded in five-minute blocks of time, five times during a class period. Stallings found that teachers interacted with males more than with females, that they asked males more questions, and that they called on males who volunteered to respond more often than females who volunteered to respond, even though females volunteered as often as males did. Teachers gave males more individual attention, as well as more praise and more encouragement. Stallings concluded that "overall, men students were treated somewhat differently than are women students in geometry classes" (p. 18).

### Summary

Differential treatment studies, with few exceptions, concluded that females and males do receive differential treatment in the classroom. Regardless of the grade level, length of observation, or observation scheme that was used, differences were found consistently. It appeared that these differences favored males, since they had more interactions with the teachers, received more help and more teacher attention, and had more informal contacts with the teachers.

There are, however, two limitations to these studies of differential treatment. First, achievement outcomes were not usually considered. The question of whether or not this differential treatment of males and females had a positive or negative effect on a student's mathematics learning in either the long or the short term was not addressed. The assumption underlying these studies was that differential treatment in favor of males positively affected their achievement, and negatively affected females' achievement, but this assumption was not adequately tested.

The second limitation of these studies is that the scope of the classroom processes observed was rather narrow. These studies focused primarily on teacher/student interactions as descriptors of classroom processes. Although, in some cases, very complex coding schemes were used and many details of the interaction were recorded, an adequate picture of the classroom processes was not conveyed. Some studies went further and collected engaged-time data or limited qualitative data regarding the classroom environment. Even with these additions, however, many aspects of classroom processes remain to be observed.

## DIFFERENTIAL EFFECTIVENESS STUDIES

Attention will now turn to studies at the next level of complexity, that is, those that continued to investigate teacher/student interaction patterns but did so within broader contexts of classroom processes. Some studies looked closely at the types of activities in which students were involved; others looked carefully at achievement outcomes. Because these studies were aimed at identifying the classroom processes most effective for teaching male students or female students, they are referred to as *differential effectiveness* studies. Most of these studies followed the model shown in Figure 6.2.

This model extends the differential treatment model by relating teacher and student behaviors and teacher/student interactions to outcome measures for females and males. Outcome measures include affective measures, such as attitude inventories, and achievement measures, such as mathematics tests. Correlations are often computed between the frequency of particular types of interactions or particular teacher or student behaviors and the outcome or product measures. Hence, these studies are often referred to as *process/product* studies.

Figure 6.2   Differential effectiveness model of classroom processes

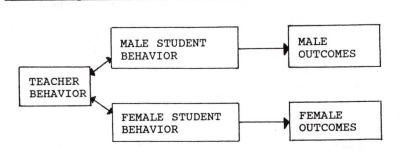

One study, by Reyes (1981), considered both differential treatment and a broader view of classroom processes, although achievement was not considered. Seventh-grade mathematics classrooms were observed, and it was found, overall, that teachers had more interactions with males, a finding similar to the differential treatment studies. However, Reyes went a step further and examined the data by class. It was found that in some classes males participated in more interactions with the teacher, while in other classes females predominated. Looking back at the observers' notes regarding the classes, it was found that classes where teachers had more interactions with males could be described as having more "teacher control."

Reyes (1981) explained that these teacher-controlled classes were those where teachers "maintain[ed] student attention on mathematics and prevent[ed] students from misbehaving" (p. 149), "kept the class actively working on mathematics" (p. 150), were "aware of what was happening with each individual in the class" (p. 150), and had a "firm control over events in the classroom" (p. 150). These classroom characteristics resemble some of the components of "active teaching," described by Good, Grouws, and Ebmeier (1983) as being effective teaching practices.

Another process/product study, conducted by Peterson and Fennema (1985) in 36 fourth-grade classes, examined the relationships between the students' classroom activities, teacher/student interaction patterns, and the mathematics achievement of the females and males on different levels of cognitive tasks. They reported that engagement by the student in a competitive mathematics activity was significantly *negatively* related to the low-cognitive-level mathematics achievement of females, but slightly *positively* related to the low-cognitive-level mathematics achievement of males. On the other hand, they found that engagement in a cooperative mathematics activity was significantly *positively* related to females' low-cognitive-level mathematics achievement, but significantly *negatively* related to males' high-cognitive-level mathematics achievement. Fennema and Peterson (1986) noted that research of this nature was indeed complex and that the observed teacher/student interactions did not lend themselves to a simple "recipe" for teachers to follow. They found that teachers behaved somewhat similarly toward males and females, but that there were different interaction patterns that were related to achievement for each gender, and also different patterns that related to high- and low-cognitive-level achievement. They suggested that teachers might promote females' high-level achievement by giving them more opportunity to engage in high-level interactions, by offering more praise and positive feedback for effort and the use of good strategies, and by encouraging them to be independent and divergent thinkers.

## THE KOEHLER DIFFERENTIAL EFFECTIVENESS STUDY

I examined the question of differential effectiveness at the secondary level in a process/product study conducted in eight beginning algebra classes (Koehler, 1985). Students were pretested on mathematics achievement in September and posttested near the end of the semester in December. Classes were observed 10 times between the two testings. Observations were made on time allocations in such categories as development (presentation of new material), review of previous day's homework, individual seatwork, and transitions. Teacher/student interactions were observed for females and males in the categories of teacher questions, teacher remarks, requests for help, and procedural and social comments. Last, teacher behaviors were rated on the categories of management, clarity, expectations, engaged time, and student involvement.

As with earlier studies, differential treatment of students in terms of teacher/student interactions did exist and was again in favor of males for the most part. Based on the usual assumptions in the differential treatment studies, it was expected that males would perform better than females in the classes where they interacted more frequently with teachers. The results, however, were not consistent with that assumption.

In six of the eight classes, males were involved in more interactions with the teacher than were females. Table 6.1 shows these results as well as the size of the discrepancy in the number of interactions, by sex, over a 10-day study period. For example, in class 1, each male was involved in eight more interactions than each female in the class, over a 10-day period. Table 6.1 also indicates which sex outperformed the other on the achievement measure, and it notes the magnitude of the difference in performance. (Effect sizes were computed according to Cohen, 1977). In only one of the six classes in which males were involved in more interactions (class 2) was the male achievement better than the female achievement. In two of the six classes (5 and 7) the female achievement surpassed the male achievement, and in three classes (1, 6, and 8) there was little or no difference in performance. There were two classes (3 and 4) where females were involved in more interactions than males; in one (class 3), females outperformed males, and in the other (class 4), males outperformed females. In other words, there was no clear-cut link between dominance in an interaction pattern and mathematics achievement.

**Table 6.1**  Interaction Patterns and Achievement, by Gender

| Class | Gender with more interactions | Number of interactions more per individual | Gender with higher achievement score | Magnitude of achievement difference |
|-------|------------------|------------------|------------------|------------------|
| 1 | Male | 8.2 | Female | Small |
| 2 | Male | 13.4 | Male | Medium |
| 3 | Female | 4.0 | Female | Medium |
| 4 | Female | 7.0 | Male | Medium |
| 5 | Male | 18.1 | Female | Medium |
| 6 | Male | 13.8 | Equal | None |
| 7 | Male | 1.0 | Female | Medium |
| 8 | Male | 8.0 | Equal | None |

These data were also analyzed by specific interaction categories, and no patterns were evident in that analysis either. This is not meant to imply that differential treatment in favor of males is not an important factor in the differential performance of females and males, but merely that it is probably not the sole factor involved.

To add further insight into my research, consider a study by Stanic and Reyes (1986). These researchers questioned the concern regarding seemingly inequitable treatment of students, when the assessment was based only on teacher/student interaction. They carried out an intensive case study in an above-average seventh-grade mathematics class with 16 students. Teacher/student interactions were recorded, interviews with students and the teacher were conducted, extensive field notes were taken, and various artifacts were collected. After a preliminary analysis of the data, they concluded that merely looking at teacher/student interaction patterns is not sufficient to understand truly how a student is being treated. In interpreting interaction patterns, they stressed the importance of considering teacher intentionality. Since teachers are taught to address individual differences in their students, they may very well *intend* to treat students differently. They point out that it is only after the teacher's intentions are considered that a particular interaction or behavior can be deemed appropriate or inappropriate for a particular student.

Stanic and Reyes (1986) also noted that, although differential student outcomes might result from differential treatment, they could also be the result of equal teacher treatment. This is because different students may "receive" the treatment differently, so that a given remark or teacher behavior might be beneficial to one student yet detrimental to another. The authors gave an example of differential reception of a teacher's homework assignments. Sometimes the teacher assigned a page to be worked on, without assigning specific problems; at other times the teacher gave one assignment and then gave a different assignment. The teacher was deliberately vague about the assignments, in the hope that the students would develop more responsibility and independence. When Stanic and Reyes interviewed the students, it was apparent that some were able to cope with this style of assigning homework, while others suffered from it.

The notion of a particular behavior being differentially beneficial to males and females was also examined in my study (Koehler, 1985). Two classes presented a particularly interesting contrast. Both were "honors" classes, that is, the students were somewhat accelerated and were covering more advanced topics. Both classes were small in size (about 15 students in each) and had about the same number of females and males. The two teachers had very similar styles of teaching. They were strong classroom managers; gave clear presentations of the material; kept their students on task; held high academic expectations for their students, as evidenced in part by the pace of the class and the assignments given; and were, in general, active mathematics teachers, as described by Good et al. (1983).

Although the two classes were similar in many respects, there was an interesting difference in achievement. Residualized gain scores were used to determine growth in achievement, and it was found that males in both classes achieved about the same, while the females in one class outperformed the females in the other. This difference, in fact, was quite large (effect size was 1.2). The question of interest, then, was, Why, in a pair of classes with so many similarities, would the females in one class (referred to as class A) perform so much better than the females in the other class (referred to as class B)?

After reviewing all the data, including all the informal field notes, differences emerged on one salient trait: help given to students by the teacher. In class B, students had more opportunity to seek help, the teacher offered help more often, and students were encouraged to seek help more than in class A. Let's look at these observations in more detail.

## Opportunity for Help

It was found that, in class B, much more time was allocated to seatwork than in class A (about 18 minutes per day, versus about 10 minutes per day). It was during this component of the class period that students could receive individual help. In addition to having more time to ask for help, it was also "easier" for students in class B to ask for help, since teacher B usually circulated in the room and was readily available for students' questions. Also, since the atmosphere in class B during seatwork was somewhat more relaxed than in class A, peers sometimes worked together, helping one another on the assignments. In contrast, teacher A did not circulate in the room, but was usually working at the teacher's desk; students had to walk up to the desk and "interrupt" the teacher in order to get help. Teacher A never appeared bothered by a student asking for help during this time, but neither did teacher A encourage students' questions.

It was noted from the interaction data that, indeed, students did ask for help more often in class B. There were about 40 student-initiated help interactions per day in class B, compared with about 11 per day in class A. Also, teacher B offered help to students more often (2.3 interactions per day) than did teacher A (1.3 interactions per day).

## Encouragement to Ask for Help

During the observation period, teacher A did not make any comments that would encourage students to ask for help, but rather made some comments that might in fact discourage such behavior. On one occasion a female student approached teacher A before class, just seconds before the bell was to ring. She said, "I had trouble with the homework." The teacher replied, "So?" To this the student said, "So, you're supposed to help me." The teacher made no response. Even though it was unrealistic for the student to expect help seconds before class was to start, had the teacher wanted to encourage the student to ask for help in the future, a better response would have been, "I'll help you later" or, "We'll go over those problems in class."

On another occasion, during the homework portion of the period, when students were asking questions about the previous night's assignment, teacher A commented, "I like the ones student Z asks — they're nice and short. Everyone else asks long, hairy ones." Although the tone of this comment was not harsh, the comment itself might inhibit some students from asking questions.

A third example involves two students who were absent one day. The next day they went up to teacher A and asked for help on what they had missed, which the teacher gave them. Students being absent is a situation that is fairly common, and a teacher will often offer help to students when they return, or at least tell them what material they missed. In this situation, although the teacher did not discourage the students from asking for help, they had to initiate the contact.

Another factor that may have inhibited students from asking questions was a fear about asking "dumb" questions. For example, when going over a chapter test, teacher A commented, "Some of you don't know a triangle has three sides!" in a tone that implied that students who did not know that were dumb. Another example occurred when students were multiplying the binomial $(x+7)(x-3)$. When one student gave the answer $8x^3+63x$ (which is far from the correct answer of $x^2+4x-21$), and another student asked incredulously, "How did she get that?" the teacher replied, "I don't care how she got it — it's *wrong*."

In contrast, teacher B appeared to encourage students to ask questions, or at least provided an atmosphere conducive to it. As stated before, the teacher moved up and down the aisles when the students were working alone. When a student raised her hand, the teacher approached that student's desk and was in the habit of saying the student's name in a questioning tone, as if to say, "How can I help you?"

Another example occurred when teacher B was going over the homework assignment. Usually students asked for one specific problem to be done; in this instance, however, a female student requested that the teacher do all the problems from #18 through #28. The teacher responded, "I'm not going to do all those," but then shortly afterward added, "If you want more help, I'll help you later."

Teacher B did not *always* encourage students to ask questions, either. During homework one day, teacher B stated, "I'm only going to spend about 10 minutes on these; I'm not going to do all of them, so make sure your question is an important one." This did not seem to intimidate the students at all — they still asked lots of questions.

## Comments

In summary then, in class B, more time was allocated for asking questions and the atmosphere was a relaxed one in which student questions were encouraged. In contrast, in class A, less time was allocated for student questions and the teacher tolerated but did not encourage questions.

This contrasting picture is intriguing. A common assumption might be that students would perform better in class B, the one with more emphasis on help. However, the data show that this is not the case. One explanation for this counterintuitive result can be found in the Autonomous Learning Behavior model suggested by Fennema and Peterson (1985) (see Chapter 4). In that model, it is hypothesized that an important factor relating to the achievement of students in mathematics is the extent to which they become autonomous learners of mathematics. Part of being an autonomous learner has to do with being an independent learner, and a facet of such independence is the ability to solve problems for oneself, without seeking help. These characteristics are thought to be especially important in the learning of high-level skills, as well as an important factor in the discrepant learning of males and females. Fennema and Peterson point out that socialization plays an important role in helping males to become autonomous learners to a greater degree than females.

The ALB model suggests that students who are given too much help may not begin to think for themselves and so may become dependent on others' help to solve problems. With respect to the students in classes A and B, the model appears valid. Students in class A, who were not given as much opportunity to seek help and were not encouraged to seek help as much, were becoming more autonomous learners. On the other hand, students in class B, where the classroom processes were more conducive to seeking and receiving help, were not becoming autonomous learners, but rather were becoming more dependent on others. (It is interesting to note that the most common question asked during seatwork by the students in class B was, "Is this right?" Most often, their answers were correct, but they needed the reassurance.)

The ALB model predicts that student achievement in class A should surpass achievement in class B. Indeed, this was the case; students in class A showed greater gains in algebra achievement than did the students in class B. The greatest differences occurred on high-level cognitive tasks and in female achievement.

## CLASSROOM ORGANIZATION

The focus of the chapter thus far has been the teacher's behaviors and interactions with students during whole-class instruction. However, in addition to what is said and done in a mathematics class, male and female performance may be affected by the organization of the classroom. In particular, two other modes of organizing for instruction, namely small groups and ability grouping, are pertinent topics for discussion.

### Small-Group Learning

There exists a fairly substantial and rapidly growing body of literature on small-group learning in mathematics. Unfortunately, as Lockheed, Thorpe, Brooks-Gunn, Casserly, and McAloon (1985) point out in their review, most research has not looked at the possible differential effectiveness of the small-group organization in terms of gender. In addition, most of the research has been done on the elementary and middle school levels, since very little small-group work currently occurs on the secondary level (Fey, 1981). Nevertheless, there are some insights to be gained that relate to gender differences.

An important characteristic of small-group work is that it is centered around the notion of working cooperatively, and in particular the seeking, giving, and receiving of help from peers. As just discussed, whether or not a student receives help, and the conditions under which help is offered, may affect the development of autonomous learning behaviors. In most small-group studies, a distinction is made between help and explanations: "Help" refers to a short response that includes the correct answer, whereas "explanation" refers to a more elaborate response that might describe a solution process. Webb and Kenderski (1984, 1985) report that most small-group studies have found that giving or receiving help is either unrelated or negatively related to achievement. On the other hand, most studies have found that giving an explanation to a peer is positively related to achievement for the giver. Receiving an explanation has usually been positively related to achievement, but Peterson, Wilkinson, Spinelli, and Swing (1984) found it unrelated to achievement. Most studies did not report whether the data had been examined for gender differences.

Two related studies involving small groups (Webb, 1984; Webb & Kenderski, 1985) did consider gender. The samples involved two above-average eighth-grade mathematics classes and two below-average ninth-grade mathematics classes. Students worked in small groups that either had a male majority, a female majority, or were gender balanced. Peer interactions within the groups were observed for a two-week period. The results differed for the high-achieving classes and the low-achieving classes. In the high-achieving classes, the males outperformed the females, the males received more explanations than females did, and the females' requests for help went unanswered at a rate double that of males. Females were more responsive to their peers and gave help more frequently. Males were helpful to other males more often than to females in their groups. Often the females (especially in groups with only one female) were ignored by the males. Females often asked more general questions, while males tended to ask questions that were more specific in nature. Both females and males tended to ask males for help more often than females.

In contrast, in the low-achieving classes, there was no significant difference in achievement, nor was there a difference in the interaction patterns of males and females. Males did not receive more help than females, and females were just as successful as males in getting their questions answered.

Webb and Kenderski (1985) commented that in the high-achieving class the males may have been exhibiting autonomous learning behaviors, as described by Fennema & Peterson (1985). They note that, by asking more specific questions, the males were perhaps more persistent than the females, since a more specific question would indicate that the problem had at least been tackled. In addition, males were more independent in the sense that they did not feel compelled to answer others' questions. It is clear that peer interactions that accompany small-group organization may provide a wealth of information regarding females' and males' learning of mathematics.

### Ability Grouping

Another mode of organizing for instruction is through ability grouping. Hallinan and Sorensen (1987) investigated the question of possible differential effectiveness of ability grouping on females and males. They conducted a study involving 48 classes in the fourth through seventh grades. Nineteen classes that used ability grouping for mathematics were contrasted with 29 classes that used whole-class instruction. The results showed that ability grouping for mathematics instruction did not have a direct effect on mathematics achievement. In addition, there was no differential effect on students' achievement by gender. However, the analyses showed that the assignment of students to ability groups did vary by sex. They found that "girls with high aptitude in mathematics are less likely to be assigned to the high-ability group than boys, and girls, in general, are more likely to be mis-assigned than boys" (p. 71). Since one of the "advantages" of ability grouping is that instruction is more appropriate in terms of level and pace, the improper assignment of females, especially high-achieving females, is a serious problem. Organizational decisions should be examined critically to make sure that they do not disadvantage females.

## SUMMARY AND CONCLUSIONS

This chapter has illuminated some of the classroom factors that could be contributing to the gap in mathematics performance between males and females. Classroom processes are indeed complex, and there is neither a single solution nor a particular style of teaching that can be uniformly recommended. There are, however, some suggestions or hints that can be gleaned from the research.

The differential treatment literature suggests that teachers promote equity by considering not only the quantity, but also the quality of their interactions with both female and male students. Teachers need to address higher-cognitive-level questions to females as often as to males. Teachers might also be encouraged to respond to requests for help with hints rather than complete solutions.

The differential effectiveness literature adds to the list of "clues" by suggesting that cooperative mathematics activities might be more beneficial than competitive ones. Further, in an effort to encourage autonomy on the part of the mathematics learners, teachers might also, on occasion, limit the amount of help they provide, with the hope that students will then become more independent problem solvers.

The question of how much help students need remains unanswered. Since each teacher knows his or her own students and their needs better than anyone else does, the classroom teacher must ultimately decide how much guidance to provide. Students may initially require different amounts of help; however, the teacher's goal should be that all students, male and female, persist and work independently in the mathematics classroom. Previously, teachers may have been enabling males to become independent, while unknowingly not enabling females to achieve autonomy. Once the importance of being an autonomous learner of mathematics is recognized, teachers will be able to focus on enabling students of both genders to become autonomous.

Last, the research on classroom organization indicates the importance of monitoring the composition of small groups in classrooms, so that all students learn to work cooperatively and have an opportunity to get the explanations and help they need. The research on ability grouping for instruction indicates the importance of accurately assigning students to groups.

In Chapter 2 in this book, data were presented regarding the gap in achievement between females and males. In reality, the gap does exist, but it is not exceedingly large. When one considers that females endure remarks from teachers or texts indicating that mathematics is not a female domain, are involved in far fewer interactions with their teachers involving mathematics, are rarely asked high-cognitive-level questions in mathematics, are encouraged to be dependent rather than independent thinkers, spend more time helping their peers and not getting helped in return, and are often not placed in groups that are appropriate to their level, it is amazing that the gap is not considerably larger.

One might speculate what females might be able to achieve with respect to mathematics if some of the imbalances that now exist in our educational environments were eliminated.[1]

## REFERENCES

Becker, J. R. (1981). Differential treatment of females and males in mathematics classes. *Journal for Research in Mathematics Education, 12*(1), 40–53.

Brophy, J. (1985). Interactions of male and female students with male and female teachers. In L. C. Wilkinson & C. B. Marrett (Eds.), *Gender influences in classroom interaction* (pp. 115–142). New York: Academic Press.

Brophy, J. E., & Good, T. L. (1970). Brophy-Good system (teacher-child dyadic interaction). In A. Simon & E. Boyer (Eds.), *Mirrors for behavior: An anthology of observation instruments* (Supple., Vol. A). Philadelphia: Research for Better Schools.

Cohen, J. (1977). *Statistical power analysis for the behavioral sciences* (rev. ed.). New York: Academic Press.

Dweck, C. S., Davidson, W., Nelson, S., & Enna, B. (1978). Sex differences in learned helplessness. Part 2: The contingencies of evaluative feedback in the classroom; Part 3: An experimental analysis. *Developmental Psychology, 14*(3), 268–276.

Fennema, E., & Peterson, P. L. (1985). Autonomous learning behavior: A possible explanation of gender-related differences in mathematics. In L. C. Wilkinson & C. B. Marrett (Eds.), *Gender influences in classroom interaction* (pp. 17–35). New York: Academic Press.

Fennema, E., & Peterson, P. L. (1986). Teacher-student interactions and sex-related differences in learning mathematics. *Teaching and Teacher Education, 2*(1), 19–42.

Fennema, E., & Reyes, L. H. (1981, October). *Teacher/peer influences on sex differences in mathematics confidence* (Final report of National Institute of Education grant NIE-G-79-0112). Madison: University of Wisconsin–Madison, Department of Curriculum and Instruction.

Fey, J. (1981). *Mathematics teaching today: Perspectives from three national surveys*. Reston, VA: National Council of Teachers of Mathematics.

Good, T. L., Grouws, D. A., & Ebmeier, H. (1983). *Active mathematics teaching*. New York: Longman.

Good, T. L., Sikes, J. N., & Brophy, J. E. (1973). Effects of teacher sex and student sex on classroom interaction. *Journal of Educational Psychology, 65*(1), 74–87.

---

[1]My thanks to Joanne Becker for enabling me to gain this insight.

Hallinan, M. T., & Sorensen, A. B. (1987). Ability grouping and sex differences in mathematics achievement. *Sociology of Education, 60,* 63–72.

Heller, K. A., & Parsons, J. E. (1981). Sex differences in teachers' evaluative feedback and students' expectancies for success in mathematics. *Child Development, 52,* 1015–1019.

Kepner, H. S., Jr., & Koehn, L. R. (1977). Sex roles in mathematics: A study of sex stereotypes in elementary mathematics texts. *Arithmetic Teacher, 24,* 379–385.

Koehler, M. S. (1985). *Effective mathematics teaching and sex-related differences in algebra one classes.* Unpublished doctoral dissertation, University of Wisconsin–Madison.

Kuhnke, H. F., (1977). Update on sex-role stereotyping in elementary mathematics textbooks. *Arithmetic Teacher, 24,* 373–376.

Leinhardt, G., Seewald, A. M., & Engel, M. (1979). Learning what's taught: Sex differences in instruction. *Journal of Educational Psychology, 71,* 432–439.

Lockheed, M., Thorpe, M., Brooks-Gunn, J., Casserly, P., & McAloon, A. (1985). *Sex ethnic differences in middle school mathematics, science and computer science: What do we know?* Princeton, NJ: Educational Testing Service.

Nibbelink, W. H., Stockdale, S. R., & Mangru, M. (1986). Sex-role assignments in elementary school mathematics textbooks. *Arithmetic Teacher,* October, 19–21.

Parsons, J. E., Kaczala, C. M., & Meece, J. L. (1982). Socialization of achievement attitudes and beliefs: Classroom influences. *Child Development, 53,* 322–339.

Peterson, P. L., & Fennema, E. (1985). Effective teaching, student engagement in classroom activities, and sex-related differences in learning mathematics. *American Educational Research Journal, 22*(3), 309–335.

Peterson, P. L., Wilkinson, L. C., Spinelli, F., & Swing, S. R. (1984). Merging the process-product and sociolinguistic paradigms: Research on small-group processes. In P. L. Peterson, L. C. Wilkinson, & M. Hallinan (Eds.), *The social context of instruction: Group organization and group processes* (pp. 125–152). San Diego: Academic Press.

Reyes, L. H. (1981). *Classroom processes, sex of student, and confidence in learning mathematics.* Unpublished doctoral dissertation, University of Wisconsin–Madison.

Rogers, M. A. (1975). A different look at word problems. *Mathematics Teacher, 68,* 285–288.

Stallings, J. A. (1979). *Comparison of men's and women's behaviors in high school math classes.* Menlo Park, CA: SRI International.

Stanic, G. M. A., & Reyes, L. H. (1986, April). *Gender and race differences in mathematics: A case-study of a seventh-grade classroom.* Paper presented at the annual meeting of the American Educational Research Association, San Francisco.

Webb, N. M. (1984). Sex differences in interaction and achievement in cooperative small groups. *Journal of Educational Psychology, 76*(1), 33–44.

Webb, N. M., & Kenderski, C. M. (1984). Student interaction and learning in
small-group and whole-class settings. In P. L. Peterson, L. C. Wilkinson,
& M. Hallinan (Eds.), *The social context of instruction: Group organization and group processes* (pp. 153–170). San Diego: Academic Press.

Webb, N. M., & Kenderski, C. M. (1985). Gender differences in small-group
interaction and achievement in high- and low-achieving classes. In L. C.
Wilkinson & C. B. Marrett (Eds.), *Gender influences in classroom interaction* (pp. 209–236). New York: Academic Press.

Wilkinson, L. C., & Marrett, C. B. (Eds.). (1985). *Gender influences in classroom interaction.* New York: Academic Press.

# 7

## Teacher/Student Interactions in the Mathematics Classroom: A Different Perspective

### GILAH C. LEDER

*In the previous chapters, students' and teachers' beliefs and practices were documented through a careful monitoring of American classrooms. In this section, Leder quantifies practices in Australian classrooms by using two different observation schedules. Similarities and differences in the information obtained through the different systems are noted. Qualitative and quantitative differences in teacher/student interactions are described. The results of three self-report measures of students' attitudes toward, and beliefs about, mathematics are also reported. Leder argues that the gender differences identified in earlier chapters are pervasive and not confined to the American culture.*

The role and behavior of mathematics teachers are closely examined in this chapter. To avoid duplication of work discussed in earlier chapters, the review of previous research is limited. Instead, data gathered in Australian classrooms are presented and discussed at some length, to determine the extent to which findings reported in previous chapters can be generalized beyond American classrooms.

### REVIEW OF RESEARCH ON INTERACTIONS

#### Frequency

As noted by Koehler in Chapter 6, findings on interaction patterns between teachers have been well summarized by Brophy and Good (1974). Their review confirmed that there were differences in the ways teachers interacted with male and female students in their classes. Males, they reported, tended to receive more criticism, be praised more frequently for correct answers, have their work monitored more frequently, and be given more contacts with their teachers. It was of interest that the sex of the teacher did not seem to affect these patterns.

More recent work has largely replicated these findings for the elementary school grades, particularly in mathematics classes. "Studies that have taken subject matter into account suggest that . . . boys may be getting more or better instruction in mathematics" (Brophy, 1985, p. 132). Observations of mathematics classes at the secondary school level (Becker, 1981; Eccles & Blumenfeld, 1985; Reyes, 1984; Stallings, 1979), as well as the work discussed in Chapter 6, have yielded varied results. While Becker (1981) reported that males had a substantially greater variety of interactions with their teachers in the classes she observed, Eccles and Blumenfeld (1985) found few consistent differences in teachers' treatment of females and males. They nevertheless reached this conclusion:

> We, like many others, have found small but fairly consistent evidence that boys and girls have different experiences in their classrooms. However, these differences seem as much a consequence of pre-existing differences in the students' behaviors as of teacher bias. Nonetheless, when differences occur, they appear to be reinforcing sex stereotyped expectations and behaviors. [p. 112]

Differences in teacher/student interactions are not confined to American classrooms. More frequent teacher attention toward males has been reported with respect to English schools by Galton, Simon, and Croll (1980) and Spender (1982); by Dunkin and Doenau (1982) and Leder (1987) in Australian classrooms; and by Moore and Smith (1980) in Papua New Guinean classrooms.

The differences in interaction patterns between teachers and certain groups of students are of more than theoretical interest. "Even if the impact on achievement scores is not immediately evident, it is quite probable that the cumulative impact over the course of the elementary school years is significant" (Leinhardt, Seewald, & Engel, 1979, p. 437). The effect on long-term motivational patterns—the development of task-intrinsic motivation or working for teacher (or peer) approval—has also been noted (Weinstein, Marshall, Brattesani, & Middlestadt, 1982). A major theme of this book is the ways in which teachers' reactions to students' behaviors in mathematics classes seem to contribute to and reinforce gender differences, notably in constructive persistence in tackling tasks, in appropriate risk-taking behaviors, and in the willingness to tackle more challenging mathematical tasks; in short, in activities that facilitate the development of high-level cognitive skills.

## Duration

Many of the studies concerned with possible differences in teacher interactions with female and male students have used an observation system based on the teacher/student dyadic interaction schedule described by Brophy and Good (1970) and discussed in some detail by Koehler in Chapter 6. In the study reported in this chapter, a modified version of this scheme was one of two classroom observation systems used. The second approach, which also falls within the process/product paradigm, relied on the methodology popularized by Rowe (1974a, 1974b). Instead of focusing on the number of exchanges between teachers and students, it emphasizes the duration of the exchange and, in particular, the "wait times" given by teachers, or taken by students, to reflect or to collect their thoughts before answering questions addressed to them.

Work within the wait-time paradigm has been carried out most frequently in science classes, somewhat less often in language and reading, and only rarely in mathematics. Two different wait times are generally identified:

> "Wait time of the species one type" may appear in two varieties. Normally, it begins when the teacher stops speaking and terminates when a student responds or the teacher speaks again. If, as sometimes happens, a teacher asks a question, pauses, or calls on a student and pauses again, the two forms are summed. Together they constitute an instance of the first species of wait time.
>
> "Wait time of the species two variety" is calculated by taking the sum of all pauses occurring on the student player side and terminates when the teacher speaks. . . . The pauses may occur within the speech of a single pupil or they may occur between the speech of a succession of pupils. [Rowe, 1974a, p. 86]

In the study reported in this chapter wait time one, engagement time between teacher and student, and overall attention time were measured. The latter measurements thus include the second kind of wait time and give a more appropriate representation of the time spent by a teacher with a specific student, once that student has been called on. It has been argued that extended interactions occur, especially with students for whom teachers have high expectations (Good, 1981). This is of particular interest for this book. As Fennema argues in Chapter 8, teachers may hold higher expectations for male students; if so, wait time for males should be higher than wait time for females.

According to Rowe (1974a), on average, students tend to be given less than 1 second to begin answering a question addressed to them. If an answer is not begun promptly, teachers usually repeat the question or call on a different student. The second variety of wait time is similarly brief, with teachers waiting, on average, 0.8 seconds before commenting on the answer, asking another question, or moving to a different topic. Consistent variations in wait times are reported when teachers' interactions with students they rate as good or poor are considered separately. Top students are allowed nearly 2 seconds to begin an answer, compared with weak students who are given less than 1 second (Rowe, 1974a).

Wait-time studies have usually investigated the effects of its manipulation on student achievement. Early studies suggested that training teachers to extend their wait time to three seconds or more led to a number of changes in students' behaviors. In particular, students' responses tended to be longer, students initiated more questions and more responses, failure to respond decreased, speculative responses were given more frequently, and the need for disciplinary comments decreased. Many of these conclusions have been substantiated in later research (Hassler, 1979; Rowe, 1986; Swift & Gooding, 1983; Tobin, 1980, 1986, 1987; Tobin & Capie, 1982). Increasing wait times has also frequently resulted in more advanced patterns of teacher questioning and reactions (Rowe, 1986). Several studies have found, not surprisingly, that teacher wait times are generally longer for higher-level questions (Arnold, Atwood, & Rogers, 1974; Fagan, Hassler, & Szabo, 1981; Rice, 1977), although this finding was challenged by the results of Gambrell (1983), who recorded shorter wait times after high-cognitive-level questions.

## STUDY OF GENDER DIFFERENCES

Gender differences have usually not been a variable of interest in wait-time studies. The work by Gore and Roumagoux (1983) is a rare exception. Their interest was not in the consequences of manipulating wait times, but rather in examining teachers' interactions in mathematics classes with their male and female students. Teachers, they reported, had a longer wait time when interacting with males. In an attempt to explore this finding further, a modified version of Rowe's observation schedule was also used in the research reported here. Specifically, careful measurement was taken of the amount of time spent by teachers interacting with students in mathematics class.

## Methodology

The study examined quantitative and qualitative aspects of the interactions between teachers and students, by gender, in mathematics classes in Grades 3, 6, 7, and 10. Two different observation schedules were used to maximize information about teacher interactions with females and males and to allow for comparisons between the two measures, an important focus of the study. Possible consistency of the findings across grade levels and across two different countries, the United States and Australia, was also a major interest.

The sample, adjusted for student absences during the lessons observed, consisted of 581 students. Of those, 52 males and 45 females were in Grade 3; 65 males and 75 females in Grade 6; 92 males and females each in Grade 7; and 80 males and 80 females in Grade 10. A total of 26 teachers from 14 different schools in the metropolitan area of Melbourne, Australia participated. As far as possible, classes at two grade levels were used in each school: a Grade 3 and a Grade 6 at the elementary level, and a Grade 7 and a Grade 10 at the high school level. The comparability of the student populations at the elementary and secondary schools was strengthened by selecting schools at the two levels in the same or similar districts. The resulting sample can be regarded as quasi-longitudinal.

Unlike the work outlined by Koehler in Chapter 6, which relied on observers seated in the class to gather data, in this study the lessons of interest were videotaped. This approach allowed the two different measures to be applied, without the need for an intrusively large number of observers.

A video camera, mounted on a tripod in one corner of the room, was used to monitor teacher/student interactions during mathematics lessons. Students were familiar with the equipment and largely ignored the camera and its operator. A built-in stopwatch allowed accurate (to one-tenth of a second) time records to be kept, with accuracy further enhanced through the use of a slow-tracking video replay facility. Apart from a request to select lessons that naturally required oral and questioning work (e.g., explanations of new work, oral revision, correction or consolidation of work previously done), no attempts were made to place any restrictions on teachers' presentation or behaviors. Classes observed included traditional, textbook-dominated lessons, lessons in which manipulatives were used, and other activity-based presentations.

Between 2.5 and 3 hours of lesson time were recorded for each teacher, giving a total recording time of some 70 hours. All relevant interactions that occurred between teachers and students were ultimately coded and timed.

The methodology employed in this study — videotaping lessons in intact classes — allowed detailed, comprehensive, and accurate records to be made of all teacher-student interactions with every student in the class. Repeated analysis of selected segments revealed high between- and within-coder reliability for each of the categories of interest.

Students' actual and perceived mathematics achievement were tapped in a number of ways. First, the operations Test in the Mathematics Profile Series (Australian Council for Educational Research, 1977) was administered to each student. The Grade-3 test consists of 20 items of graded difficulty, while the others contain 30 items, 30 items, and 40 items, respectively, for Grades 6, 7, and 10. (To allow comparisons across grade levels, raw scores were converted to brytes, the unit of measurement used in the test.) An example of an easy item on the Grade-6 test is $7 \times 8 = 8 \times \underline{?}$, while $(40-8) \times 4 = (40 \times 4) - (\underline{?} \times 4)$ is a more difficult item. As well as standard, basic recall of fact questions, each test includes items that require understanding and application of underlying principles.

In addition, teachers were asked to categorize students in their class in terms of below-average, average, good, and excellent achievement. Finally, in selected classes, students' perceptions of their own mathematics achievement and ability were tapped using three paper-and-pencil instruments. These were a simple self-report scale (Where would you rate yourself in mathematics, compared with your classmates? What is your academic ability, compared with your classmates'?); the Mathematics Attribution Scale (Wolleat, Pedro, Becker, & Fennema, 1980), described in detail in Chapter 4; and a 30-item Likert scale based on the Fennema-Sherman Mathematics Attitude Scales (Fennema & Sherman, 1976), also discussed comprehensively in Chapter 4.

As noted earlier, two different observation systems were used. In the first, teacher/student dyadic interactions were categorized using the approach of Brophy and Good (1970). Interactions were coded according to the type of question addressed to the class (low or high cognitive level), whether there was a single question or a sustained question set, the nature of any other exchange (procedural, discipline, or work-related), the setting (public or private), and the initiator of the exchange (teacher or student). Many of the work-related exchanges occurred in a private setting.

Low-cognitive-level questions were defined as routine recall quesions; high-cognitive-level questions required students to synthesize, generalize, or make abstractions. A conservative approach was used for coding the relatively small number of ambiguous questions as being of a low rather than high cognitive level. Procedural exchanges were those that described routine matters ("Organize yourselves into groups of six," "Use a colored pencil for that") or were personal comments ("I hope your mother is feeling better again"). Disciplinary exchanges, questions, or comments are self-explanatory. Work-related exchanges (i.e., interactions concerning the subject matter at hand) were further divided into teaching or monitoring exchanges for the seventh- and tenth-grade samples. For these samples, student-initiated high- and low-cognitive-level questions were coded separately from other student-initiated interactions. Exchanges clearly audible to the whole class were categorized as public, while more intimate, face-to-face exchanges were coded as private. For Grade 7 only, qualitative differences in teacher/student interactions were also examined.

The second observation scheme, based on that of Rowe (1974a, 1974b) involved monitoring time intervals. For teacher-initiated questions, these included wait time, the engagement time per subsequent single exchange, and the overall attention time (see Figure 7.1). In this study, wait time described the pause $(X_1X_2)$ or pauses $(X_0X_1 + X_1X_2)$ following an initial question by the teacher and directed at a specific student. As can be seen in Figure 7.1, for single questions, the subsequent engagement time consisted of the time taken by the student to answer the question, the subsequent wait time, and the teacher's response, if one was provided $(X_2X_3 + X_3X_4 + X_4X_5)$. The corresponding overall attention time included the initial wait time as well and was thus designated by $(X_0X_1 + X_1X_2 + X_2X_3 + X_3X_4 + X_4X_5)$. For sustained question episodes, additional cycles of this model were added, as appropriate. Figure 7.1 shows the total engagement time for an initial question plus one follow-up question to the same student. The initial wait time $(X_0X_2)$ or $(X_1X_2)$ was added to this sequence for the overall attention time. For other exchanges, only overall attention time was measured. Single-word or very brief disciplinary comments were not timed at all.

### Results of Mathematics Achievement Measures

The Operations Test results are shown in Table 7.1. There were no statistically significant differences in the performance of males and females in Grades 3, 6, and 7. At the Grade-10 level, however, males achieved significantly better than females $(t_{169} = 2.48, p < .05)$. The steady increase in students' scores from Grade 3 to Grade 10 is worth

Figure 7.1   Representation of time intervals (in
seconds)

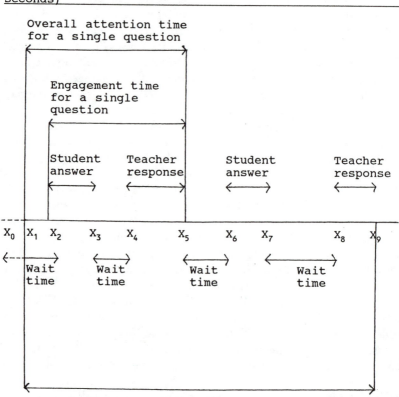

Categories of time intervals measured for teacher-
initiated questions in the second (Rowe) observation
scheme

noting. The quasi-longitudinal composition of the sample allows one to
conclude that students' mathematical knowledge, as measured by the
Operations Test, increases with increase in grade level.

In general, the test scores obtained coincided with the teachers'
perceptions of students' ability. The relationship between the two measures of achievement can be summarized by stating that, at each grade

**Table 7.1**   Operations Test Results, by Gender[a]

|  | MALES | | FEMALES | | |
| GRADE | $n$ | *Mean* | $n$ | *Mean* | $t$-TEST |
| --- | --- | --- | --- | --- | --- |
| 3 | 55 | 41.8 | 48 | 41.6 | $t_{101} = .21$ |
| 6 | 65 | 51.8 | 80 | 50.8 | $t_{143} = .74$ |
| 7 | 96 | 53.3 | 100 | 54.3 | $t_{194} = -1.28$ |
| 10 | 87 | 65.5 | 84 | 63.6 | $t_{169} = 2.48^b$ |

[a]The data for students absent from some of the lessons videotaped are included in this table.
[b]Significance level: $p < .05$.

level, the mean score for students rated as below average was less than the mean score of students rated average, which, in turn, was less than the mean score of students rated good. Students rated as excellent had the highest mean score. Yet, when students in three Grade-7 classes, in which the performance of males and females on the Operations Test was comparable, were asked to indicate whether they considered themselves above average, average, or below average in mathematics, compared to their classmates, males and females responded differently. Approximately 65% of the males rated their mathematics ability as above average, compared with approximately 20% of the females. Similar results were obtained with respect to academic ability: 62% of the males, compared with 18% of the females, considered themselves to have above-average academic ability, compared to their classmates.

Responses to items on the Likert scale are suggestive of further gender differences in students' beliefs (Leder, 1988). Items that elicited significantly stronger agreement from males than females included

> Mathematics is one of the most worthwhile and necessary subjects to take.
> I have a lot of self-confidence when it comes to mathematics.
> I am confident I can get good marks (grades) in mathematics.
> I study mathematics because I know how useful it is.
> One of my highest priorities is to be an outstanding student in mathematics.
> It is very important to get good marks (grades) in mathematics.
> Mathematics is enjoyable and stimulating to me.
> Being regarded as smart in mathematics is a great thing.

The following items, on the other hand, drew significantly stronger agreement from females than males:

> I'm not good at mathematics.
> I'm not the type to do well in mathematics.
> Figuring out mathematics problems does not appeal to me.
> I do as little work in mathematics as possible.

Gender differences in students' beliefs about their mathematics ability and their confidence in coping with mathematics are further reinforced by their responses on the Mathematics Attribution Scale. Significant differences occurred for three of the eight components: success due to ability, failure due to ability, and failure due to difficulty of task. Males, more often than females, attributed their success to ability, while females were more likely than males to attribute failure in mathematics to ability and to the task difficulty.

It is worth recalling that these gender differences in students' internal beliefs about themselves as learners of mathematics were expressed by two groups of students who performed equally well on the mathematics achievement test. Moreover, these mathematics scores were substantiated by the teachers' ratings of their students' mathematics ability. The incongruencies tapped by the three self-perception instruments parallel the findings reported by Meyer and Koehler (Chapter 4 in this volume) with American samples. Students' internal beliefs are shaped by factors beyond actual achievement.

### Findings on Frequency of Interaction

It is appropriate to turn now to the data gathered through the observation schedules. Frequency of interaction findings are summarized in Table 7.2. The quasi-longitudinal format of the data allows for some general observations. Teachers asked more low- than high-cognitive-level questions, with the discrepancy being greatest at Grades 6 and 7. With the exception of the Grade-10 students, the proportion of low- to high-cognitive-level questions was similar for females and males. Students themselves asked few cognitive questions but instead approached teachers for general assistance. Elementary teachers seemed to ask proportionately more public high- and low-cognitive-level questions; private exchanges were more common at the secondary level. Public, teacher-initiated exchanges formed the bulk of the data. At three of the four grade levels monitored, the ratio of teacher- to student-initiated exchanges was remarkably similar for males and females: 8.1:1

TEACHER/STUDENT INTERACTIONS IN THE MATHEMATICS CLASSROOM 159

**Table 7.2**   Mean Number of Interactions, by Gender and Grade Level

|  | GRADE 3 | | GRADE 6 | | GRADE 7 | | GRADE 10 | |
|---|---|---|---|---|---|---|---|---|
|  | M | F | M | F | M | F | M | F |
| *Interaction category* | | | | | | | | |
| Low cog. Q | 9.9 | 8.3 | 9.2 | 9.0 | 7.6 | 7.6 | 7.2 | 7.4 |
| High cog. Q | 1.9 | 1.7 | 1.3 | 1.2 | .9 | .9 | 2.0 | 0.6 |
| Proced. exch. | 1.8 | 1.4 | .8 | .6 | 2.0 | 1.9 | 2.0 | 1.2 |
| Discip. exch. | 2.5 | 1.0 | .7 | .3 | 1.9 | 1.2 | 2.6 | 0.5 |
| Work-rel. exch. | 6.6 | 6.3 | 3.6 | 1.8 | 6.4 | 5.5 | 7.1 | 6.0 |
| (Teaching) | | | | | (1.6) | (1.4) | (2.3) | (2.4) |
| (Monitoring) | | | | | (4.8) | (4.1) | (4.8) | (3.5) |
| Student Q | | | | | .2 | .1 | 0.7 | 0.3 |
| Total | 22.7 | 18.7 | 15.6 | 12.9 | 19.0 | 17.2 | 21.6 | 16.0 |
| *Interaction setting* | | | | | | | | |
| Public | 18.6 | 14.9 | 13.5 | 11.7 | 13.4 | 12.4 | 14.4 | 9.7 |
| Private | 4.2 | 3.4 | 2.5 | 1.4 | 5.6 | 4.7 | 7.0 | 6.3 |
| Total | 22.8 | 18.3 | 16.0 | 13.1 | 19.0 | 17.1 | 21.4 | 16.0 |
| *Interaction initiator* | | | | | | | | |
| Teacher | 20.3 | 16.4 | 13.6 | 12.0 | 14.7 | 13.4 | 15.9 | 12.1 |
| Student | 2.5 | 2.2 | 2.0 | 1.1 | 4.3 | 3.6 | 5.5 | 3.9 |
| Total | 22.8 | 18.6 | 15.6 | 13.1 | 19.0 | 17.0 | 21.4 | 16.0 |

*Key:* Low-cog. = Low cognition; High-cog. = High cognition; Proced. exch. = Procedural exchange; Discip. exch. = Discipline exchange; Work-rel. exch. = Work-related exchange.

and 7.5:1 for Grade 3; 6.8:1 and 10.9:1 for Grade 6; 3.4:1 and 3.7:1 in Grade 7; and 2.9:1 and 3.1:1 in Grade 10. Thus, students' initiatives reflected teacher focus on them.

The significance of these data and the groups attracting more interactions are specified in Table 7.3. It not only illustrates that males interacted with their teachers more frequently than females, but also highlights the interaction categories for which this occurred. No clear trend emerged for low- and high-cognitive-level questions, though, most significantly at the Grade-10 level, males attracted more high-cognitive-level questions ($\chi_1^2 = 58.74$, $p < .0001$). While males dominat-

**Table 7.3**   Gender Receiving Significantly Greatest Number of Teacher
Interactions, by Grade Level

|                              | GRADE 3 | GRADE 6 | GRADE 7 | GRADE 10 |
|------------------------------|---------|---------|---------|----------|
| *Interaction category*       |         |         |         |          |
| Low cognition Q              | Males[b] | NS | NS | NS |
| High cognition Q             | NS | NS | NS | Males[d] |
| Procedural exchange          | Males[a] | NS | NS | Males[c] |
| Discipline exchange          | Males[d] | Males[b] | Males[c] | Males[d] |
| Work-related exchange        | NS | Males[d] | Males[b] | Males[b] |
| (Teaching)                   |  |  | (NS) | (NS) |
| (Monitoring)                 |  |  | (Males[a]) | (Males[c]) |
| Student Q                    |  |  | Males[b] | Males[b] |
| All categories               | Males[d] | Males[d] | Males[c] | Males[d] |
| *Interaction setting*        |         |         |         |          |
| Public                       | Males[d] | Males[b] | Males[a] | Males[d] |
| Private                      | NS | Males[d] | Males[b] | NS |
| *Interaction initiator*      |         |         |         |          |
| Teacher                      | Males[d] | Males[b] | Males[a] | Males[d] |
| Student                      | NS | Males[d] | Males[a] | Males[d] |

[a] $p < .05$.    [b] $p < .01$.    [c] $p < .001$.    [d] $p < .0001$.

ed public interactions at each grade level, this was true for private
interactions between teacher and students only at Grades 6 and 7.

Teachers' greater focus on males was further reinforced by the tendency for the latter to initiate more interactions in Grades 6, 7, and 10
($\chi_1^2 = 19.47$, 5.13, and 21.23, respectively) and to ask more cognitive
questions in Grades 7 and 10 ($\chi_1^2 = 5.58$ and 10.99, respectively). While
males attracted more disciplinary exchanges at each grade level, removing this category from the total number of exchanges monitored still left
males with significantly more interactions at each grade level.

Some interesting gender differences emerged when the data for the
seventh- and tenth-grade students were correlated with teacher ratings.
Seventh-grade students who were rated as excellent had fewer interactions overall with the teacher than did any other group (males-17.4,
females-14.5), while females rated as below average had more interactions (27.5) than any other group. Tenth-grade females who were rated
as excellent had more interactions (21.1) than the other three groups of

females, but significantly fewer than males similarly rated ($\chi_1^2 = 10.58$, $p < .005$).

## Findings on Qualitative Differences

The transcripts for all seventh-grade teachers were examined for explicit attributions made by teachers for students' successes or failures during the lessons, according to whether performance was attributed to student ability or effort, the task difficulty, or other factors. Examples identified included

"You might show more understanding if you listened" (failure attributed to effort).

"That's good. You got these easy ones right" (success attributed to difficulty of task).

A total of 46 such comments, 25 to males and 21 to females, occurred during the 32 lessons observed (approximately 20 hours of lesson time). Almost all the attributions referred to the task difficulty or to student effort. The following ability attribution was a notable exception:

"That's brilliant, Richard, really excellent" (success attributed to ability).

On average, teachers made approximately two attributive statements per teaching hour. There was no appreciable difference in the numbers of females and males who attracted such comments on mathematical tasks, nor in the balance of effort and task attributions given to them.

## Findings on Time Variables

Details of the length of time spent on different interactions were gathered using the second observation schedule (refer to Figure 7.1). Means are shown in Table 7.4; significant differences and groups attracting more time, in Table 7.5.

As can be seen in Table 7.4, for low-cognitive-level questions, teachers' wait times typically exceeded 2 seconds. Longer wait times, ranging from 2.6 to 4.3 seconds, were given for high-cognitive-level questions. Not only did high-level questions attract more time per unit of exchange, overall attention time per exchange set was also longer

**Table 7.4**  Mean Time (in Seconds) Spent on Interaction, by Gender and Grade Level

| | WAIT TIME | | SUBSEQUENT TIME/QUESTION | | ATTENTION TIME/EXCHANGE | |
|---|---|---|---|---|---|---|
| | M | F | M | F | M | F |
| *Grade 3* | | | | | | |
| Low-cog. Q | 1.9 | 2.2 | 3.9 | 4.3 | 6.5 | 7.5 |
| High-cog. Q | 3.4 | 2.7 | 6.4 | 8.9 | 11.9 | 16.6 |
| Proced. exch. | | | | | 15.3 | 12.2 |
| Discip. exch.[a] | | | | | 8.0 | 4.3 |
| Work-rel. exch. | | | | | 12.3 | 30.7 |
| *Grade 6* | | | | | | |
| Low-cog. Q | 2.2 | 2.0 | 4.6 | 4.5 | 8.0 | 7.7 |
| High-cog. Q | 2.6 | 2.7 | 6.8 | 4.7 | 13.4 | 8.8 |
| Proced. exch. | | | | | 71.7 | 35.1 |
| Discip. exch.[a] | | | | | 12.6 | 4.3 |
| Work-rel. exch. | | | | | 34.7 | 35.2 |
| *Grade 7* | | | | | | |
| Low-cog. Q | 2.1 | 2.3 | 4.7 | 4.6 | 7.9 | 7.6 |
| High-cog. Q | 3.7 | 2.8 | 8.5 | 7.5 | 12.6 | 14.0 |
| Proced. exch. | | | | | 5.6 | 6.8 |
| Discip. exch.[a] | | | | | 4.3 | 3.2 |
| Work-rel. exch. | | | | | 19.6 | 17.2 |
| (Teaching) | | | | | (45.7) | (40.6) |
| (Monitoring) | | | | | (10.6) | (8.5) |
| Student Q | | | | | 17.8 | 8.5 |
| *Grade 10* | | | | | | |
| Low-cog. Q | 3.0 | 3.4 | 5.0 | 5.8 | 9.9 | 13.0 |
| High-cog. Q | 3.4 | 4.3 | 8.4 | 7.8 | 16.4 | 13.6 |
| Proced. exch. | | | | | 9.1 | 9.3 |
| Discip. exch.[a] | | | | | 3.4 | 4.1 |
| Work-rel. exch. | | | | | 22.1 | 22.9 |
| (Teaching) | | | | | (46.7) | (40.7) |
| (Monitoring) | | | | | (9.2) | (10.2) |
| Student Q | | | | | 18.7 | 19.5 |

[a]Very brief (e.g., single-word) disciplinary comments were not timed.
*Key:* Low-cog. = Low cognition; High cog. = High cognition; Proced. exch. = Procedural exchange; Discip. exch. = Discipline exchange; Work-rel. exch. = Work-related exchange.

**Table 7.5**   Gender Receiving Significantly Greatest Amount of Teacher Time, by Grade Level

|  | WAIT TIME | SUBSEQUENT TIME/QUESTION | ATTENTION TIME/EXCHANGE |
|---|---|---|---|
| *Grade 3* | | | |
| Low-cog. Q | Females[a] | NS | NS |
| High-cog. Q | NS | Females[a] | Females[a] |
| Proced. exch. | | | NS |
| Discip. exch. | | | NS |
| Work-rel. exch. | | | Females[a] |
| *Grade 6* | | | |
| Low-cog. Q | NS | NS | NS |
| High-cog. Q | NS | Males[d] | Males[b] |
| Proced. exch. | | | Males[a] |
| Discip. exch. | | | Males[a] |
| Work-rel. exch. | | | NS |
| *Grade 7* | | | |
| Low-cog. Q | NS | NS | NS |
| High-cog. Q | NS | Males[a] | NS |
| Proced. exch. | | | Females[a] |
| Discip. exch. | | | NS |
| Work-rel. exch. | | | NS |
| (Teaching) | | | (NS) |
| (Monitoring) | | | (NS) |
| Student Q | | | NS |
| *Grade 10* | | | |
| Low-cog. Q | NS | Females[d] | Females[d] |
| High-cog. Q | NS | NS | NS |
| Proced. exch. | | | NS |
| Discip. exch. | | | NS |
| Work-rel. exch. | | | NS |
| (Teaching) | | | (NS) |
| (Monitoring) | | | (NS) |
| Student Q | | | NS |

[a]$p<.05.$    [b]$p<.01.$    [c]$p<.001.$    [d]$p<.0001.$
*Key:* Low-cog.=Low cognition; High-cog.=High cognition; Proced. exch.=Procedural exchange; Discip. exch.=Discipline exchange; Work-rel. exch.=Work-related exchange.

than for low-level questions. Students' own questions attracted reasonably long attention times.

The data in Table 7.5 are less readily summarized. Overall, females and males were more often given equal time than unequal time. Noteworthy is the longer time given to females on a number of interactions at Grade 3 and on low cognitive questions at Grade 10. Males were given a longer time for certain high cognitive exchanges at Grades 6 and 7.

Analysis of seventh- and tenth-grade data by gender as well as by teacher rating revealed two significant differences for Grade 7, and one for Grade 10. For the highest-rated students in Grade 3, subsequent time per low-cognitive-level question was longer with females than males, but it was longer with males in the other three rating groups ($F_{3,1358} = 5.99$). Grade-3 students received similar attention times per teaching exchange, except for the lowest-rated males, with whom the teacher spent approximately three times as long as with any other group.

## DISCUSSION

Classroom observation schedules typically involve the monitoring, by in-class observers, of teacher interactions with selected students for discrete time intervals within a lesson. In the study reported here, however, continuous monitoring of all teacher interactions with all students was achieved through videotaping intact classes during complete lessons.

The resulting statistics help to sketch a general picture of the lessons observed. Despite a request for a maximum amount of oral work, the cycle of oral group work followed by private seatwork, followed by more oral work, described by Brophy and Good (1985) for American mathematics classrooms, was typical as well of Australian classrooms. Also as was the case for American classrooms, in my study relatively few explicit attributive statements for students' success or failure on mathematical tasks were made by teachers. However, the initial wait times I recorded came closer to the ideal of three seconds or more advocated by Rowe (1986) than has been reported in studies of American classrooms.

The broad findings I obtained using the modified Brophy and Good (1970) observation schedule were consistent with those reported with the more traditional approach to gathering data (recording events during parts of the lesson and for only some of the students). In Chapter 6, Koehler provides further evidence for this. Overall, males interacted more frequently than females with their teachers at each of the four

grade levels observed. Statistically significant differences were uniformly in this direction. Differences in total numbers of interactions monitored ranged between males having just over 10% more interactions
than females did with teachers at the Grade-7 level to over 30% more at
the Grade-10 level. While such a summary statement masks within- and
between-class differences, it nevertheless reflects the overall classroom
climate experienced by students over a longer period.

As in much of the work reviewed by Brophy (1985), the differences
in interaction patterns were subtle. Teachers, by and large, addressed as
many questions to females as to males. They admonished males more
often, however, and had more work-related exchanges (particularly
monitoring exchanges) with them, accepted more cognitive questions
from males, and responded more frequently to other requests for assistance. The overall consistency of the data at the different grade levels is
striking. The pervasiveness of males' domination of teacher attention in
Australian mathematics classrooms, in terms of frequency of interactions, is highlighted by the similarity of such findings in contemporary
American classrooms.

The discrepancies in teachers' interactions with males and females
preceded gender differences in mathematics achievement. Only at the
Grade-10 level, where differences in frequency of teachers' interactions
with males and females were most pronounced, did males outperform
females on the mathematics achievement test. This treatment of females
and males cannot be explained in terms of response to unequal student
achievement.

The inadequacy of capturing the complexity of the classroom climate with any one observation schedule becomes apparent when the
findings of the two different schemes applied to the present data are
compared. While there were no differences in the incidence of high- and
low-cognitive-level questions teachers addressed to males and females, 8
of the 12 significant interactions with respect to time spent with students occurred for these categories. Above Grade 3, females were more
likely to get extra time on the routine, low-cognitive-level questions,
males on the more difficult and challenging high-cognitive-level questions. Inspection of the data in Table 7.4 indicates that nonsignificant
differences were generally consistent with this trend. Can one infer that
these differences in allocated times are reflective of teachers' beliefs that
females should be encouraged particularly on low-level, routine questions (which are less useful as a preparation for advanced mathematics
courses), at least once a certain level of proficiency has been reached,
while males need to practice skills required for advanced mathematics
studies? The relatively few significant differences scattered over the four

grade levels preclude a more intensive interpretation of the data. The finding of Gore and Roumagoux (1983) that teachers had longer wait times when interacting with males than females was not confirmed in this study.

## CONCLUSION

The nature and extent of gender differences in interaction patterns between teachers and students are subtle and their description is clearly not independent of the methods for gathering data. Taken together, however, the two sets of data examined in this chapter point to a greater and more constructive involvement between mathematics teachers and their male students. It is important to remember, however, that schools do not function in a vacuum. They reflect the dominant cultural values and expectations of the society they serve. There is abundant evidence that females and males are not always treated equitably in the wider society outside schools; in fact, differences in treatment of the sexes may well be more pronounced outside than inside the classroom. The teachers observed in the study described in this chapter were caring individuals, anxious to maximize the potential of all their students. The interaction patterns quantified should be interpreted in this context.

The data presented suggest ways in which teachers can monitor their own behavior and make adjustments, if necessary, so that they facilitate and enhance the learning of mathematics for all their students.

## REFERENCES

Arnold, D. S., Atwood, R. K., & Rogers, V. M. (1974). Question and response levels and lapse time intervals. *Journal of Experimental Education, 43,* 11–15.

Australian Council for Educational Research. (1977). *Operations test.* Hawthorn, Victoria: Author.

Becker, J. (1981). Differential treatment of females and males in mathematics classes. *Journal for Research in Mathematics Education, 12,* 40–53.

Brophy, J. (1985). Interactions of male and female students with male and female teachers. In L. C. Wilkinson & C. B. Marrett (Eds.), *Gender influences in classroom interaction* (pp. 115–142). New York: Academic Press.

Brophy, J., & Good, T. (1970). The Brophy-Good dyadic interaction system. In A. Simon & E. Boyer (Eds.), *Mirrors for behavior: An anthology of class-*

*room observation instruments: 1970 Supplement, Vol. A.* Philadelphia: Research for Better Schools.

Brophy, J. E., & Good, T. L. (1974). *Teacher-student relationships: Causes and consequences.* New York: Holt, Rinehart & Winston.

Brophy, J. E., & Good, T. L. (1985). Teacher behavior and student achievement. In M. C. Wittrock (Ed.), *Handbook of research on teaching* (3rd ed.) (pp. 328–375). New York: Macmillan.

Dunkin, M. J., & Doenau, S. J. (1982). Ethnicity, classroom interaction, and student achievement. *Australian Journal of Education, 26,* 171–189.

Eccles, J. S., & Blumenfeld, P. (1985). Classroom experiences and student gender: Are there differences and do they matter? In L. C. Wilkinson & C. B. Marrett (Eds.), *Gender influences in classroom interaction* (pp. 79–114). New York: Academic Press.

Fagan, E. R., Hassler, D. M., & Szabo, M. (1981). Evaluation of questioning strategies in language arts instruction. *Research in the Teaching of English, 15,* 267–273.

Fennema, E., & Sherman, J. (1976). Fennema-Sherman mathematics attitude scales: Instruments designed to measure attitudes toward the learning of mathematics by females and males. *JSAS Catalog of Selected Documents in Psychology, 6,* 31. (MS No. 1225).

Galton, M., Simon, B., & Croll, P. (1980). *Inside the primary classroom.* London: Routledge & Kegan Paul.

Gambrell, L. B. (1983). The occurrence of think time during reading-comprehension instruction. *Journal of Educational Research, 77*(2), 273–275.

Good, T. L. (1981). Teacher expectations and student perception: A decade of research. *Educational Leadership, 28,* 415–422.

Gore, D. A., & Roumagoux, D. V. (1983). Wait time as a variable in sex-related differences during fourth-grade mathematics instruction. *Journal of Educational Research, 76*(5), 77–80.

Hassler, D. M. (1979). *A successful transplant of wait time and questioning strategies to children's oral language behaviors.* ERIC Document Reproduction Service No. ED 205-951.

Leder, G. C. (1987). Teacher-student interaction: A case study. *Educational Studies in Mathematics, 18,* 255–271.

Leder, G. C. (1988). Teacher-student interactions: The mathematics classroom. *Unicorn, 14,* 161–166.

Leinhardt, G., Seewald, A. M., & Engel, M. (1979). Learning what's taught: Sex differences in instruction. *Journal of Educational Psychology, 71,* 423–439.

Moore, D., & Smith, P. (1980). Teacher questions: Frequency and distribution in a sample of Papua New Guinea High Schools. *Australian Journal of Education, 24,* 315–317.

Reyes, L. H. (1984, August). *Mathematics classroom processes.* Paper presented at the Fifth International Congress on Mathematical Education, Adelaide, S.A., Australia.

Rice, D. R. (1977). The effect of question-asking instruction on preservice elementary science teachers. *Journal of Research in Science Teaching, 14*, 353–359.

Rowe, M. B. (1974a). Wait-time and rewards as instructional variables, their influence on language, logic, and fate control. Part 1: Wait-time. *Journal of Research in Science Teaching, 11*, 81–94.

Rowe, M. B. (1974b). Relation of wait-time and rewards to the development of language, topic, and fate control. Part 2: Rewards. *Journal of Research in Science Teaching, 11*, 291–308.

Rowe, M. B. (1986). Wait-time: Slowing down may be a way of speeding up! *Journal of Teacher Education, 37*(1), 43–50.

Spender, D. (1982). *Invisible women.* London: Writers and Readers Publishing Cooperative.

Stallings, J. (1979). *Factors influencing women's decisions to enroll in advanced mathematics courses: Executive summary.* Menlo Park, CA: SRI International.

Swift, J. N., & Gooding, C. T. (1983). Interaction of wait-time feedback and questioning instruction on middle school science teaching. *Journal of Research in Science Teaching, 20*, 721–730.

Tobin, K. G. (1980). The effect of an extended wait-time on science achievement. *Journal of Research in Science Teaching, 17*, 479–485.

Tobin, K. G. (1986). Effects of teacher wait-time on discourse characteristics in mathematics and language arts classes. *American Educational Research Journal, 23*, 191–200.

Tobin, K. G. (1987). The role of wait-time in higher cognitive level learning. *Review of Educational Research, 57*, 69–95.

Tobin, K. G., & Capie, W. (1982). Relationships between classroom process variables and middle school science achievement. *Journal of Educational Psychology, 14*, 441–454.

Weinstein, R. M., Marshall, H., Brattesani, K., & Middlestadt, S. (1982). Student perceptions of differential treatment in open and traditional classrooms. *Journal of Educational Psychology, 74*, 678–692.

Wolleat, P., Pedro, J. D., Becker, A., & Fennema, E. (1980). Sex differences in high school students' causal attributions of performance in mathematics. *Journal for Research in Mathematics Education, 11*(5), 356–366.

# 8 Teachers' Beliefs and Gender Differences in Mathematics

## ELIZABETH FENNEMA

*Fennema explores an area that has not been investigated in relation to gender differences in mathematics. She argues that teachers' beliefs and knowledge are gaining recognition as important influences on the development of gender differences in mathematics. She identifies several teacher beliefs as being critically important: expectancies, causal attribution, usefulness of mathematics to both females and males, and stereotyping of females and males as learners of mathematics. Data are presented that give validity to the idea that more investigation in this area would prove beneficial to the achievement of equity in mathematics for both genders.*

What teachers do in classrooms has been the focus of many studies concerned with gender differences in mathematics. Overt behaviors of teachers have been carefully coded and related in a variety of ways to what females and males do in classrooms and what they learn. (See Chapters 6 and 7 in this book for a complete discussion.) Less attention has been given to the beliefs teachers have and how these beliefs influence the decisions that teachers make as they plan for and carry out instruction.

Teachers work and make decisions in a complicated environment. Not only is classroom planning complex, but the actual interactions between teacher and student demand that teachers make decisions quickly and continually. There is a rapid flow of events that teachers must apprehend and process before deciding how to respond. Teachers need to decide such things as whether the pacing of the lesson is appropriate, whether the activity selected is working to achieve stated goals, what child to call on when a question is asked, how to respond to the answer, how to motivate a bored student quickly, and how and when to reprimand certain students. The decisions that teachers make have a strong influence on what their students learn and how they feel about themselves as they learn. These decisions are influenced by teachers' beliefs. The purpose of this chapter is to explore how teachers' internal belief systems impact on decisions and thus on the development of gender differences in mathematics.

As more evidence has been gathered about teachers' cognitions, the importance of teachers' beliefs has been increasingly recognized. The rationale for studying teachers' cognitions was presented most clearly in a report produced by one of the panels of the National Conference on Studies in Teaching, which was convened in the United States in 1974 by the National Institute of Education. The panelists argued,

> It is obvious that what teachers do is directed in no small measure by what they think. Moreover, it will be necessary for any innovation in the context, practices, and technology of teaching to be mediated through the minds and motives of teachers. To the extent that observed or intended teacher behavior is "thoughtless," it makes no use of the human teachers' most unique attributes. In so doing, it becomes mechanical and might well be done by a machine. If, however, teaching is done, and in all likelihood, will continue to be done by human teachers, the question of the relationships between thought and action becomes crucial. [National Institute of Education, 1975, p. 1]

Since the publication of this panel's report, there has been an increasing amount of research on teachers' thought processes. Comprehensive reviews of this research have been written by Shavelson and Stern (1981) and Clark and Peterson (1986). Before discussing what this work has to say about gender differences in mathematics, I will briefly summarize Clark and Peterson's conclusions.

First, they concluded that research shows that teachers' thinking plays an important part in teaching. They concluded that the image of a teacher as a reflective professional is not far-fetched. As such, teachers have more in common with physicians and lawyers than with technicians. Second, the research shows that teachers plan for instruction in a rich variety of ways and that these plans have real consequences in the classroom. Third, during interactive teaching, teachers are continually thinking, and they report making decisions frequently — once every two minutes. Fourth, teachers have theories and belief systems that influence their perceptions, plans, and actions in the classroom. Concurring with this last point were Peterson and Barger (1985), who stated that teachers' behavior is "guided by . . . a personally held system of beliefs, values and principles" (p. 287).

Fennema, Carpenter, and Peterson (in press) have suggested a model that illustrates how teachers' knowledge and beliefs influence learning, shown in Figure 8.1. As can be seen, the final outcome, students' learning, is directly influenced by children's cognitions and behaviors, which in turn are influenced by classroom instruction. More important for the concern of this chapter, however, is the fact that classroom instruction is determined by the decisions that teachers make, which are directly influenced by their knowledge and beliefs. There is consider-

Figure 8.1   The influence of teachers' knowledge and beliefs on students' learning

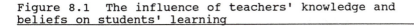

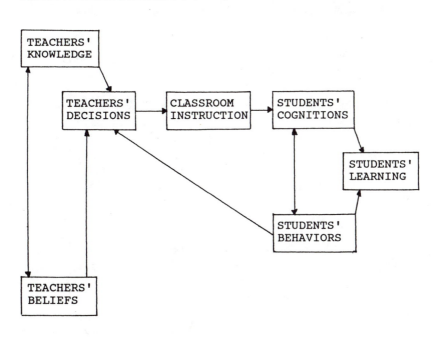

From Fennema, E., Carpenter, T. P., & Peterson, P. L. (in press). Teachers' decision making and cognitively guided instruction:  A new paradigm for curriculum development.  To appear in K. Clements, & N. F. Ellerton (Eds.), Facilitating change in mathematics education. Geelong, Victoria, Australia:  Deakin University Press.

able evidence that this model has validity. (Carpenter, Fennema, & Peterson, 1988; Carpenter, Fennema, Peterson, & Carey, 1989; Peterson, Fennema, Carpenter, & Loef, 1989). One could substitute "gender differences in mathematics" for "students' learning" in the last box of the model, to illustrate the main thesis of this chapter: partly based on what teachers know and believe about gender differences in mathematics, decisions are made about what each female and male should do in the classroom; these, in turn, influence what that female or male learns in mathematics.

Since knowledge about gender differences in mathematics and differential treatment of females and males by teachers has been covered in previous chapters, the major concern here is identification of those teacher beliefs that are important influences on the development of gender differences in mathematics. Also included is some discussion of how instructional decisions, made as a consequence of these beliefs, influence classroom instruction.

## ANALYSIS OF TEACHER BELIEFS ABOUT GENDER AND MATHEMATICS

Simply put, beliefs are what one believes. They are based on one's values and are developed by the experiences that one has had. They come from parents, peers, the media, the church, the country that one lives in, what one reads, and all the various experiences of living. They are often covert and not easily identified, measured, or studied.

There are some specific teacher beliefs that appear to be important influences on the way teachers interact with females and males and organize their classes for instruction. Teacher expectancy for students has received much attention in areas other than gender. In addition, certain beliefs identified in Chapter 4 as being important for students are also relevant to teachers: perception of the usefulness of mathematics, the sex-role congruency of mathematics, and attributional style. An additional category that was not considered there is teachers' beliefs about equity as explored in Chapter 1 of this book.

When one considers teacher beliefs, the concern is not about the belief that is held about oneself (as is the case with student beliefs), but the belief that is held about others (i.e., males, females, and mathematics). Do teachers have different expectancies for the mathematics learning of males and females? Do teachers believe that mathematics is going to be equally useful for males and females? Do teachers believe that the learning of mathematics is congruent with both the male and female sex role? Do teachers believe similar things about the causes of females' and males' successes and failures in mathematics? How should equity for males and females be defined and achieved? While these are not beliefs that are independent of each other, for clarity's sake, each will be considered separately.

## Different Expectancies

Reyes and Stanic (1988) suggest that the important teacher beliefs that influence the development of gender differences in mathematics are their attitudes about "the aptitudes of students and the appropriateness of their achieving at a high level in mathematics that differs on the basis of . . . sex" (p. 30). They also hypothesize that these attitudes are reflected in the expectancies that teachers hold for females' and males' learning.

Teacher expectancies and their influence on learning have been studied for some time, and the complexity of issues related to them is recognized by Dusek, who has edited a major book reviewing the research (Dusek, 1985). He concludes that teachers do form expectancies about their students' learning and that they are correlated with student learning. However, not many studies have addressed the problems of differential teacher expectancy for females and males and whether or not these are a partial explanation of existing gender differences in achievement. Good and Findley (1985) also have reviewed the literature about gender and expectancy carefully and conclude that the research is so sparse that "it becomes difficult to draw any conclusions with confidence. There do seem to be indications, though, that teachers variably perceive and evaluate male and female students' abilities. The precise nature of these variations is open to question" (p. 278). Certainly the area of teacher expectancies about females and males is a fertile area of investigation. While it would be easy to conclude that differential teacher behavior is a reflection of different expectancies, there are few data to support such a conclusion.

The entire research area of teacher expectancy, as already noted, is extremely complex and has often been oversimplified. There are many unanswered questions that are beyond the scope of this book. Perhaps including sex of subject as a variable when research is done on teacher expectancy would increase both our knowledge about gender and the relationship of teacher expectancy to student outcomes.

## Usefulness of Mathematics

If teachers believe that mathematics is useful or will be useful to the student in the future, it seems reasonable to assume that they will work harder to ensure that their students learn mathematics. In addition, as mathematics becomes an elective subject or when students are placed in various tracks in secondary education, if a teacher believes that a particular student's career path will be facilitated by mathematics, then that teacher will make decisions about what mathematics class is most appropriate for that student. Teachers do talk to their students about why mathematics is useful and why it should be learned. There is no doubt that teachers influence students in their beliefs and in their motivation to persist. There has been some indication that teachers select males, more often than females who have the same learning problems, for participation in remedial mathematics programs. Could this be an indication that teachers believe it is more important for males to learn mathematics?

If teachers believe that mathematics will not be as useful for females as it will be for males, it will have an influence on the expectations that they have for the learning of mathematics by each gender. While there are no empirical data that support the hypothesis of such differential teacher beliefs, there is much informal knowledge that supports the hypothesis. Consider the following vignette, shown in the Multiplying Options series (Fennema, Becker, Wolleat, & Pedro, 1980).

> SCENE: A secondary school coed class of year 3 mathematics students with about two-thirds male students.
> MALE: Miss J, do I need to take fourth-year mathematics in order to get into college?
> MISS J: No, you don't need fourth-year math to get into college. However, if you boys want to go on in science or get into something like the space program you will need fourth-year math as a prerequisite for courses you will need in college.

This scene seems innocent enough. A teacher indicates awareness that fourth-year mathematics will increase her students' options for college majors. However, note that the comment was addressed to the males. How the females in the class would interpret such a remark is unknown, but it seems reasonable to assume that it is a reflection of the teacher's beliefs that consideration of a career that requires advanced math is not important for females. Thus males are actively encouraged to persist in math while females are not.

Many people have reported that the opportunities for females to take advanced mathematics are more limited than for males. For example, some females' schools in Australia have a more limited mathematics curriculum and fewer mathematics-related courses. Is this not another indication that teachers do not believe that advanced mathematics is very important for females? Others have reported that scheduling problems often prohibit females from taking advanced mathematics classes. Females are often forced to choose between taking advanced classes of other types that have wide appeal to them (such as music or foreign language) and advanced mathematics. Since females themselves often do not perceive that mathematics is particularly useful to them (see Chapter 4), they often choose not to take advanced courses, rather than object to the conflict. Is this scheduling problem yet another sign that schools and teachers downplay advanced mathematics for females?

Another indication regarding usefulness of mathematics is the way teachers often encourage females to perform well in routine mathematics and offer them less encouragement to work hard at mathematics that is more cognitively demanding (see Chapters 6 and 7 in this book). In addition, teachers may expect conformity and dependence on the part of females, which may prohibit them from learning to do high-cognitive-level tasks such as problem solving. For example, Grieb and Easley (1984) conclude from extensive case studies that certain boys "have a distinct advantage over . . . girls with similar mathematical creativity: they can develop habits of independent thinking in mathematics from early primary grades because they are not being expected by most teachers to conform to the social norms of arithmetic" (p. 317). Females in the primary grades in this study were doing what the teacher asked them to do. Their papers were neat, complete, and accurate, while in many cases the males' papers were not. While the females were becoming increasingly proficient at computational, rule-bound tasks and more dependent on the teacher, the males were becoming increasingly proficient at problem solving and working independently. Is this an indication that teachers believe that females will only need to understand routine, rule-bound arithmetic?

Casserly (1975) reported similar expectations of precocious females in advanced mathematics in the secondary school. Many females in her studies reported that teachers often became fearful that the females would fail and become emotionally upset if they were unable to solve difficult mathematics problems. Often the teachers would tell them how to solve the problems. This was done with all good intentions of preventing tears and negative emotions; however, what happened was that the females were prohibited from having a successful problem-solving experience. They themselves reported that the teacher appeared to believe that mathematical problem solving was not useful for them.

It is to be hoped that most teachers do not overtly tell students that mathematics is useful for males and not useful for females. If teachers do have such a belief, however, it is reasonable to assume that they communicate it in subtle ways to students as they interact with them. Teachers' belief in the usefulness of mathematics for females and males is an important variable to be considered.

## Attributions for Success and Failure

Certainly teachers are concerned with many kinds of behavior, but probably none is more important than learning behavior. What is it that causes some to learn and others not to learn? Teachers believe, rightly or wrongly, that when they understand what causes a child to learn they can decide how and what that child can learn. Learning environments are structured with this knowledge in mind. For example, if the reason that a child is unable to learn is because she comes to school hungry, then if food is provided the child will learn better. If a child learns well because she is highly intelligent, then she should be provided with a stimulating environment where much cognitive activity is expected. If a student learns well because he works very hard and is conscientious about doing the assigned work, then he should receive praise or other rewards of various kinds. If a student does not learn because he is learning disabled, then the pace or structure of the lessons should be adapted so that learning does occur. If someone does not learn because of lack of motivation, then stimulating activities of high interest to the learner should form the basis of the curriculum. Thus, the causal attributions that teachers make regarding the success and failures of their students are highly important.

As discussed earlier in this book (see Chapter 4), attributions of the causes of learners' successes and failures can be put into four categories: ability, effort, task difficulty, and luck (or environment). Ability and effort fall under internal control, while task difficulty and luck are under external control. Further, ability and task difficulty are considered stable factors, while effort and luck are seen as unstable. This categorization scheme is one proposed by Weiner (1974); readers may refer to Figure 4.1 for a graphic of these relationships. The validity of this scheme for understanding teachers' expectancies of their students is well recognized, and reviews of the research dealing with it have been done by Clark and Peterson (1986) and Peterson and Barger (1985). Several conclusions from these reviews are relevant here.

First, Clark and Peterson (1986) concluded, "The most important beliefs that teachers have about students are those that deal with the teachers' perception of the causes of students' behavior" (p. 281). Second, if teachers attribute successes or failures of students to themselves (i.e., the teachers), then they will do something to alleviate the failure. If, on the other hand, the reason that students succeed or fail lies within the students, then the teachers do not feel as much responsibility for dealing with failure. Overt teacher behavior is directly related to how the teacher attributes causation of successes and failures. Peterson and Barger (1985) further concluded that "students who are perceived by teachers as expending effort . . . are rewarded more and punished less by teachers than students who are perceived as not really trying" (p. 175).

Studies on teachers' attributions of males' and females' successes and failures have reported somewhat mixed results. Clark and Peterson (1986) concluded that the sex of the student has not been shown to be a significant factor affecting teachers' attributions. Dweck, Davidson, Nelson, and Enna (1978) reported that evaluative feedback on the part of teachers differed significantly. For males more than females, (1) positive feedback was addressed to the intellectual quality of the work; (2) less negative feedback was addressed to the intellectual competence of the work; and (3) males' failure tended to be attributed to effort. From this work, Dweck et al. concluded that children tend to be reinforced in such a way that males perceive that failures are due to insufficient effort and females perceive that failures are due to insufficient ability.

Belief in the stability or instability of the internal cause of success or failure is what is being developed. Thus, Dweck et al.'s (1978) results indicate that males are reinforced in such a way that they come to believe they can control their own learning. Since effort is unstable, if they decide to exert more effort, then they will be able to learn. On the other hand, females are rewarded in such a way that they come to believe that their failures are due to lack of ability and their successes due to effort. Since effort is unstable, they can continue to succeed only if they continue to exert the same or greater effort in the future. There is little chance to develop confidence in their ability, and there is fear that they might fail. Further, if females believe their failures are due to insufficient ability, a stable attribution, and they do experience failure, they may come to believe that they cannot control or overcome it.

While Heller and Parsons (1981) report that they were unable to replicate these results of differential teacher attribution, this pattern was found among the female students, by Fennema, Peterson, and Carpenter (in press), and is discussed at length in Chapters 4 and 5. It appears clear that *something* is causing females to believe that success in mathematics is due to effort and failure is due to ability. It is at least a reasonable hypothesis that teachers may contribute to the development of this pattern of attributions in females.

The Fennema, Peterson, Carpenter, and Lubinski (in press) study investigated, among other things, teacher attributions of their male and female students' learning of mathematics. Thirty-eight first-grade teachers were asked to select their four most and four least-capable mathematics students (two females and two males in each case). They were then asked to select, from a list, the causes of those students' successes and failures. Table 8.1 lists the percentages of these students who were placed in each attribution category.

Teachers selected ability as the cause of their most capable males' success 58% of the time, and the cause of their best females' success only 33% of the time. Most capable females' successes were due to effort 37% of the time, while best males' successes were due to effort only 12% of the time. It is also interesting to note that teachers said that their least-successful females' failures were due to ability 29% of the time, while their least-successful males' failures were due to ability only 22% of the

**Table 8.1**   Percentage of Teacher Attributions for Performance to Various Categories, by Gender and Success Rating

| SUCCESS RATING | ATTRIBUTION CATEGORY | CAUSE FOR SUCCESS | | CAUSE FOR FAILURE | |
|---|---|---|---|---|---|
| | | Females[a] (%) | Males (%) | Females (%) | Males[b] (%) |
| *High* | Ability | 33 | 58 | 8 | 3 |
| | Effort | 37 | 12 | 24 | 25 |
| | Intrinsic motivation | 18 | 25 | 4 | 3 |
| | Task difficulty | 3 | 1 | 40 | 45 |
| | Teacher helped | 7 | 4 | 16 | 16 |
| | Others helped | 3 | 0 | 0 | 1 |
| | Other causes | 0 | 0 | 9 | 8 |
| *Low* | Ability | 9 | 8 | 29 | 22 |
| | Effort | 32 | 24 | 28 | 33 |
| | Intrinsic motivation | 12 | 11 | 8 | 12 |
| | Task difficulty | 16 | 21 | 28 | 20 |
| | Teacher helped | 24 | 35 | 3 | 3 |
| | Others helped | 5 | 1 | 1 | 2 |
| | Other causes | 2 | 0 | 4 | 7 |

[a]Total attributions=76 per sex.
[b]Data missing from one teacher.

Adapted from Fennema, E., Peterson, P. L., Carpenter, T. P., & Lubinski, C. (in press). Teachers' attributions and beliefs about girls, boys, and mathematics. *Educational Studies in Mathematics*. Reprinted by permission.

time. It appears that teachers attribute success and failure in much the same way that Dweck et al. (1978) reported that they made overt attributional statements. Males, more so than females, are perceived to succeed because of their ability, and females are perceived to succeed more often because of effort.

While this is a study of only first-grade teachers, it appears that these teachers believed that males and females succeeded or failed for different reasons. What might be the consequences of such a belief on teacher behavior with learners? It would probably affect how teachers interact with learners. If they believe that females' successes are caused by effort, then they will encourage females to work hard. While it is difficult to fault the idea that hard work is rewarded by learning, as noted earlier, this may have detrimental effects on females. On the other hand, if males are encouraged to work by being told their success is due to ability to do the mathematics, then they will likely come to believe that they will always be able to learn mathematics.

In Table 8.1, for low-achieving males and females, a differential pattern of attributions can be seen for the category referring to teacher help. This may reflect the amount of responsibility these teachers were willing to assume for the mathematics learning of their least-successful students. Teacher help was chosen most frequently as the reason for low-achieving males' successes 35% of the time, compared to only 24% of the time for low-achieving females. As the cause for the failures of these students, teacher help was selected 12% of the time for males, compared to 3% of the time for females. Peterson and Barger (1985) suggested that, if teachers attribute success and failure of students to themselves, then they will do something about correcting it. Evidently these first-grade teachers attributed success and failure in mathematics of low-achieving males more to themselves than the success and failure of low-achieving females. There is no direct evidence available that these teachers actually did more about the mathematics learning of low-success males than they did for low-success females, but it is a reasonable hypothesis.

The evidence is far from conclusive that teachers believe that the causes of successes and failures in learning mathematics are different for males and females. All the evidence that is available, however, suggests that, if there is a difference in teachers' beliefs about causation, the more positive belief is held about males than about females. There is also no conclusive evidence that such a belief influences teachers as they make instructional decisions; however, this, too, is a reasonable hypothesis that could be profitably investigated.

## Sex-Role Congruency of the Domain of Mathematics

Most human beings in this world hold stereotypic beliefs about gender, and teachers are no exception. Unfortunately, these stereotypic beliefs probably influence the cognitive development of males and females. Nash (1979) has suggested that the perception of cognitive consistency with one's sex-role identity influences acquisition of various kinds of knowledge. When a male or a female perceives that the learning of a subject is consistent with how his or her sex-role identity has been defined, then he or she will work harder to learn the subject. For example, if a female perceives that it is feminine to learn to speak a foreign language, then she will work to learn the language. Conversely, if a male perceives that it is not masculine to learn about poetry, then he will resist learning about poetry. In other words, sex-role identity includes competence in various cognitive endeavors and precludes it in others.

The sex-role congruence of various subjects is communicated in a variety of ways to males and females, and certainly teachers are part of the society that communicates it. Do teachers believe that certain subjects are more appropriate for males than for females? The evidence suggests that they do. Dusek and Joseph (1985) report one study in which teachers rated anonymous students with masculine and feminine characteristics, on various cognitive traits. Students with masculine characteristics were rated higher on intelligence, independence, and logic. Mathematics appears to be one subject that is stereotyped as masculine, and this influences the learning of mathematics by females.

When teachers stereotype mathematics as masculine, does it influence the decisions that they make and their interactions with learners? Good and Findley (1985) have reviewed the literature on sex-role expectations and achievement and conclude that "there are signs that teachers' sex-related beliefs about children may influence teachers' classroom behavior" (p. 271). While research on beliefs about appropriate behavior of males and females by teachers is scanty, there seem to be indications that teachers do perceive and evaluate females and males differently and that these beliefs do influence classroom behavior of teachers as they interact with females and males. (See Chapters 6 and 7 for more on how teachers interact differently with females and males in mathematics.) There is also evidence that teachers interact differently with males and females in various subject areas. For example, Leinhardt, Seewald, and Engel (1979) reported that teachers paid more attention to females in reading (a female-stereotyped subject) and more attention to males in mathematics (a male-stereotyped subject). Certainly, males receive more encouragement in mathematics and mathematics-related courses than do females (Stage, Kreinberg, Eccles, & Becker, 1985).

While there is no conclusive evidence that teachers believe that mathematics is more appropriate for males than for females, wherever evidence exists, it indicates that teachers tend to stereotype mathematics as a male domain. Such stereotyping results partially in differential treatment of males and females in classrooms and undoubtedly influences the development of gender differences in mathematics.

### Sex-Role Stereotyping of Mathematics-Related Characteristics

The study reported on earlier, by Fennema, Peterson, Carpenter, and Lubinski (in press), also investigated whether teachers held different beliefs about their best male and best female mathematics students. Information on this was collected using a questionnaire that was an adaptation of the Broverman, Broverman, Clarkson, Rosenkrantz, and Vogel (1970) Sex-Role Stereotype Questionnaire. Sixteen personality descriptors that seemed to be relevant to achievement in the mathematics classroom were selected from the original instrument. Four new behavioral descriptors were added that permitted ratings of actual behaviors in the mathematics classroom (seldom or often volunteers answers to mathematics problems, does not enjoy or enjoys mathematics, very dependent or independent in mathematics, does not persist or is very persistent on very hard mathematics tasks). These 20 items, each of which consisted of a pair of statements, formed an "adjective checklist" to which teachers responded on a five-point Likert scale. A response of "1" indicated strong agreement with the first of the pair of statements; "5" indicated strong agreement with the second.

The results from this checklist are shown in Table 8.2. Significant differences in the responses were found on items 7, 8, 10, 11, 17, 18, and 19. These correspond to the factors of competitiveness, logicalness, adventurousness, loudness, volunteering of answers, enjoyment of mathematics, and independence in mathematics. For all these descriptive phrases, teachers rated their male students as displaying higher levels of those traits.

Several interesting things are apparent. First, overall, the teachers did not strongly stereotype their best male or female mathematics students as masculine or feminine. Of the 16 phrases selected from the Broverman et al. (1970) scale, only 3 were seen as differentially describing the best males and females: competitiveness, logicalness, and adventurousness. Second, there were significant differences on three of the four items that were added to the adjective checklist, which were specif-

**Table 8.2**  Adjective Checklist for Sex-Role Stereotypes: Descriptive Statistics and t-Tests, by Item

| ITEM | BEST MALE STUDENTS | | BEST FEMALE STUDENTS | | t-TESTS |
|---|---|---|---|---|---|
| | *Mean* | *SD* | *Mean* | *SD* | |
| 1. Not aggressive/very aggressive[a] | 2.68 | 1.45 | 2.61 | 1.33 | .27 |
| 2. Not independent/very independent | 3.95 | 1.01 | 4.26 | .83 | -1.53 |
| 3. Very subjective/very objective | 3.79 | .91 | 3.34 | 1.05 | 1.86 |
| 4. Very easily influenced/not very easily influenced | 3.95 | .84 | 3.76 | 1.05 | .85 |
| 5. Very submissive/very dominant | 3.79 | .84 | 3.63 | 1.05 | .76 |
| 6. Very passive/very active | 3.89 | 1.03 | 3.71 | 1.11 | .79 |
| 7. Not at all competitive/very competitive | 4.11 | 1.01 | 3.68 | 1.09 | 2.25[a] |
| 8. Very illogical/very logical | 4.55 | .65 | 4.21 | .78 | 2.59[b] |
| 9. Very indirect/very direct | 3.89 | .89 | 3.68 | 1.14 | 1.07 |
| 10. Not at all adventurous/very adventurous | 3.66 | 1.15 | 3.26 | 1.03 | 2.16[a] |
| 11. Very quiet/very loud | 3.21 | 1.12 | 2.76 | 1.15 | 1.82 |
| 12. Has difficulty making decisions/makes decisions easily | 3.89 | .98 | 4.11 | .89 | -1.11 |
| 13. Almost never acts as leader/almost always acts as leader | 3.55 | 1.13 | 3.45 | 1.03 | .43 |
| 14. Very strong need for security/very little need for security | 2.92 | 1.12 | 3.13 | 1.19 | -.84 |
| 15. Not at all self-confident/very self-confident | 3.84 | .86 | 3.89 | .98 | -.25 |
| 16. Very uncomfortable about being aggressive/not uncomfortable about being aggressive | 3.18 | 1.18 | 3.18 | 1.37 | .00 |
| 17. Seldom volunteers answers to mathematics problems/often volunteers answers to mathematics problems | 4.66 | .94 | 4.08 | 1.34 | 2.77[c] |
| 18. Does not enjoy mathematics very much/enjoys mathematics very much | 4.89 | .31 | 4.47 | .65 | 3.60[c] |
| 19. Very dependent in mathematics/very independent in mathematics | 4.74 | .60 | 4.29 | .87 | 2.90[c] |
| 20. Does not persist on hard mathematics tasks/very persistent on hard mathematics tasks | 4.13 | 1.04 | 3.97 | .75 | .81 |

[a]Score greater than 2.5 indicates more agreement with the phrase on the right.  [b]p < .05.  [c]p < .01.
From Fennema, E., Peterson, P. L., Carpenter, T. P., & Lubinski, C. (in press). Teachers' attributions and beliefs about girls, boys, and mathematics. *Educational Studies in Mathematics.* Reprinted with permission.

ic to mathematics. Females were perceived as volunteering answers to problems less often, enjoying math less, and as being more dependent than were males. Third, while males were not seen as more independent overall than were females (see item 2), in mathematics males were seen as more independent. Furthermore, some other traits that could be seen as essential to the learning and use of mathematics (competitiveness, logicalness, and adventurousness) were perceived as more descriptive of males than females. Thus, while avoiding overall sex stereotyping, these first-grade teachers did stereotype their best students in the domain of mathematics. Overt behavior, such as volunteering answers and enjoyment of math, were rated as descriptive of males, and independence, which was discussed in the introduction as being strongly influential in continued growth in high-cognitive-level mathematics learning, was also more descriptive of males.

Another way to look at the responses on this adjective checklist is to examine those phrases that received the highest and lowest ratings for females and males. These are listed in Table 8.3. These sets are practically identical for females and males, with some switching in rank order. One exception is that for the highest-rated descriptors, females

**Table 8.3**   Adjective Checklist Descriptors Receiving Highest and Lowest Ratings, Rank Ordered by Gender

| MALES | FEMALES |
|---|---|
| *Highest ratings* | *Highest ratings* |
| Enjoys mathematics (4.89) | Enjoys mathematics (4.47) |
| Very independent in math (4.74) | Very independent in math (4.29) |
| Often volunteers answers (4.66) | Very independent (4.26) |
| Very logical (4.55) | Very logical (4.21) |
| Very persistent in math (4.13) | Often volunteers answers (4.08) |
| Very competitive (4.11) | Very persistent in math (3.97) |
| *Lowest ratings* | *Lowest ratings* |
| Objective (3.79) | Objective (3.34) |
| Adventurous (3.66) | Adventurous (3.26) |
| Comfortable with aggression (3.18) | Comfortable with aggression (3.18) |
| Loud (3.21) | Little need for security (3.13) |
| Little need for security (2.92) | Loud (2.76) |
| Very aggressive (2.68) | Very aggressive (2.61) |

From Fennema, E., Peterson, P. L., Carpenter, T. P., & Lubinski, C. (in press). Teachers' attributions and beliefs about girls, boys, and mathematics. *Educational Studies in Mathematics*. Reprinted by permission.

got high scores for overall independence, while males got high scores for competitiveness. Teachers often gave their best male math students higher ratings than they did their best female math students; that is, they saw the same traits in both males and females, but rated them as being stronger in males.

In summary, while there is not always conclusive data about teachers' beliefs in relationship to females, males, and mathematics, when data are available they indicate that teachers' beliefs are somewhat negative about females and the learning of mathematics. Care should be taken not to overgeneralize the data and thereby conclude that teachers are overtly biased against females. Nonetheless, it appears that there are some negative consequences of what could be interpreted as negative teacher beliefs.

## ACHIEVING EQUITY IN MATHEMATICS

Why do teachers hold beliefs about males, females, and the learning of mathematics that appear to have such a detrimental effect on the learning of mathematics by females? It is not because they are insensitive people who really don't care about their female students. It appears, at least to me, that most teachers are caring individuals who are working in a difficult, complex situation and trying to make their instructional decisions in such a way so that each of their students is treated fairly. However, I feel that the long-term results of their treatment are basically inequitable.

Teachers try to make their classrooms pleasant places to be. In particular, they are concerned that their female students be comfortable and not subjected to much stress. But, in so doing, they fail to permit their female students to develop a real sense of pride in their own ability to do mathematics and to continue to learn mathematics. Females are not permitted to become independent learners of mathematics, do not come to believe that the reason they succeed in mathematics is because of their ability, and do not develop adequate self-esteem in mathematics.

It should also be pointed out that teachers often believe that what they are doing is necessary. When asked why they spend more time with males than with females, teachers often reply it is because the males demand more time. Sometimes, if attention is not paid to the males, they become unruly and often disrupt the entire classroom. At other times, teachers report that they can depend on a male for a response that will enable the class to move forward.

In Chapter 1, equity was defined in three ways: as the legal right to equal access to mathematics; as equal treatment in the mathematics class; and as equal educational outcomes. It appears that, if teachers' actions totally reflect their beliefs, then they must believe that equity is achieved when all learners have equal access to mathematics. Teachers don't treat both genders the same, nor do females and males have equal educational outcomes. However, a more optimistic explanation of teachers' actions is that they reflect lack of knowledge. Presented in Figure 8.1 was a model of curriculum development suggesting that teachers' decisions are influenced by the interaction of their knowledge and beliefs. This model indicates that, when teachers have knowledge, their beliefs might change and enable them to make decisions to enable all their students to learn mathematics.

As in most cases, it is easier to identify where problems exist than it is to solve them. However, teachers are skilled professionals who are better able to solve the problems they meet in the classroom than is anyone else. Thus, it is very important for teachers to have knowledge about gender differences in mathematics, so they will be able to construct approaches that will enable those problems to be solved.

## REFERENCES

Broverman, I. K., Broverman, D., Clarkson, F. E., Rosenkrantz, P. S., & Vogel, S. (1970). Sex-role stereotypes and clinical judgments of mental health. *Journal of Consulting and Clinical Psychology*, 34(1), 1-7.

Carpenter, T. P., Fennema, E., & Peterson, P. L. (1988, April). *Effects of cognitively guided instruction on students' problem solving*. Paper presented at the annual meeting of the American Educational Research Association, New Orleans.

Carpenter, T. P., Fennema, E., Peterson, P. L., & Carey, D. (1989). Teachers' pedagogical content knowledge of students' problem solving in elementary arithmetic. *Journal for Research in Mathematics Education*, 19(5), 385-401.

Casserly, P. L. (1975). *An assessment of factors affecting female participation in advanced placement programs in mathematics, chemistry, and physics* (Grant No. GY-11325). Washington, DC: National Science Foundation.

Clark, C. M., & Peterson, P. L. (1986). Teachers' thought processes. In M. C. Wittrock (Ed.), *Handbook of research on teaching* (3rd ed.) (pp. 255-296). New York: Macmillan.

Dusek, J. B. (Ed.). (1985). *Teacher expectancies*. Hillsdale, NJ: Lawrence Erlbaum.

Dusek, J. B., & Joseph, G. (1985). The bases of teacher expectancies. In J. B. Dusek (Ed.), *Teacher expectancies* (pp. 229–250). Hillsdale, NJ: Lawrence Erlbaum.

Dweck, C. S., Davidson, W., Nelson, S., & Enna, B. (1978). Sex differences in learned helplessness. Part 2: The contingencies of evaluative feedback in the classroom. Part 3: An experimental analysis. *Developmental Psychology, 48*, 268–276.

Fennema, E., Becker, A., Wolleat, P. L., & Pedro, J. D. (1980). *Multiplying options and subtracting bias*. Reston, VA: National Council of Teachers of Mathematics.

Fennema, E., Carpenter, T. P., & Peterson, P. L. (in press). *Teachers' decision making and cognitively guided instruction: A new paradigm for curriculum development*. In K. Clements & N. F. Ellerton (Eds.), *Facilitating change in mathematics education*. Geelong, Victoria, Australia: Deakin University Press.

Fennema, E., Peterson, P. L., Carpenter, T. P., & Lubinski, C. (in press). Teachers' attributions and beliefs about girls, boys, and mathematics. *Educational Studies in Mathematics*.

Good, T. L., & Findley, M. J. (1985). Sex role expectations and achievement. In J. B. Dusek (Ed.), *Teacher expectancies* (pp. 271–302). Hillsdale, NJ: Lawrence Erlbaum.

Grieb, H., & Easley, J. (1984). A primary school impediment to mathematical equity: Case studies in role-dependent socialization. In M. Steincamp & M. L. Maehr (Eds.), *Women in science. Vol. 2: Advances in motivation and achievement* (pp. 317–362). Greenwich, CT: JAI Press.

Heller, K. A., & Parsons, J. E. (1981). Sex differences in teachers' evaluative feedback and students' expectancies for success in mathematics. *Child Development, 52*, 1015–1019.

Leinhardt, G., Seewald, A. M., & Engel, M. (1979). Learning what's taught: Sex differences in instruction. *Journal of Educational Psychology, 79*(4), 432–439.

Nash, S. C. (1979). Sex role as a mediator of intellectual functioning. In M. A. Wittig & A. C. Petersen (Eds.), *Sex-related differences in cognitive functioning* (pp. 263–302). New York: Academic Press.

National Institute of Education. (1975). *Teaching as clinical information processing: Report of Panel 6, National Conference on Studies in Teaching*. Washington, DC: Author.

Peterson, P. L., & Barger, S. A. (1985). Attribution theory and teacher expectancy. In J. B. Dusek (Ed.), *Teacher expectancies* (pp. 159–184). Hillsdale, NJ: Lawrence Erlbaum.

Peterson, P. L., Fennema, E., Carpenter, T. P., & Loef, M. (1989). Teachers' pedagogical content beliefs in mathematics. *Cognition and Instruction, 6*(1), 1–40.

Reyes, L. H., & Stanic, G. M. A. (1988). Race, sex, socioeconomic status, and mathematics. *Journal of Research in Mathematics Education, 19*(1), 26–43.

Shavelson, R. J., & Stern, P. (1981). Research on teachers' pedagogical thoughts, judgments, decisions, and behavior. *Review of Educational Research, 51,* 455–498.

Stage, E. K., Kreinberg, N., Eccles, J., & Becker, J. R. (1985). Increasing the participation and achievement of girls and women in mathematics, science, and engineering. In S. S. Klein (Ed.), *Handbook for achieving sex equity through education* (pp. 237–268). Baltimore: Johns Hopkins University Press.

Weiner, B. (1974). *Achievement motivation and attribution theory.* Morristown, NJ: General Learning Press.

# 9 Gender Differences in Mathematics: A Synthesis

GILAH C. LEDER
ELIZABETH FENNEMA

This volume began with a discussion of equity and justice. Do all students have equal opportunities to learn, or are certain groups—for example, females—disadvantaged? Can we be confident that contemporary educational practices achieve equal treatment for all students, or are certain groups currently receiving inadequate instruction? If some groups are, in fact, disadvantaged in either of these ways, then it is unlikely that the third dimension of equity—equal educational outcomes—will be satisfied.

In this chapter, we intend to look both backward and forward: backward to determine how the work described in this volume has added to our pool of existing knowledge so that we can address the issues just raised more sensitively and constructively; forward, to canvass areas that are worthy of further explorations. The dimensions of equal opportunity to learn and equal educational practices dominate this work. Equal educational outcomes are considered implicitly throughout.

## SUMMARY OF RESEARCH PRESENTED

Spatial ability is one of the factors most consistently linked to gender differences in mathematics achievement, one dimension of educational outcome. The conflicting findings—exacerbated by definitional confusion—that have characterized much of the research suggest the need for carefully structured and clearly described further study. Longitudinal research is rare in education. The strength of the research directed by Fennema and presented by Tartre in Chapter 3 lies in its application of precisely this approach: it formed precise definitions and used interview data to supplement information elicited through paper-and-pencil instruments.

Just what did Tartre report? Two groups of Grade-6 students performed equally well on a series of mathematics problems. Differences emerged, however, when approaches to problem solving were examined. Certain students (those who had scored high on a test of verbal skill, as measured by a vocabulary test, but low on a test of spatial visualization (measured by their facility in making transformations from two to three dimensions) seemed to draw on their verbal strengths in their description of the problems. They also focused on verbal clues for their solution. Another group of students (those with low verbal but high spatial visualization scores) relied on visual, pictorial cues for their descriptions and solutions. Division of the two groups on the basis of sex yielded some further interesting distinctions. A mathematics test was administered in each of the three years of the study. The group who consistently obtained the lowest scores on the tests consisted of females with high verbal but low spatial skills. Yet, the corresponding males' · group (those with high verbal but low spatial scores) obtained the highest number of correct solutions to the problems in each of the three years. Low spatial skills seemed to be related differently to the mathematics achievement of males and females. The study further addressed the possibility that the groups relied differently on their spatial skills. How easy was it for males and females who relied on verbal cues to be forced into a visual/pictorial solution? The answer to this question was defined in terms of how much help was needed to translate verbal information into an equivalent pictorial representation. While there was relatively little difference in the amount of help needed by the two male groups, the group needing most help was the females with low spatial scores; the group requiring least help, the females with high spatial scores.

How can we extrapolate from this to the regular classroom setting? What happens to students whose preferred mode of learning is at variance with the manner in which their teachers structure their lessons? The findings in Chapter 3 suggest that females may be more disadvantaged; that some of them may have unnecessary difficulty in following the solution and strategies discussed in class; that, for them, there is no equality of opportunity to learn. Some support for this conjecture is given by the finding that, of the four groups, those whose performance changed most over the three-year period comprised the females with high verbal but low spatial scores. They, in fact, fell further behind the other three groups.

Constructive ways of enriching the classroom dialogue are suggested by Tartre's final study. Approaches to problem solving were examined for constituent strategies, especially those that required spatial or verbal skills. Some strategies seemed to be used spontaneously and with equal facility by males and females. Can we infer from this that instructional explanations that rely on those solution processes are meaningful for both females and males, or are some more relevant and meaningful for one gender than the other? Further explorations that maximize congruence between the teaching of mathematics and students' preferred mode of learning are required before the ideal of equal opportunity to learn can be realized.

Implicit in the foregoing discussion is the notion that equal educational treatment does not necessarily result in equal opportunity to learn. This assertion is tested further in Chapters 4 and 5, which focus on ways in which students exposed to superficially equal educational treatments may not have equal opportunity to learn. The Autonomous Learning Behavior (ALB) model (Fennema & Peterson, 1985), with its emphasis on the crucial part that internal beliefs play in the process of learning mathematics, serves both as a unifying theme for the work discussed in these two chapters and is simultaneously challenged and supported by them.

Longitudinal data were also presented in Chapter 4 by Meyer and Koehler. Once again, paper-and-pencil measures were supplemented and enriched by interview data. Internal beliefs of particular interest included confidence, students' perceptions of mathematics as a male domain, students' perceptions of teachers' expectations for them in mathematics class, students' own expectations for success and failure in mathematics, and students' reactions to these outcomes. Do these internal beliefs affect mathematics learning, as predicted by the ALB model? Do they change over time? Are certain measures more effective in quantifying them?

Two groups of students, differentiated by the way they responded to items on the confidence-in-learning-mathematics subscale (Fennema & Sherman, 1976) performed differently on mathematics tests administered in Grades 6 and 8. At both grade levels, students who indicated that they considered themselves confident learners of mathematics performed better. Examination of the data separately by sex revealed few differences. An intriguing finding, however, was that the mean achievement of the females in the high-confidence group changed most over the three years. They started out as the group with the highest achievement in Grade 6, but their performance relative to the other groups dropped somewhat. By Grade 8 they still performed well, but not as well as males who were equally confident about their ability to do mathematics. Why should confident females, but not confident males, do less well in mathematics over time? Did the two groups of students perceive themselves as having equal opportunities to learn? A series of carefully planned interviews, described fully in Chapter 4, indicated that both females and males believed more strongly over time that males were more likely to succeed in mathematics; furthermore, females' beliefs in females' ability to succeed in mathematics decreased over time. Yet, no significant achievement differences were found between males and females in either Grade 6 or 8. What influences, either inside or outside the classroom, might have contributed to such changing expectations?

A close look at the interview data proved revealing. At least some of the students showed themselves aware of the cultural stereotypes about males' and females' ability to do mathematics and who most required it in life beyond school. It is interesting to speculate to what extent such views were reinforced as they were being expressed to the interviewer. How often must such ideas be read, processed, or repeated before they are accepted by students as facts? What is the cost of this acceptance to females, in terms of beliefs in their own mathematics ability?

A further longitudinal study provided some useful insights. It followed students from Grade 6 to Grade 12. Various instances of unequal educational outcomes were noted, particularly on more demanding conceptual items. Evidence was found of stereotyping of mathematics as more appropriate for males, particularly by the males. It appeared that their female classmates were sensitive to such views, for Meyer and Koehler documented a number of instances in which the relationships between achievement in mathematics and selected internal belief variables changed between Grade 6 and Grade 12 for females, but not for males. Over time, for the females, achievement seemed more affected by their beliefs about the perceptions others held of them as learners of mathematics. The complexity of the relationship between achievement and an internal belief variable such as confidence is highlighted by the finding that confidence was both a predictor of achievement and a result of it.

How internal beliefs interact with achievement was explored from a somewhat different perspective by Kloosterman in Chapter 5. In this view, a close link between confidence and motivation is seen as exemplified by the Expectancy X Value view of motivation. Thus, the motive to achieve is defined as a function of the value to the individual of the end goal, as well as the individual's expectation (and confidence) of attaining that goal. Might differences in the ways females and males react to prior experience, such as success and failure in mathematics, contribute to gender differences in mathematics achievement? Are comparable events interpreted differently by females and males, so that an ostensibly equal educational environment ceases to be such? A careful examination of students' reaction to failure in mathematics, Kloosterman hypothesized, should help answer this.

A first experiment, devised to assess students' performance following induced and recognized failure (PFF) on mathematics problems, indicated that females appeared less resistant to the failure experience than males. While the performance of the males on a comparable set of mathematics problems improved after the artificially induced failure experience, the performance of the females deteriorated. Furthermore, for females but not for males, more general mathematics achievement appeared related to the PFF measure. Females most affected by the induced failure experience on a specific and artificially controlled occasion had lower scores on an unrelated mathematics test than those not so affected. The inclination to generalize from this first study about the long-term cumulative effects of a common classroom experience, failure in mathematics, is counterbalanced by Kloosterman's second study, in which PFF was examined in connection with attributional variables. Those students, both males and females, whose attributional style seemed to make them the most susceptible to the immediate effects of induced failure were the highest achievers on a general mathematics test.

Can the PFF notion help our understanding of gender differences in mathematics achievement, or is it too vague a measure and merely an intriguing theoretical notion without practical applicability? Are there perhaps such individual differences in reactions or attributions of failure that further refinements are needed? No gender differences were found in attributional style, as defined by Kloosterman, nor in the relationship between attributional style and failure-induced performance decrements. Yet, attributional style and general mathematics achievement were found to be correlated.

Kloosterman's research illustrates particularly well how difficult it is to examine the effects of internal belief variables that appear, intuitively at least, to have great influence on learning. The conflicting and frequently nonsignificant findings might suggest that the notion of performance following failure is irrelevant to our understanding of gender differences in mathematics. On the other hand, might more refined measures, less reliance on paper-and-pencil assessment, more carefully delineated contexts, and, above all, more realistic classroom settings tap subtle relationships still hidden? Further work along these lines may provide some answers. While the work presented in Chapters 4 and 5 provides some validity for the ALB model, alternate research strategies may yield additional confirmatory or challenging evidence.

Throughout this synthesizing discussion, so far, it has been made clear that students face and interpret actions, events, and opinions around them. The emphasis has been predominantly on the students' own feelings and beliefs. It has become apparent that students' perceptions of the experiences they have may detract from potential equal educational treatment and opportunities to learn. The extent to which teachers, who occupy a central place in classrooms, contribute to this was examined in the remainder of the book.

There is both overlap and divergence in the work discussed by Koehler in Chapter 6 and Leder in Chapter 7. There is overlap in that both asked whether all students received equal educational treatment from teachers and were given equal opportunities to learn; the divergence is because of the distinctly different samples and methodologies used.

The issue of equal treatment is addressed by Koehler's first study and substantiated by Leder's work. Typically, males had more interactions with their teachers than did females, both in American and Australian classrooms and at a wide range of grade levels. The somewhat different observation methods employed in the two studies gives added weight to the accuracy of this finding. But, how important are different interaction patterns? Do they facilitate, or perhaps hinder, the mathematics learning of those with frequent teacher contacts? Koehler's data revealed that, at least in beginning algebra classes, overall frequency of interactions was not simply or directly related to achievement, nor could contacts in any one particular interaction category be linked to differences in performance. Might an intensive investigation provide more constructive leads? To explore this issue in depth, Koehler selected two classes with many similar characteristics, including class size, balance of females and males in each class, and readily observable teacher behaviors. Significantly, while the performance of the males in the two classes remained comparable, that of the females diverged with time.

Koehler wondered whether any, perhaps less readily observable, behaviors could be identified in which the two teachers differed. Relying in particular on informal field notes taken during classroom observation periods, Koehler singled out a number of such behaviors, summarized as helping behavior on the part of the teacher. Males' achievement in mathematics did not seem to be affected by the ease with which help was given or the encouragement for seeking it. For females, on the other hand, some discretion in withholding help seemed beneficial. They did better in mathematics in the class in which students both received and asked for help less often. Koehler's own interpretation of the data — namely, that withholding help encouraged and nourished characteristics required for independent thinking and that this, in turn, led to the higher performance of females — cannot be discounted. Consistent with this is Leder's finding that, for Grade 7 students (i.e., students of an age close to those in Koehler's sample), the group with the most interactions with the teacher were, in fact, the females with the lowest performance in mathematics. Suggestive, too, is the finding that females perceived as excellent by their teachers had fewer teacher interactions at the Grade-7 level, when no gender differences in mathematics achievement were observed, whereas, at the Grade-10 level where more interactions were observed, males outperformed females. Carefully documented further work with larger samples seems warranted.

Worthy of further exploration, too, is the effect on students of the rather blunt way in which failure was pointed out, at least on some occasions. Did students' reluctance to expose themselves to such statements reduce the number of times they received public and private failure feedback, and did this affect the mathematics performance of females? Once again, intensive study of selected classes might lead to further insights. Whatever the ultimate explanation or, most probably, explanations, Koehler's work highlighted the notion that females seem more susceptible to certain teacher behaviors. Equal educational treatment, it seems, does not necessarily lead to equal opportunities to learn.

The difficulty of capturing the classroom environment, alluded to in Koehler's work, is made explicit by Leder's research. Substantially different classroom descriptions emerged from two different observation schedules used. If differences in frequency of interactions with males and females are not closely tied to gender differences in mathematics achievement, as argued by Koehler, is it more helpful to consider the actual time that students spend interacting with their teachers? No direct investigation of this hypothesis was offered, though the quasi-longitudinal composition of the sample allowed an indirect assessment. The differences in time spent on cognitive questions, with females receiving somewhat more time on low-cognitive-level questions and males on higher ones, were suggestive of differential teacher expectations of the two groups. Overall, however, there were few substantive indications that student gender influenced the time teachers spent with students. Whether this reflects equity of educational treatment, at least in this dimension, or whether the observation scheme used was too blunt to identify inequities of treatment, remains an open question at this stage. Far more telling were the students' own beliefs about their ability to do mathematics. At a time (Grade 7) when there was no evidence of unequal educational outcomes as measured by a mathematics achievement test, there were substantial differences in females' and males' perceptions of their mathematics and overall abilities, their confidence about doing well in mathematics, their expressed liking of mathematics, and their perceptions of its usefulness. Leder's study confirmed the assertions of Meyer and Koehler that males and females have different beliefs about learning mathematics, and to that extent it provides support for the ALB model.

The overlap between the findings presented in Chapters 4, 6, and 7 are of more than incidental interest. The subtle yet consistent differences in internal beliefs about mathematics learning expressed by females and males in American schools were shared by students in Australian schools and were tapped by a wide range of instruments. Furthermore, the identifiable differences in teacher treatment of males and females were found in widely divergent classrooms in different countries. Given these consistencies, it seems more profitable for future work to concentrate, not on the existence or magnitude of these differences, but rather on how they interact with the learning of mathematics.

The data presented by both Koehler and Leder indicate that readily observable teacher behaviors, such as frequency of interactions with students, cannot be explained in simple terms of teacher responsiveness to differences in the mathematics achievement of males and females. Subtle gender differences were revealed when students' beliefs were examined. How fruitful a parallel examination of teachers' beliefs might be was explored by Fennema in Chapter 8.

Teachers' beliefs have attracted considerable research attention; however, correlating them with the development of gender differences in mathematics has rarely been done. Fennema provided some pertinent evidence, based on the responses of a sample of first-grade teachers. It is worth recalling that gender differences in mathematics achievement are typically not reported for this grade level. Yet these teachers of very young children differed, it seems, in the ways they thought about their students' successes and failures in mathematics. Males' success in mathematics was explained in terms of ability more often than occurred for females; females' success was described more often in terms of effort than males. Further differences emerged when teachers were asked to comment on failure in mathematics. Lack of teacher help was considered a more likely explanation for males' than for females' failure.

Two of the findings reported in this book raise an interesting question about certain teachers' beliefs that may influence their interactions with females and males. Leder reported that seventh-grade teachers spent three times longer with the males they perceived as the lowest achievers than with any other group. Fennema noted teachers' indications that, when males fail in mathematics, it is because the teachers failed to help them. Could these findings indicate that teachers believe they can or should help males more than females to learn mathematics?

The similarity between the patterns of attributions by teachers for their students' successes and failures and those of students themselves (albeit a different, older sample), as described in Chapters 4 and 7, is inescapable. Could this similarity perhaps be due to the similarity in instruments used? Would a different instrument give different results? Fennema uncovered further subtle differences when she probed teachers' beliefs in a different way. Several descriptors, including competitiveness, logicalness, volunteering of answers, enjoyment of mathematics, and independence in mathematics were seen as more applicable to the best young male mathematics students. Yet, few differences were found in the descriptors used most and least frequently by teachers for the most- and least-capable students. Crucial with respect to these findings is the extent to which the students themselves were sensitive to these very subtle differences. In the absence of more direct evidence, it may be useful to refer to Leder's finding that differences in the frequency of teacher interactions with their male and female students tended to be reflected in the rates with which students themselves initiated interactions. Much further work with teachers of young, as well as older, students is required before we can be confident that we know enough about how teachers' beliefs are reflected in the educational environment they provide for their students.

Gender differences in mathematics has been a fertile area of investigation, and the problem has been well described and documented in this book. Characteristics of learners, such as motivational variables, which are both related to and predictive of future learning, were measured and studied in a variety of ways. The differential treatment of males and females within classrooms was well documented, and, in some of the studies described, indications were given as to which classroom characteristics might improve outcomes of mathematics education for both females and males. Within reported studies of both learners and classrooms there was some consistency of findings, and this has led us to conclude that we know a great deal about gender differences in mathematics.

However, there is a great deal more that needs to be known. We have collectively worked in the area for over 25 years, and each of us is growing more and more aware of the complexity of the problem. Naïvely perhaps, we had assumed that if important, alterable variables could be identified, then the problem of females and mathematics could and would be eliminated. This has not been the case. It appears to us that, while most of the important variables have been identified, and while the problem is somewhat diminished, gender differences in mathematics still exist and still inhibit females from taking their rightful place in society.

Knowledge about gender and mathematics gained through educational research has been a change agent in some cases. It has provided knowledge to educational agencies, focused public attention on gender differences in mathematics, and pointed the way to educational intervention. To conclude this book, we present a discussion of additional types of research that might prove beneficial.

## DIRECTIONS FOR FUTURE RESEARCH

While the monitoring of outcomes of mathematics education in the affective as well as cognitive areas in the general female and male populations is still essential, most research should not be focused on this type of work. Instead, we need to ask more specific questions, such as, On what type of mathematics do gender differences exist for students with certain characteristics? For example, do high-achieving females achieve as well as high-achieving males in algebra? Is the situation the same for geometry? Are low-achieving females more confident in one kind of mathematics than in another kind? Are all classrooms the same for high-achieving males and females as for low-achieving ones? For too long, researchers have lumped all mathematics as well as all females (and males) into one large category. Not all males learn mathematics well, nor do all females have trouble with mathematics. Such an obvious truism should no longer be ignored as we try to gain information about characteristics of learners who either have or do not have trouble achieving important mathematical outcomes.

More explicit information is also needed with respect to characteristics of specific schools and classrooms. Research to date has dealt mainly with the typical school and classroom. While researchers have recognized the wide diversity of classrooms and schools, the reported research has not been concerned with how classrooms or schools differentially influence students. The Fennema and Peterson (1985, 1987) studies represent an initial attempt to identify classrooms that are differentially effective for females and males. Future research should focus on questions such as, What are the characteristics of schools and classrooms where no gender differences in mathematics exist? Why do some schools have many more females than males enrolled in upper-level mathematics classes? Even within schools where overall gender differences in mathematics are evident, there are some classrooms where the differences are not present. Why is this? In order to gain profitable information about successful schools and classrooms, it may be necessary to supplement standard research paradigms with methodologies like ethnography. Knowing about the characteristics of successful schools and classrooms might lead to the design and testing of interventions, which in turn may lead to elimination of gender differences in mathematics.

Investigations of the variables in a personal belief system which enables one to approach, to work hard in, and ultimately to learn mathematics have been a major focus of this book and, indeed, of much other research about gender and mathematics. One overwhelming conclusion that must be reached after thorough study is that a belief system, and its development and influence, are extremely complex. In Chapter 1 we proposed that autonomy was a unifying variable which resulted from both external and internal pressures and enabled or inhibited one from achieving important educational outcomes. The Autonomous Learning Behavior model (Fennema & Peterson, 1985) appears to be an important starting point for further investigations. There are few data that contradict the model and many data that support it. This model does take into consideration the complexity of personal belief systems, their development, and their influence. Whether or not researchers choose to use the model as suggested, it appears that defining components and investigating their influence on each other and on educational outcomes will result in important new knowledge. There may be other components that need to be identified and included; however, only as researchers recognize the intricacies of the issues with which they are dealing will they be able to develop and verify models that will lead to increased understanding.

Perhaps a major modification of current research paradigms on gender and mathematics would be profitable. There have been many important studies of large populations, which have utilized strong statistical techniques for analyzing their data. We also need studies on a more micro level; these would attempt to understand the cognitions of teachers and learners, which ultimately influence the learning of mathematics and the development of a beneficial internal belief system. Such studies may utilize cognitive science methodologies, which have so dramatically increased our knowledge about how children learn and why teachers teach as they do.

Not until we somehow get into the "black box" of the learner's mind will we know whether many of the things that are assumed to be detrimental or helpful are indeed influences on a learner. For example, is it really detrimental to females that the teacher spends more time with males? Or is the major detriment a single critical incident involving overt sexism? Not until we know what the learner is thinking can we answer such questions. Why do teachers spend more time with males? Not until we find out what the teacher really believes and knows about gender and mathematics can this be answered. Some of the research techniques currently being utilized in the study of teachers' thinking would be extremely helpful in gaining an understanding of teachers' beliefs about gender and mathematics. Use of stimulated recall techniques or in-depth interviewing of a few teachers may provide important information and testable hypotheses for future studies.

Research can and should provide important knowledge that enables teachers and schools to eliminate gender differences in mathematics. Throughout this book, we have attempted at all times to delineate clearly our values and the reasons why we have pursued and reported on the kind of research that we have. Our values have provided the questions. The authors' knowledge and abilities as scholars have provided the studies and conclusions. The studies have not always resulted in conclusions that we have anticipated or liked; however, we feel confident that the studies were properly implemented and the conclusions were drawn objectively. It is our hope that these and future studies will ultimately contribute to the achievement of equity and justice for all in mathematics education.

## REFERENCES

Fennema, E., & Peterson, P. L. (1985). Autonomous learning behavior: A possible explanation of gender-related differences in mathematics. In L. C. Wilkinson & C. B. Marrett (Eds.), *Gender-related differences in classroom interactions* (pp. 17–35). New York: Academic Press.

Fennema, E., & Peterson, P. L. (1987). Effective teaching for girls and boys: The same or different? In D. C. Berliner & B. V. Rosenshine (Eds.), *Talks to teachers* (pp. 111–125). New York: Random House.

Fennema, E., & Sherman, J. (1976). Fennema–Sherman mathematics attitude scales: Instruments designed to measure attitudes toward the learning of mathematics by females and males. *JSAS Catalog of Selected Documents in Psychology*, 6, 31. (Ms. No. 1225).

**Index
About the Contributors**

# Index

# About the Contributors

**Elizabeth Fennema** holds a joint appointment as Professor in the Department of Curriculum and Instruction and in the Women's Studies Program at the University of Wisconsin–Madison. She also is a co-director of the National Center for Research in Mathematical Sciences Education. Well known for the Fennema–Sherman Studies on gender-related differences in mathematics learning, the Fennema–Sherman Mathematics Attitude Scales, her research on gender issues in education, and her commitment to equity issues, Dr. Fennema is equally respected for her contributions to the study of teaching. Her current research in Cognitively Guided Instruction concerns teacher knowledge and beliefs about children's cognitions in addition and subtraction and their impact on learning.

**Mary Schatz Koehler** is an Associate Professor in the Department of Mathematical Sciences at San Diego State University. Her research focuses on gender and race differences in mathematics achievement, attitude, and participation. In particular, she is interested in the classroom processes that may directly affect the differential achievement of females and males in high school mathematics classes. Dr. Koehler is actively involved with several programs designed to interest girls from disadvantaged backgrounds in mathematics and science, and to give professional support to mathematics teachers in schools with high minority populations, high dropout rates, and high numbers of students from low-income families.

**Peter Kloosterman** is currently an Assistant Professor in the Department of Curriculum and Teacher Education at Indiana University in Bloomington, Indiana. His research focuses on the relationships between personal beliefs, motivation, and problem-solving achievement in mathematics. Dr. Kloosterman's latest publications concern self-confidence, motivation, and the phenomenon of learned helplessness among secondary school students. He has also been involved with several multi-disciplinary research and teacher training projects designed to improve instruction in science and mathematics in secondary schools.

**Gilah Leder** is an Associate Professor of Education at Monash University, Clayton, Victoria, Australia. Her research has focused on the impact of affective variables on mathematics learning, gender differences, and exceptionality, and she is widely published in each of these areas. Most recently, Dr. Leder has co-edited the book *Educating Girls: Practice and Research*, has served as a joint guest editor of a special bicentennial issue of the *Australian Journal of Education*, and has written a chapter on gender for the forthcoming *Handbook of Research on Mathematics Teaching and Learning*.

**Margaret R. Meyer** is a Faculty Associate in the Department of Curriculum and Instruction at the University of Wisconsin–Madison. Her research interests concern the role of affect in the teaching and learning of mathematical problem solving, as well as the investigation of gender differences in mathematics achievement, participation and affect. Dr. Meyer's recent publications include an analysis of the results of the Fourth Mathematics Assessment of the National Assessment of Educational Progress for gender differences in mathematics, and a discussion of equity issues in mathematics education.

**Lindsay Anne Tartre** is an Associate Professor in the Department of Mathematics at California State University–Long Beach. She is widely known for her research on the differential use of spatial skills by females and males. Dr. Tartre's current research is investigating the relationship of spatial skills to problem solving in mathematics, particularly to geometry. She is equally committed to teacher education and helping teachers to become aware of the impact of spatial skills on students' learning of mathematics.